God's Plan:

Obedience & Results

Bob McCauley (signature)

Bob McCauley

FIRST EDITION

ISBN: 9798574960547

Imprint: Independently published

Table of Contents

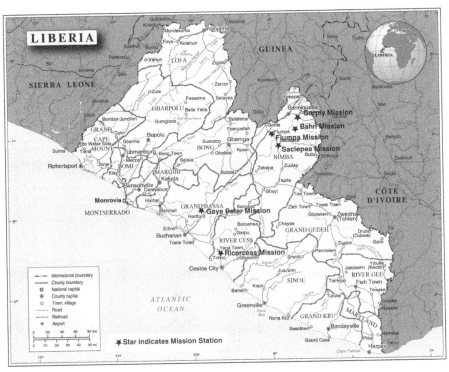

Introduction

"God's Plans: Obedience & Results" is a true story written by a man who died as the result of an accident in Africa. Immediately after his spirit left his body, he saw the Lord or an angel waiting to take him to Heaven. The man asked the Lord to give him a little longer to preach and He gave him his request. His spirit came back into his body and he preached the Word of God in America, Canada, Africa, and Russia. Later in his life God led him to write his first book, "The Still Small Voice: A Journey in Listening." Then the Lord led him to write another book called, "God's Faithfulness: A Journey in Trusting." He never thought he would write the third book, but the Lord led him to write this one. The theme of this book is to show that God has plans for every person and if they are obedient to Him, the results are very good.

The book is about two brothers God used for His service. One actually died, as was said above, and the other was at the edge of death, but God healed him. The death and near-death experiences were unexpected, but they both had another death experience that they knowingly and willfully planned for. They committed their lives as a holy living sacrifice to God. It could be said this way, "They had a 'death to self' experience and lived a holy life." This was their reasonable service to God and He used them much like we read about in the Book of Acts.

The Bible verse on this is shown below:

Romans 12:1 *(KJV)* ***I beseech you therefore, brethren, by the mercies of God, that ye <u>present your bodies a living sacrifice, holy, acceptable unto God, which is your reasonable service.</u>***

The brothers knew that living in obedience to God included living a holy life. As they did that God could use them in His perfect plans.

v

The brothers grew up in very adverse conditions due to alcohol. The author is one of them, but he has chosen to write the book in the third person. He experienced the miracles and adventures told about in this book, including the time when he had the death experience. Since he has experienced dying and having God give him back his life, he tells what it is like to die and that there is joy and absolutely no fear in dying in Jesus Christ. Few in the world have died and then been able to write about the experience, but he can and does. He also testifies to the fact that all of the miracles in the book of Acts are still for us today. He and his brother have experienced nearly all of them and you will read about these in this book.

The author was a senior engineer for General Motors, who resigned from his job and became a missionary jungle pilot in Africa. The book contains many jungle flying adventures and other adventures that God took the brothers through as they served Him at home and in Africa. It includes the Baptism of the Holy Spirit, a death experience, confrontations from witch doctors who tried to kill them, an aircraft engine failure over the jungle, a weather changing miracle, and other stories of adventure including one of saving a girl from drowning in a riptide in Florida. The adventures include a true heart wrenching story of a little girl who was carried to a remote place in Africa and left to die and how God used the brothers' obedience to save her. In addition to that, you will read about God's miracle of giving direction through His spiritual gifts and providing hundreds of thousands of dollars for the brothers' ministries.

This book is the author's testimony about God's plans for us in five different areas of our lives. The first is that God loves and has good plans for every person, but He wants them to obey Him in everything. This includes living a holy life. The second is that the miracles in the book of Acts are for us today. The third is that no matter how we grow up, God can use us if we accept Jesus Christ as our Savior and are obedient to Him. The fourth is that God is faithful and will meet all of our needs throughout all of our lives, and this is true even when we get old. The fifth is the fact that having a crisis does not mean we are living in sin or disobedience.

Chapter 1
Left Her to Die

A little African girl was lying unconscious on the ground in a remote area with no hope of survival. She had no clothes on and was laying in her own feces with insects crawling over her little body and fly eggs in her eyes, nose, ears, and mouth. No one seemed to care about her physical condition and where she was. Her parents believed she was dying and they carried her out of the village to a remote area and left her to die alone tormented by sickness, insects, hunger, and thirst rather than taking her for medical help. She was dying and only a few miles away was a mission clinic where they could treat the child, but her parents would not take her there. There was absolutely no one in her life, family, or village who would help her and most certainly she could not help herself.

The little girl had been living in very harsh conditions since her birth because her mother and father were nearly always drunk as a result of drinking their home brewed beer made from maze. Now, due to her parents living this kind of life style, she was dying a terrible death.

Even in this terrible and hopeless state of facing certain death, God loved her with a love that we cannot even comprehend. The poor child was one of His beloved and He had plans for her. However, dying as she was in this remote area was not in His perfect plans for the little girl. From God's Word, we know that His plans would have included her parents raising her properly. Why weren't they doing that? This question could be answered in one word, "Sin!" They were living to satisfy the lust of this world or the acts of the flesh. In Galatians 5:19-21 we see that drunkenness is one of the acts of the flesh and that controlled nearly everything her parents did.

The child's parents had treated their own daughter very despiteful, but, as we said above, God still had good plans for her. We could say, "How could it be possible for God's plans for her to come about?" It certainly was not going to come from her parents or the village she came from. It was part of their culture. It was against their culture for someone else to interfere with her parent's decision.

God was going to help her because no one else would. Also, His help would have to come quickly because she was near death. It was nearly

1

impossible for this little girl to live, however, God can and does do the impossible. It is nearly always impossible for us to correctly predetermine how He will do it and this was so in the case of this little girl. Yes, God had a plan to save the child, but it would take obedience from another person for God's plan to come about.

Later it would be found that the little girl's name was Zenzele, so we will refer to her by that name. No person could have known, if they looked at this little dying girl, that someday she would be the highest qualified nurse in the nation where she lived and be in charge of the entire nursing program in her country. Also, that she would marry a young police officer and later he would be in charge of all the police in their country. Then most important of all, both of them would be very dedicated Christians serving Jesus Christ with all of their heart and having a lovely family of their own.

Yes, God had plans for Zenzele, and it was not because she would someday be a respected woman in a high government position, but because she was a person whom He loved and His Son died for.

Jeremiah 29:11 (NIV) *For I know the plans I have for you," declares the LORD, "plans to prosper you and not to harm you, plans to give you hope and a future.*

In Isaiah 46:11, God says He will summon a man from a far-off land, or even a bird from the east to fulfill His purpose. Then He promises to bring about what He has said and He will do what He has planned.

Isaiah 46:11 (NIV) *From the east I summon a bird of prey; from a far-off land, a man to fulfill my purpose. What I have said, that I will bring about; what I have planned, that I will do.*

If God called a man from a far-off land, how could he get there to save Zenzele before she died? When we think about a situation like this, we need to understand that God knew every detail about Zenzele before the earth was formed. He can see the present, past, and future at the same time. He is not bound with time as we know it. Therefore, even before we need it, He can prepare help for us so they will be there when we go through our troubles! In Jeremiah 1:5 we see that God is saying He knew and appointed Jeremiah as a prophet to the nations before he was born.

Jeremiah 1:5 (NIV) *"Before I formed you in the womb I knew you, before you were born I set you apart; I appointed you as a prophet to the nations."*

Isaiah is saying in Isaiah 49:1 that the Lord called him and spoke his name before he was born.

Isaiah 49:1 (NIV) *Listen to me, you islands; hear this, you distant nations: Before I was born the LORD called me; from my mother's womb he has spoken my name.*

We, as humans, can give a child a name and, with medical science, we can see if the child is a boy or girl before they are born.

However, we do not know the future of the child, but God can see our entire life at the same time and He can see it even before we are born. Also, He gives all of us a free will and He knows the choices we will make.

An example of this is with Israel and a Persian king named Cyrus. Due to Israel's disobedience, her people ended up as slaves in a foreign country. Two hundred years before Israel was to be delivered from her slavery and returned to her own country God gave a prophecy through Isaiah telling the name of the person who would deliver them. Then God raised Cyrus up so that he would do this when God was ready to set the nation of Israel free. We can see one prophecy on this below.

Isaiah 45:13 (NIV) *I will raise up Cyrus in my righteousness: I will make all his ways straight. He will rebuild my city and set my exiles free, but not for a price or reward, says the Lord Almighty."*

It was never in God's plan for Israel to go to Persia as slaves. Over and over God warned them through His prophets about their sin and they refused to repent. As a result, God punished them. As was said above in Jeremiah 29:11, God had plans to bless and prosper them, but they had to make the right choice and repent for this to come about.

Also, it is not God's will or in His plans that any should go to hell.

2 Peter 3:9 (KJV) *The Lord is not slack concerning his promise, as some men count slackness; but is longsuffering to us-ward, <u>not willing that any should perish,</u> <u>but that all should come to repentance.</u>*

The sad thing is, many shall go to hell because they made the wrong choice and were disobedient.

God is so multifaceted that He can and usually does many things at the same time He is preparing a person for a special task. This was so in the case of having Cyrus in his position to free the Jews when God was ready. The events surrounding King Cyrus includes the life of Queen Esther and all that happened to her. We won't get into this now, but the events are all related.

It is very clear from Scripture that God can and does have plans for our future and does prepare people to fit into His plans even before they are born. This was the case for Zenzele. Yes, God had plans for her and some day she would be a highly respected Christian woman in her country.

Chapter 2
A Harsh Childhood

To better understand how God brought about His plans for Zenzele, and many others, we need to go back in time to the lives of two brothers who grew up in very harsh conditions. The brothers had this in common with Zenzele because she and the brothers suffered greatly due to alcohol.

Bob and Jim McCauley grew up on a farm in mid-northern Indiana and life should have been good for them, but it was very harsh because of the disobedience of their father. He was one of the largest farmers in the area and was wealthy from the stand point of making a lot of money. There was a problem however. He became an alcoholic early in life and this contributed to extreme difficulties for the brothers and their mother.

The boy's mother was a four foot ten-inch-tall beautiful woman who loved her husband very much, but he did not return the love. Jim and Bob both remember how their father would get dressed up every evening after the day of farming was over and drive away in his car. The brothers' mother wanted him to stay at home or take all of them with him, but he would not do it. During those nights their mother would stand at a kitchen window looking down the road to see if her husband was returning home. Jim and Bob well remember how sad she looked as she stood there night after night.

The boy's parents argued every day and most of it centered around their father's drinking and also their mother felt he was being unfaithful to her. Their father would not stop going out at night and their mother became increasingly bitter about it. Then one day their father told their mother he would take her with him when he went out if she would start drinking. Jim and Bob were shocked by his remark, but they had no idea of the results it would bring about. The boy's mother loved their father very much and wanted desperately to have his affection, even if it required drinking with him. As a result, when Bob was about seven and Jimmy five years old, their mother started going to the taverns with their father. After that the brothers were often left home alone to fend for themselves.

After their mother started going to the taverns with their father things did not improve in their relationship. In fact, they got much worse and their daily arguments intensified. Jim and Bob cannot remember one single meal without a major argument between their parents. Usually the meal ended up with broken dishes and food all over the floor and walls. When the boys were younger their parent's arguments were mainly verbal, but as time went on, they developed into physical violence. Jim and Bob watched this time after time, helpless to stop them, but sick in their hearts because they loved both of their parents.

There were times after an argument when the brothers' mother would look at Bob and say, "This is all your fault." In Bob's young mind he could not figure out how he had caused his mother and father to have all of their arguments. This made Bob feel badly and he would try to reason how it was his fault, but could not come up with an answer. This left him very confused and hurt.

As an adult, Bob well remembers when he was in the first grade, sitting at his desk in his little farm community school house praying. He should have been thinking about his subjects, but he could not get out of his mind the fight his mother and father had the night before. He grieved over their fights more than any child should have. He simply could not get over hearing the terrible words his parents spoke to each other nearly every time they were together. Even though Bob was just a little boy, this was an ongoing event and it was impossible for him to understand why they were always fighting. Bob's prayer was always, "God, help mother and daddy to get along."

God no doubt heard little Bobby's prayer and had compassion on him. Also, it was not in God's plans for both boys to be living like they were. Their father and mother had both grown up in Christian homes and rebelled against the teaching of their parents when they were young. Their disobedience and rebellion was causing unhappiness for them, but also mental pain for their children. The brothers were suffering because of something they did not cause or want.

Jim and Bob still remember one evening when their father brought five gallons of gasoline into their house threatening to burn the house down with all of them in it. It was a very fearful experience for the brothers. Both boy's nerves were extremely on edge because they knew their father might strike a match and blow the house up with them in it. The can of gas sat there in the kitchen with its fumes filling the room as their parents continued to scream at each other. To the brothers' relief, finally their mother got their father under control and the boys carried the gas out of the house.

Both of the brothers well remember another evening when their mother and father got in an argument and their father grabbed his 12 Gage shotgun. It seemed obvious to the boys and their mother that their father intended to shoot their mother right then. As their father was swinging the gun around towards their mother, she lunged forward towards their father and managed to grab the barrel with her right hand and the butt of the gun with her left hand. Immediately their father tried to yank the gun away from their mother's grip and a fight was on, each trying to get the gun away from the other.

Bob was only a few feet away from them when this happened. He knew their mother was not as strong as their father and soon he would get the gun. Bob fully believed their mother would be shot and killed. Immediately he determined to help their mother get the gun away from their father. He quickly saw that the gun's barrel was being swung by his mid-section and he knew he was in extreme danger of being killed himself if the gun went off. Regardless of this Bob started to jump into the fight when the gun was pointed a little to his right side. He had his eyes focused on the end of the barrel when a flash of fire came out of it along with a very loud explosion. The shotgun went off and the shot missed Bob by just a few inches. Immediately he looked down at the rocking chair he was standing next to and saw that the whole arm was gone.

Quickly Bob looked back at their mother and father to see if they were still fighting over the gun. He saw a very startled look on their faces as they seemed to realize they nearly killed him. The fighting had stopped and the boy's father was holding the gun at his side. Their mother ran out of the house and hid all night in the back seat of their neighbor's car. Jimmy says he could hardly believe what he just saw. His brother was nearly killed right in front of him because of their father's violence. Also, his mother would have been killed if she had not grabbed the gun in time. After she ran away Jim and Bob were left with a drunken father, but he seemed to settle down after he realized what he almost did. Then he got in his car and left.

One day when Bob was with a group of people he knew, a woman spoke out very loudly and pointed at Bob and said, "Your mom and dad got married and six months later you came along." All of the people there looked at Bob and laughed and he stood there trying to be calm, but suddenly realizing what his mother meant when she said that it was his fault that they were having the arguments. Then he did some checking and found that the woman's statement was true.

Bob did some more checking and found that after their mother knew she was pregnant she wanted to get married. The brothers' dad told their mother that he would marry her, but as soon as the kid grew up, he was leaving her. Then all of the pieces came together in Bob's mind as to why his mother and father had a terrible marriage. Bob realized that in his mother's mind, her troubles with her husband came about because he was conceived and born. He also realized that his father probably hated his mother because he had to marry her.

This new knowledge that Bob was suddenly aware of was very disturbing to him. He had to process it in his mind and come to a conclusion as to how he would react to it. He knew he was the product of sexual sin. Also, he could not help being alive and blamed for all of the problems between his parents. He was still a person who was born and had a life to live. Bob also knew he had a choice of how he reacted and lived after knowing how he was conceived.

During their years of growing up, Jim and Bob experienced so many difficult events that, in some ways, their lives were like living in a horror movie. Many in the community were wondering how the brothers would turn out since they were raised in an alcoholic and violent home. "Like father like son," was a famous saying at that time and some thought the brothers would end up in life the same way that their father had. Was this to be true or was there another factor involved in this that hardly anyone knew or thought about?

The brothers had Christian grandparents and neighbors praying for them. Also, God Almighty had plans for them. The fact that God had plans for their lives never entered the brothers' minds and it probably never entered the minds of any in the community. Years later, some of the people would say, "We never thought it possible for Bob and Jim to be what they are."

By the time Jim and Bob were in their mid-teens they hated alcohol and what it did to their parents and also to them. They also had a very strong dislike for taverns, which they called beer joints. Every person they knew of who went to the beer joints had grief and trouble in their lives. This dislike for the lifestyle of those who drank alcohol caused Jim and Bob to want nothing to do with it.

When Bob was seventeen years old, he had no idea that God had a plan for his life and that it was good. He did however have a God given choice to either live as his parents had or to live for God as his grandparents did. After thinking seriously about this for a time, he went to a church down the road about a mile and a half from his home on a Sunday morning with the plan to become a Christian. Bob listened closely to the message given by a young pastor named Johnny Mayes. After the message, Bob told the pastor he wanted to get right with God. Pastor Mayes then questioned Bob to see what he knew about the Word of God. The pastor quickly found that Bob knew very little about the Bible and that he did not understand God's plan of salvation at all. He had Bob sit down and he took about an hour to explain the plan of salvation starting with Adam and Eve and their sin and through Jesus Christ dying for man's sin.

After the pastor was satisfied that Bob clearly understood God's plan of salvation, he led Bob in the sinner's prayer. Immediately Bob knew he was born-again and he felt like a great weight was removed from him and he felt very good inside. Bob had just accepted Jesus Christ as his Savior and was born-again according to John 3:3.

John 3:3 (NIV) *Jesus replied, "Very truly I tell you, no one can see the kingdom of God unless they are born again."*

Pastor Mayes then mentored Bob every Sunday afternoon for four months. By this time in Bob's life he knew the Word of God fairly well and he became very active in serving the Lord in his church and witnessing for Him to nearly every person he could.

Right after Bob accepted Jesus Christ as his Savior he started to pray for his brother and talk to him about the Lord. Jim started going to church with Bob and he also made the right choice and accepted Jesus Christ as his Savior. Bob was delighted when this happened.

The brothers could have followed the same example that they saw from their mother and father as they were growing up. According to statistics, about 75% of children who grow up in alcoholic and violent homes live the same way when they become adults. It had just the opposite effect on Bob and Jim. It caused them to hate that kind of life style and to have a great compassion and desire to help children and

9

adults who were hurting. This compassion for hurting people and the desire to help them would be a driving force within them for the rest of their lives. Satan meant their difficult childhood for evil, but God was going to use it in bringing about His plans to send the Gospel to the world and to help hurting children and adults in many different countries. One of these hurting children would be little Zenzele.

God's plans for Bob and Jim were far beyond anything they could ever have thought of. His plans would require the brothers to leave their homes, land, and jobs, to follow Him. The only thing that would stop God's plans from coming about would be their disobedience or refusal to obey. If the brothers obeyed, the results for the Kingdom of God would be fabulous.

Bob and Jim 1942

Chapter 3
The Riptide

Bob and Jim got into a difficult situation in their latter teen years that they did not see coming, did not cause, did not plan for, did not want, and it took them where they did not want to go. It is hard to imagine, but this was in God's plan for the brothers. They had experienced emotional difficulties that they did not cause or want, but this was a physical difficulty. It was something that they had never heard of called a riptide.

Riptides are narrow fast flowing currents of water flowing outward from a beach. The water in them can be flowing eight feet per second. The riptide area looks almost the same as the rest of the sea so it is nearly impossible for the normal person to tell where they are. Many people have drowned as a result of getting into a riptide because they were swept far out to sea and they tried to swim back against the current and could not do it. Riptides almost always occur when there are high breaking waves causing a certain area along the beach to have water that is rapidly flowing back out to sea. To get out of a riptide a person needs to swim parallel to the shore for a ways and then swim towards the shore at an angle.

The brothers got in a riptide in the Gulf of Mexico, but there are also what I call riptides of life. Many people, who get into a riptide of life, need someone to get into it with them to help them get out of it with the least possible amount of damage or scars. Nearly always a riptide of life leaves many scars on the person who was in it. Also, many times it leaves scars on the person or people who go to the aid of the person in the riptide. The scars can be physical, but usually they are emotional scars that are difficult to get rid of. To get out of a riptide of life nearly always requires every bit of strength the one in it has and also complete dedication and endurance from the one who goes to their rescue.

A thirteen-year-old girl named Marj was playing in the water at Fort Myers Beach in Florida. Her mother and father were on the beach watching her and they had no idea that a tragedy was about to happen to their beloved daughter. Then it happened! Marj was quickly swept about sixty yards outward from the beach and was still going farther out. She was not a good swimmer and started screaming for help. Her father and mother were terrified as they watched this and were helpless to save their daughter because they did not know how to swim. They knew she was going to drown if someone did not come to her aid.

God had wonderful plans for this thirteen-year-old. They included being happily married, raising a family, teaching piano, and her family ministering in song and music at many different churches. This girl would also be a wonderful witness for Jesus Christ wherever she went. Satan, no doubt, wanted to stop her in her youth from what God had planned for her and he got her into a riptide.

Riptides of different sorts come into many people's lives. Seldom are they an actual riptide as Marj's was, but many times they are impossible to get out of without some help. Some examples are financial problems, sickness, unfaithfulness, drugs, alcohol abuse, and suffering from injustice etc. Often there is only one person who can help them and if that person does not do it the person who is in the riptide of life will suffer. Sometimes they will even die.

In Luke chapter ten we see the story of a man who was robbed and beaten so badly he could not help himself. He needed someone to help him and a priest came along. It would have been in God's plan for the priest to help the man, but he did not want to get involved so he passed on by him. Then a Levite came along and did the same thing. Later a good Samaritan came by and helped the man.

Luke 10:33-37 (NIV) [33]*But a Samaritan, as he traveled, came where the man was; and when he saw him, he took pity on him. [34]He went to him and bandaged his wounds, pouring on oil and wine. Then he put the man on his own donkey, brought him to an inn and took care of him. [35]The next day he took out two denarii and gave them to the innkeeper. 'Look after him,' he said, 'and when I return, I will reimburse you for any extra expense you may have.' [36]"Which of these three do you think was a neighbor to the man who fell into the hands of robbers?" [37]The expert in the law replied, "The one who had mercy on him." Jesus told him, "Go and do likewise."*
When some people see a person in a riptide of life they don't want to get involved and walk away like the priest and Levite did. The good Samaritan stopped and helped the injured man even when it cost him time, effort, and money. Let me be so bold as to say this. At times a person can need help that is even beyond what

the good Samaritan did. You might say, "How can that be possible?" The good Samaritan helped the man after the robbers had beat him and taken all of his money. What if the good Samaritan had come along earlier and saw the robbers beating and robbing the man? Would he have stepped in and fought the robbers at the possible cost of his own life? We don't know, but there are times when a person should get involved and defend someone, even if it possibly could cost their own life. Here is an example of this.

One time in South Africa Bob suddenly found that he was the only person to stop a murder, but if he tried to do it, he would probably be killed. The man, who was about to be murdered, suddenly had a riptide in his life that he could not get out of without someone coming to his aid. When Bob saw what was about to happen, he immediately reacted in a way he had never planned for, did not want, and knew beyond any doubt that his own life could end within seconds because he was going to get involved in trying to save the man's life. The full story will be told later in this book.

There can be other times when coming to someone's aid is not so traumatic as what Bob experienced, but greatly needed, such as defending someone against some untruth or injustice. Bob and Jim both have taken stands on this and they know from experience that few stood with them and this made it very difficult.

God knew Marj would need someone to save her life and He already had someone in place to do it. There was no one on the beach that morning except Marj, her mother and father, and four teenage boys. One of them named Bob Dugan was about forty yards down the beach from where Marj was playing in the water and the McCauley brothers were about ten yards farther away. The fourth man was about another thirty yards farther away. Bob Dugan heard Marj screaming for help and he yelled at Bob and Jim and told them the girl was yelling for help. The three young men started swimming towards Marj as fast as they could. As was said above, they had never heard of a riptide, but quickly they were in one without knowing it. The swift current took them rapidly away from the shore and towards Marj.

Bob Dugan got there first and saw Marj slowly go under, but he could still see her long hair at the surface as she was going down. He grabbed her hair and tried to pull her back up, but he was pulled under. The brothers got there just in time to see Bob Dugan come back to the surface with Marj. He had taken in some water and he was coughing so badly that he could hardly swim. He did however manage to keep Marj above water long enough for Bob to reach out with his right hand and grab Marj's arm under her left shoulder. Almost instantly Jim did the same thing, grabbing her with his left hand.

Both brothers instantly saw that Bob Dugan was in bad shape because of his violent coughing and would be of no help in saving Marj. They yelled at Bob and said, "Let us swim with her, and you get to shore." Bob Dugan did as the brothers suggested and headed toward the shore alone. After that the brothers had their full concentration on saving Marj.

By this time the brothers, along with Marj, were about eighty yards straight out from the beach and, though they were swimming as hard as they could, they found it impossible to make any progress in getting closer to the shore. Both Bob and Jim were strong swimmers and they could not understand this. They could not tell for sure, but it looked like they were getting farther away from the shore and the waves seemed to be larger or worse out where they were. They could also see that the waves were not flowing straight towards the shore, but at an angle towards it.

Marj was nearly unconscious when Bob Dugan brought her to the surface. She remained in that condition even after Jim and Bob took hold of her. After they swam as fast as they could to get to her, they were already very tired. Marj was a small girl and probably weighed only about eighty pounds, but with her extra weight and with the brothers swimming with only one arm, they had difficulty keeping her above the waves. Each wave, with its whitecap of rolling water, would break over their heads. They had to hold their breath while they were underwater and then, when the wave had passed over, they would have to get their breath and swim as hard as they could for a few seconds before the next wave came. The waves would nearly roll the three over with their tremendous force. When they were under water, the brothers had to exert a tremendous amount of effort to hold on to Marj and to stop themselves from rolling over with the waves.

15

Bob and Jim were getting some water down their windpipes during the process and they knew Marj probably was also. Both brothers started to feel extremely tired. They kept swimming as hard as they could, but were not getting closer to the shore. They were, however, being carried farther away from the area where they had started due to the waves carrying them somewhat parallel to the beach.

Bob and Jim started to get numb and their muscles seemed to be shutting down. However, they were still able to keep Marj above the water except when the waves broke over them. Both brothers were very concerned about her being able to hold her breath while they were underwater. To make matters worse, there was no way they could keep her above the waves when they broke over them.

Both brothers started to realize that they might not be able to make it; however, they were determined that they would keep going as long as God gave them strength. Although Jim and Bob couldn't discuss it, they both knew they would never let go of Marj to save their own lives. That was out of the question! Without talking to each other, both of them had made a strong decision that they would die before they would let go of Marj!

As the three were moved farther down the shore, they came closer to a pier that extended out into the water about one hundred yards. By that time the current had carried them farther out and they were about one hundred yards from the shore. The pier was about twenty feet above the water and supported by poles about twelve inches in diameter. When they were about fifty yards from a pole at the end of the pier, both brothers determined, at about the same time, to swim toward that pole, rather than trying to swim to shore. If they could get to the pole and hold onto it, it might save their lives.

Changing their direction of swimming did help conserve their strength some, but both brothers were feeling very numb and could hardly move the arm they were swimming with. The numbness in Bob's left arm and Jim's right arm was getting worse with each stroke of swimming. Bob was holding on to Marj with his right hand, so all the strength it took to swim was coming from his left arm. He was right-handed and much stronger in his right arm than his left. Jim was left-handed and was swimming with his right arm, so he was in the same situation. Both brothers had started out opposite of what they should have.

In their haste to take Marj from Bob Dugan, Bob had reached out to her with his right hand and Jim with his left. They did not think about the results of this seemingly small decision at the time. Now the results were showing up, but they could not change it. The brothers were so busy fighting to keep on top of the water between the waves that it was impossible to take time to trade places so they could swim with the other arm.

The brothers, along with Marj, were spending less and less time above the water between the waves. This meant that they all had to hold their breath longer and longer as the waves broke over their heads. It was constantly on the brothers' mind about Marj being able to hold her breath when they were under water. By this time Marj was less conscious than when Bob Dugan brought her to the surface. Then the brothers heard her start to pray between the waves and say over and over, "God save me, God save me!" Jim and Bob were agreeing with her prayer, even though they were not praying out loud.

The three kept getting closer to the pole at the end of the pier, but Bob's strength was almost finished. It was taking extreme concentration on his part just to keep swimming. He kept thinking, "Don't give in, keep moving, keep moving. We have to save her, we must save her." Jim was thinking about the same thing. From the time the brothers took a hold of Marj it took all of the effort they could put into each stroke to keep themselves and Marj from going under. Now that they were very tired, they still had to make each stroke as powerful as they did in the beginning. This was getting more and more difficult and the brothers knew that saving Marj was totally up to them, but they had to have God's strength to accomplish it. Bob knew that if he failed, Jim and Marj would also drown because Jim would try to save both of them if he had any strength left.

Bob's muscles became completely numb. By the time the pole was just a few feet away, he had to start telling himself, "You can do just a few more strokes." Jim was struggling as well and he was swimming deeper and deeper in the water with only his face surfacing enough between the waves to get a few breaths of air before they were under water again.

Without an ounce of strength to spare, the brothers finally reached the pole, but when they grabbed it, they found they had just traded one problem for another. The pole was covered with little razor-sharp shells that they later found were barnacles. The brothers' hands were cut instantly upon touching the pole. And to make matters worse, they were suddenly hit by a huge wave that slammed all three of them hard against the sharp, barnacle-covered pole. Instantly the water all around them was red as all three of their bodies were cut in hundreds of places. Bob and Jim could instantly see that Marj's face and upper body were covered with cuts and they were bleeding badly. Also, each of the brothers could see that the other one was bleeding badly, but that did not bother them nearly as much as it did to see Marj bleeding.

They were too tired to let go of the pole and swim farther, and the pain was almost too much to bear staying where they were. However, there were no other choices, so in spite of the pain they continued to hold onto the pole and each wave would cause the barnacles to cut their bodies more severely. Marj was getting cut up so badly that the brothers decided to rotate her location on the pole so she was on the side opposite the direction of the waves. They did this so that the waves would pull her away from the pole rather than slamming her against it; however, the waves were pulling her away from them, and they had to hold on even tighter so she would not be torn from their grip. The brothers were afraid she might go under immediately if they lost their hold on her. With all the pain and the force of the waves, holding onto the pole and onto Marj took all their strength and concentration.

Where was God in all of this? He had given the brothers strength to make it to the pole, but now they were in pain, bleeding badly, and the water around them was red with their blood. Both brothers knew that blood in the water could quickly attract sharks, which could cause them another very dangerous problem. Even with this in the back of their minds they had to continue holding to the pole because they were too tired to try swimming on to the shore. God, however, had help on the way for them.

The waves were so high that they could hardly see anything on shore, and they were left hanging high on the pole as the water dropped below them. As time wore on, they wondered what happened to Bob Dugan. After what seemed like a very long time, they saw him swimming through the waves toward them with a car inner tube.

The brothers found out later that when Bob Dugan finally made it to shore, he saw that some people had come to the beach with a concession stand and they had inner tubes to rent for swimming. He ran to the stand and took one without taking time to pay for it. He said they were screaming at him to bring it back, but he kept running. The three were so glad to see him! The brothers put Marj's arms through the center of the tube so they could hold on to her arms below the tube. Then they were able to swim easily to the shore with Marj in tow. Soon their feet touched the bottom, and it felt so good to be able to stand on solid sand. Marj could not walk by herself, so the brothers picked her up and carried her to her parents, who were standing at the edge of the water waiting on them.

Marj was covered with so much blood that her mother screamed in terror when she first saw her, and her father looked like he was ready to cry. Both, however, were so thankful to have their little girl back safe. Jim and Bob were covered with blood and exhausted, but they made it! Marj's parents took her to the hospital for a checkup and she was okay except for the cuts, which they treated. Thank You, Jesus!

Was it worth it? You bet! Did they make a difference in Marj's life? Yes, they did! For years Marj and her entire family sang together at many churches. Over forty years later Marj, her husband, and her children were doing a musical concert at a church with about 400 people present. Bob and Jim were attending the concert and also Marj's father was there. During a short break time in the service, Marj's father stood up and, with tears in his eyes, pointed at Bob and Jim and loudly said, "My daughter would not be doing this concert if it had not been for those two guys, Bob and Jim McCauley, saving her from drowning many years ago in Florida."

God had plans for Marj's life and they were good. Those plans did not cease when she was screaming for help and then went under the water. In God's plans, He had three teenagers there to save her from drowning. It took a full commitment on their part to do it. Two of them nearly drowned themselves plus they ended up with many cuts and covered with blood. The brothers and Marj had scars on their bodies for years as a reminder of that fearful day.

You will, no doubt, have opportunities to help people who are in riptides of their life. You may be the only person who can come to their aid. If you see a riptide in some one's life, it is almost always God's plan for you to come to their aid! God's perfect plan for you and them might not come about if you do not do it.

God blessed the brothers and they were over comers of the large waves and extreme exhaustion. The one thing they had to do however was to exert every ounce of strength they had to be over comers and then God gave them the rest of the strength they needed to get to the pole. When they got to the pole, they had no strength left, but they made it. This is the same thing people have to do when they face difficulties and temptations. They must be willing to exert all of the strength they have to overcome them. It is in God's plans for every person to be an over comer, but they have to also help themselves the best they can and trust God to give them the added strength they need.

At any point in the process of saving Marj, Bob Dugan and the brothers could have given up to save their own lives. If that would have happened, Marj would have drowned. Then God's plans for her and her descendants would not have come about. Also, if Marj had fought or struggled against the brothers in any way as they were trying to save her the three of them would have drowned. This often happens when a person is trying to save someone from drowning. When a person is trying to help or save a person who is in what I have called a riptide of life it is all too common for that person to fight or turn against the one who is trying to help them. It is critical that the person who is being helped submits to those who are trying help to them just as Marj fully submitted to the brothers when they were trying to save her.

Chapter 4
Jim's Drive and Goals

During Jim's high school years, he had a desire to be a farmer and to own the land. He had no money to bring this about, but he did have a tremendous drive and willingness to work hard to reach his goal. He kept this in the back of his mind and would occasionally day dream about having a loving wife and raising their children on their farm. His dreams always included loving and treating his wife well and having a home of peace for their children, which was much different than the one he grew up in.

When Jim was a senior in high school the boy's father helped him buy a used Harley Davidson motor cycle. Jim loved it, but one evening shortly after his high school graduation in 1953 he was in an accident while riding it and was hurt very badly. His parents, along with Bob, took him to the hospital and they examined him. After the examination, a doctor reported to his parents and Bob that his back was fractured, one lung was injured so badly that he would lose half of it, and one kidney was torn so badly that it would have to be removed. The doctor gave Jim little hope of living and he said that he would never again be able to do physical work if he lived.

Even though Jim was seriously injured, he was not knocked unconscious. As a result, he overheard the surgeon talking about removing his kidney. Even though he was in extreme pain, Jim said to the surgeon, "Don't remove it, fix it." The surgeon took Jim's request seriously and decided to try it. He told Jim, his parents, and his brother that they had never done any operation like that in Kokomo, but they would try. Jim and his family agreed with this. During the surgery they removed the kidney and repaired it and put it back in Jim. They could not repair the lung and he lost half of it. The fracture in his back did not require an operation. However, after the kidney operation the surgeon gave Jim's family little hope that he would live.

Even though Jim was near death and fighting for his life, God's plans for him did not include him dying as a result of his injuries. Many Christians were praying for him and he slowly improved. After about a month in the hospital he was released even though he could hardly walk and was very weak. However, at that time no one, including Jim, knew if he could ever again do physical work. Jim did not give up, but drove himself as much as he could to build up his strength. About six months later he was fully back to the strength and ability to walk and work as he had before being hurt so badly.

Before Jim's accident he met a Christian girl in his church named Mary Golliday and they were married shortly after she graduated from high school in 1954. God blessed and they were able to start farming right after they were married. Jim allowed himself four hours of sleep each night and pushed hard the rest of the time in their farming operation. As time went on, Jim and Mary became large farmers and they purchased a lot of farm land, which included two houses. Jim and Mary lived in one of them and their hired hand and his wife lived in the other one. During the years they had three children named Belinda, Mark, and Debra. Jim also became one of the largest pork producers in their area of Indiana. He was very successful in his farming and especially in his hog production and by the time he was thirty years old he and Mary were quite wealthy. During those years Jim also got a job working in skilled trades as a tin smith for General Motors.

Jim's loss of half of one lung put him in a status of being physically unfit for the army so he was never drafted and was able to fully pursue his goal with no interruptions of being sent off to war. During those years Jim continued to drive himself very hard, but he and Mary always found time to be active in their church and spent quality time with their children, whom they loved very much.

God had plans for the Apostle Paul, but before this could come about, He had to redirect Paul's tremendous drive to get him to do what He wanted. This was the same in Jim's case. He was going to church and involved in it some, but his focus and goal was almost entirely on making money. God had plans for Jim, and He was going to use his drive and endurance to bring about a tremendous ministry in Africa. First however, God had to get Jim's goal and drive focused on total obedience to Him.

Also, God had plans for Zenzele and Jim's drive and endurance would someday be a key factor in saving her life.

Left to right Debbie, Mary, Mark, Jim and Belinda McCauley

Chapter 5
Honor and Sacrifice

In many old movies the hero was always a man of honor. His honor meant more to him than the possibility of death. He might be a man of heavy drinking, fighting, hard to get along with, and many other such traits, but he wanted to always be a man of honor. This meant that he was always honest in his dealings with other people and would fight to protect his honor and the honor of others.

God wants all of His servants to be honest and honorable. A very important point in this is being honest when no one else will ever know except God and the person themselves. It is easy to think of one's self as being honest, but you can prove it to yourself when a very difficult situation arrives and a lie would seem to bring about better results than telling the truth. Or perhaps your honesty could further be tested when being truthful could greatly endanger your life, or to possibly cause you to lose it. Then there is another aspect to this. If something is not true and you keep quiet about it to protect yourself you are entering into a lifestyle of living a lie. Bob thought of himself as an honest person and a man of honor, but his honesty and honor was going to be tested shortly after he graduated from high school.

When Bob was a Freshman in high school only one person could beat him in the 100, 220, and 440-yard dashes. He was a Senior and would be graduating that year so Bob would not be running against him during his last three years of high school. Also, Bob got faster and he was the fastest in his school during his last three years and one of the fastest in his area of Indiana. He won many ribbons and most of them were for first place. Bob could also quickly do fifty push-ups, fifty sit ups, and twenty-five chin ups so he felt he was in very good physical condition. He also played basketball and had tremendous endurance in all kinds of physical activities.

During Bob's high school graduation ceremony, he was shocked when the American Legion called him to the platform and gave him their award for honesty and honor. Yes, Bob thought of himself as being honest and honorable, but he had never thought about others seeing this in him. He later learned that the students and teaching staff had chosen him as the student to receive this award. This was very touching to him and still is to this day. However, he had no idea that his honor was about to be tested.

The Korean War was going on when Bob graduated from high school in 1952. During that time all of the boys who graduated with Bob knew there was a very good possibility they would be drafted and sent to Korea. Shortly after graduation Bob received a letter from the draft board to get a physical exam for induction into the army. From his youth, Bob loved and was very dedicated to his country. He was in the first grade when the Second World War started and he saw some of his family and neighbors go off to war.

Bob also saw firsthand how people worried about their husbands, fathers, uncles, and sons being wounded or killed. Every now and then he would hear a report about the death of some young soldier. His own extended family had one son who was killed. Even at a young age Bob developed a great love and respect for the soldiers who went to war, risking their lives to keep his country free.

A few days after receiving the letter from the draft board Bob reported at 6:00 in the morning at the court house in Kokomo, Indiana. He and about thirty other young men were taken to Indianapolis, Indiana where they received their physicals for the draft. Bob thought he would easily pass his physical because he was in excellent condition. A few days after he took his physical, he receives a letter from the draft board and he fully expected it to say he was put in 1A and fit for the draft. After opening the letter and looking at the results Bob was shocked to see that he was put in 4F, meaning he was physically unfit for the army and would not be drafted and sent off to war.

When Bob was in the sixth grade, he got an infection in his lungs called Histoplasmosis. It is noncontagious and caused by inhaling spores found in the droppings of birds and chickens. Bob quickly got over this, but it left many white spots on his lungs. The military medical examiners saw those white spots on Bob's x-rays and put him in 4F as a result.

This meant that Bob could continue working at his job and make very good money with many benefits. Also, he would never have to go to Korea and possibly get killed. He could legally stay home and not be thought of as a draft dodger because he was declared physically unfit for the army.

25

Bob knew some people did everything they could to get out of being drafted and some of the things were very dishonorable. One such incident happened with one of the young men in his graduation class who lived on a farm a few miles from where Bob grew up. The day before he was to get his physical examination he went into his barn and threw dust into the air all day and heavily breathed it in until he was totally stopped up. When he took his physical, they noticed his difficulties in breathing and put him in 4F. The young man later bragged to Bob how he got out of being drafted. Bob felt this was very dishonorable.

Bob was devastated by his 4F classification because he knew it was not right. He knew it was very unfair for him to not be drafted because he was probably in better physical condition than most of the men who went off to war. There was no question in his mind that he needed to be honest and do everything he could to correct his draft status.

Bob most certainly did not want to be killed in the Korean War, but he could not live with himself if he was not honest and try to get his 4F status changed to 1A. Even though Bob knew some who were dishonest and did things to get out of the draft, he could not do it. Yes, he could only live with himself if he did everything he could to get his draft status changed from 4F to 1A.

Bob thought about what he could do, but did not have a plan. He could not remove the white spots on his lungs. They were there for the rest of his life so that thought was out. Possibly he could go to his family doctor and ask him to write a letter to the draft board saying he was physically fit for military service. There was no other way he could think of to be honest and get his status changed. He did this and the doctor gladly wrote a letter saying he was fit for the draft. Bob took the letter to the draft board and requested that they change his physical status to 1A.

The Draft Board reviewed the doctor's letter and changed Bob's classification from 4F to 1A, which meant he would be drafted. Bob knew he could face some very difficult times in Korea and possibly get killed as a result of this, but being honest with himself was worth more to him than any dangers that might lay ahead.

Bob was dating a Christian girl named Pat Lamb and they decided to get married even though they knew he would eventually be drafted. At that time Bob was working in production for Delco Radio, which was a division for General Motors. God blessed and he got a job in skilled trades as an apprentice tool and die maker for Delco. He was working 60 hours a week making very good money with many benefits.

Four months later Bob was drafted into the army and started his basic training in preparation to go to Korea. His salary went from making very good money and having medical insurance to only making sixty dollars a month with no insurance. This was very little for Pat to live on and during Bob's military service their son, Michael, was born and there was no money from the military to pay for the hospital bill. Bob could do nothing to help them financially and Pat had to handle it herself. She hired a baby sitter and got a job as a teller in a bank and sold Tupperware to pay the bills. Even with this she had to borrow a lot of money for her and Michael to live. It was very difficult for Bob to be away from Pat and his son and he felt badly that they had so little money.

Bob found that his basic training was fairly easy for him physically. Near the end of his basic training they had a battalion competition test on physical fitness. It was an extremely difficult physical endurance test doing things like running long distances, push-ups, pull-ups, and getting through obstacle courses as quickly as possible. Bob knew it would be very difficult to win this competition, but he wanted to do it. He put all of the energy into it that he could, but a man from Puerto Rico beat him. Bob was disappointed, but he felt he did well by coming in second. He felt it proved that he was right in believing he was fit for the draft and that he did the right thing in being honest and getting his physical status changed from 4F to 1A and fit for the army.

During the last few days of Bob's first eight weeks of training all of the soldiers were given a series of written tests and he scored very high on them. Bob did not know it at the time, but some government men went to his home area and questioned many people to determine if he could have a special clearance for the job they wanted him to do in Korea. The men were satisfied with the answers they received and Bob was put into a special high security unit and sent to Korea.

Bob and about 3,000 other soldiers got on a 300-foot-long ship, built in 1917, which took them on a three-week cruise across the Pacific to Korea. Then, on a cold rainy day in January, their ship anchored about one mile out from the city of Inchon. The troops then climbed down the side of the ship into a landing craft, which held about 35 troops. From there they were taken to the edge of the city and, for the first time, Bob walked on the soil of a foreign country. The war had finished before he got there, but he saw that it had left the country in devastation and the Korean people very poor.

Bob was stationed near Inchon for a short time and then taken to Osan Air Base where he started working with his special unit. The American soldiers in that area were on daily maneuvers in the country and they occasionally found a hungry and very dirty child laying by a rice paddy or in other remote places. Nearly always the soldiers stopped what they were doing and tried to find the child's parents or ask some Korean family to take the child. The answer would usually be, "We don't have enough food for our own children and we cannot take them."

The soldiers from the United States were some of the best in the world. They were usually eighteen or nineteen-year-old who were taught to fight and kill for their country in time of war. This extreme training could have made them so hard that they would not have cared about a starving child laying in filth on some hill side. However, the culture within nearly every one of the soldiers was not changed because of their training and they cared enough that they wanted to help every hurting child they found. The military base was not set up to take orphans in and there seemed to be no way the soldiers could help them.

Two soldiers decided to try and make a difference for the children and they asked Bob to join them. The three soldiers were very busy with their jobs in the army, but found time to rent a large Korean house and hire a woman to care for the orphans. Then they asked the other soldiers to give money to buy food, pay the rent, and to pay the house mother. The generosity of the American soldiers was amazing and they gave month after month to support their orphanage. After the orphanage was started the soldiers had a place to bring each homeless child they found. They ended up with about thirty-five orphans.

As far as Bob and the other two soldiers knew, they had the first orphanage in Korea that was started and run by soldiers. Soon the military officers became happy that the men under them had started the orphanage and it became a bragging point for them to the officers of other companies. After that, many other companies across Korea started and ran orphanages. This all became a very good public relations benefit to the American Army and also to America. There is no way of knowing how many orphans were helped through the years, but it is certain that each one of them was loved by God and He had a plan for their lives. He used the American soldiers to help bring about that plan.

The orphans were always fearful and hungry before some soldier found them. Bob had never been hungry, but he did grow up in fear of the next fight between his parents and what would happen. He could relate to a child living in fear and God used that to help him reach out to children living in fear in Korea. In a way God used Bob's memories of a tragic childhood to reach out and make a difference in children living in crisis.

When the North Korean Army attacked South Korea and fought their way to the southern tip of Korea, they executed about 3,000 Christian pastors. The Communists hated Christianity and wanted to wipe it out. Syngman Rhee was the president of South Korea when the war started and he was a devout Christian. His army had a very high number of devout Christian chaplains and Christianity was flourishing in South Korea when the North Koreans attacked.

Satan, in his hate for God and His Son Jesus Christ, tried to stop Christianity in Korea, but God intervened and today they are free to serve the Lord and obey His Great Commission to take the Gospel to the world.

God had a special plan for the South Korean Christians, which included their nation sending out thousands of missionaries going into countries all over the world preaching the Gospel. God used the United States of America to help bring about His plan for South Korea and also used Bob to be a part in helping the homeless South Korean children.

When Bob and the other two soldiers went home after being in Korea a year and a half other soldiers took their place and the orphanage continued to operate. Bob does not know what later happened in the lives of these children, but he knows God had good plans for each of them just as He has good plans for everyone. He also knows today that his honesty of telling the draft board that he was physically fit for the military helped bring about food, shelter, and a good place to grow up for each of the Korean orphans.

After Bob's term was finished in the army, he received an honorable discharge and went back home to his wife and son. The reunion was delightful and especially for him to see and hold his son Michael. Bob had not been able to be a father to Michael for nearly the first two years of his life, but now he wanted to make up for that. Bob loved him very much and wanted to spend quality time with him to make up for those two years he was away. Even though Bob enjoyed his time with Michael very much he could not help but think about the many soldiers who could never again be with their sons and daughters because they lost their life in Korea. This was a painful thought in Bob's mind that was with him for years and it would play a major part in a future decision. After a few days of being home Bob went back to work and resumed his job as an apprentice tool and die maker at Delco Radio.

Even though Bob was back working again and making money he was faced with needing to pay off a large debt. While he was in Korea, he made ninety dollars a month, but that was not enough for Pat to live on and raise a baby. With Bob's consent through correspondence, Pat went to the bank and asked for a loan for living expenses until Bob got out of the army. The bank was very helpful and gave her the funds she needed, trusting Bob to pay the money back after he got out of the army. When he returned home from Korea the bank loan was up to $7,000, which was a tremendous amount in the 1950s. Even though Bob was faced with this debt he was still glad he was able to serve his country and did not complain about it. By working ten hours a day at his tool and die job and six hours a day at a second job rebuilding electric motors he was able to pay the debt off within three years.

Was Bob foolish to get his draft status changed from 4F to 1A? Many people would say so. It is now over sixty years later and he knows he did the honorable and honest thing and he would do it again.

Bob in Korea   With war orphans

Chapter 6
Secrecy and Deceit

God prospered Bob on his job and, after becoming a journeyman tool and die maker, he was promoted to a tool designer. By this time in his life he was making very good money and he and Pat were able to purchase a fifty-seven-acre farm. Three years later they purchased an eighty-acre farm with a beautiful home on it. During this time Bob was promoted again to a junior engineer making more money with many benefits. Two years later he was promoted to a senior engineer. His salary increased, plus he and Pat could drive a new car every year for very little cost. Also, during those years, they were buying all of the G.M. stock they could and the company was adding one dollar for each dollar they invested.

God was truly blessing Bob and Pat and they had a huge income, money in the bank, G.M. stock, two farms, and a lovely home that was about 300 yards back off of the road. There was a creek between their house and the road and the boys loved to fish in it plus they each had a pony and Bob had a horse they loved to ride on the farm. Tony also had a St. Bernard dog he rode like a pony. At that time Bob was an expert in sheet metal stamping dies. He was responsible for leading the design and building of millions of dollars' worth of tooling. His job also required that he travel a lot over the mid-west getting the tools properly designed and built.

One morning Bob went to work as usual expecting his day to be normal. At about 9:00 o'clock that morning Bob's engineering supervisor said to him, "Two men want to talk to you at 10:00 o'clock in a certain conference room, be there." His supervisor seemed to have no idea what it was about and Bob certainly did not either. About two minutes before 10:00 o'clock Bob arrived in the designated conference room and at exactly 10:00 o'clock two very well-dressed men walked into the room. The men immediately identified themselves as being agents with a special department of the American government. Bob was quite surprised that these agents wanted to talk to him.

Bob immediately knew this meeting was very serious and these men wanted something very special from him. They were very serious and got right to the point of their meeting. The agents told Bob they wanted him to be an engineer for them on a very secret manufacturing project.

They also said the job required a very high government secret clearance and they told him what it was. Bob was surprised because it was even higher than the one he had while he was in Korea.

The Vietnam War was going on at the time and they told Bob that thousands of American soldier's lives would be saved as a result of the project. They told him the job was so secret that, if he took it, he could not even tell his wife or anyone else he was working on the secret project. He would have to travel to different cities and he would not be allowed to tell his supervisor or wife where he was going. Also, he would not be able to make a phone call from that city or stay overnight there. He would only be allowed to give his wife a contact telephone number in case of an emergency. They would know where he was and would contact him if needed.

The men also told Bob that his wife's life would be in danger if certain people in America found out he was working on the secret project and they would kidnap and kill her immediately. Then they would try to get Bob to give them the secret in an effort to get his wife back. The agents warned Bob that keeping the secret would be very difficult and they gave him a stern warning. If he took the job and told anyone what he was doing, and they found out about it, they would consider it treason and he would be sent to prison for the rest of his life.

It was obvious to Bob that the project was ultra-serious. Doing the tool engineering on the project would not be a problem because he knew he could do it. Keeping the secrecy from his wife would be the difficult part. How would his marriage stand up to his secret life if he took the job? When Bob traveled to different cities and businesses, he always told Pat what city he would be at and the name of the business he was going to. He knew Pat would ask him where he was going when he traveled and what would he say to her when she did? The fact that he could not even tell her he was working on a secret project would make it worse. Bob told the men he was married and asked how could he keep his travels from his wife? They said, "That is not our problem, it is yours!"

There was another problem. Bob was a Christian and he could not lie to his wife. All kinds of problems were flying through Bob's mind with no answers about how to handle them and the men were leaving it entirely up to him as to how he took care of them. It was his responsibility to keep the secret if he took the job.

Bob thought about the sacrifices many soldiers made for his country's freedom. He knew thousands of American boys lost their lives in Korea where he was stationed for a year and a half. He also thought about himself making a sacrifice to save thousands of soldier's lives. This one fact became the driving factor in Bob's decision. He could not think of himself as being honorable if he refused to make a sacrifice to save other men's lives. He had to take the job or else he could not live with himself.

The men knew Bob had the qualifications needed for this job. In Bob's heart, he also knew he had them. He had a special government clearance in the army, was a veteran and understood the military and the need for secrecy, he was a tool and die maker, tool designer, and tool engineer. He had also managed the building of tools at his company and at other tool and die shops. Bob understood every step in producing tools and dies for manufacturing parts. He knew there was not one other person in his company who had all the qualifications they wanted for this job. Also, there were very few in America who had them, so it would be very difficult for these men to find someone else to do the job.

The men wanted an answer right then. They were not going to give Bob a few days to think it over. One of the things they wanted in the person who was going to do this job was the ability to quickly evaluate a situation, make a decision, and stick with it. Bob was a person who could do that and he made the decision right then and said, "I will do it." His decision was not based on money for it was never mentioned. It certainly was not for fame, because no one would even know what he was doing. Bob based his difficult decision on three things. The first was his love and dedication to his country and to save American soldier's lives. The second was he would do the job in respect of the young soldiers who paid the full price of giving their lives for his country. The third was he had to do it because he could not live with himself if he knowingly and willfully refused to make the sacrifice and other men's lives were lost as a result.

When Bob said he would accept the job the men pulled out a detailed contract, which included all of the warnings of breaking the secrecy of the job. He was surprised that they already had his name on the contract. He was also surprised to see that the government intelligence had already checked him out for the high-level secrecy and he had

34

passed it. Bob believed that somehow, they must have believed he would accept the job to have already made the contract out with his name on it. He knew the seriousness of signing the contract but, even with his concerns, he signed it. The men then explained the details of the secret project to Bob. When he heard the details, he was amazed at what this project could do in saving many soldier's lives. It was almost staggering in his mind how some person came up with such a good idea and Bob felt it was an honor to be asked to be an engineer on building it.

He also saw how massive the project was and how it had to be a secret to save lives. The agents told Bob that a contact person would be calling him with a special code giving him directions on where they wanted him to go to start on the project. They also told him of a person he could contact for airplane tickets, car rentals, hotels, and cash that he needed for his travels. Bob was to just tell the person what he needed and they would get it for him with no questions asked. Also, there would be no expense report for him to make out.

The next day Bob received his first message from his contact. It was a woman who sounded to be around fifty years old and she immediately gave him the code so he would know she was working with the government agents on the secret project. She told Bob they wanted him to go to a manufacturing business in a distant city the next day and to another business in another city the following day and they were trusting him to do the proper engineering on what they were making.

Bob was somewhat shocked that they wanted him to start traveling so quickly. It had only been about 24 hours since the two agents talked to him and he had not worked out in his mind how he could make the secret trips without his supervisor and wife knowing about them. Bob had to quickly come up with a way to make the trips for the secret project without his supervisor knowing about it. This was totally new territory for Bob as he had never made plans to deceive someone before. Also, it was very serious and he had to do it right or he would be caught and probably lose his job with his company. Thoughts were flashing through Bob's mind like lightening because he had only a few hours to make arrangements to fly out the next morning.

A plan of deceit formed in Bob's mind and he felt it would work. He had some tools and dies being built in Detroit. He would tell his supervisor he was going to Detroit the next day to follow up on his tools and dies and he would be gone two days. He was confident his supervisor would be okay with him doing that. He would fly to Detroit early in the morning and go to one of his tool shops. Then he would hurry back to the airport and fly about 500 miles to another state to do engineering on the secret project. After that he would fly back to Detroit and go to his motel and call Pat and his supervisor from there. They would think he had been in Detroit all day. The next day he would fly to another state and help with the engineering of what they were making for the secret project. After that he would fly back to Detroit and then back home.

Through the years Bob had made many plans for trips to follow up on tools and he was happy with every one of them, but not this one. It contained deceit and Bob hated it, but he had to do it. He was compelled to do it to save lives and he was going to do it with all of the engineering ability God had given him.

After Bob had the plan for his secret travels settled in his mind, he had to get his plane tickets, cash, and car rentals so he went to the person they told him about to get them. The contact was a woman and she got him what he needed with no questions asked.

Bob had formed a plan on how to deceive his supervisor and peers, but he failed to have a plan to keep his wife from knowing about his secret trips. He always told Pat where he was going and why he had to stay overnight. Now Bob could find no way to be truthful with Pat and still keep the secret from her and everyone else.

By this time Bob knew what the project was and how valuable it would be to certain ruthless people if they learned about it. It would be worth millions to them and they would kill a person in an attempt to get it. Bob knew Pat's life would be in danger, just as the agents said, if word got out that he was working on this project. The best way he could protect Pat's life was to make sure she and no one else knew what he was working on.

Bob decided to just tell Pat he was going to be gone for two days and to call a certain phone number if an emergency came up. The next morning, shortly before he left, he did this and Pat immediately wanted to know where he was going.

Bob tried to avoid her question and that made things worse. She demanded to know where he was going. The more Bob tried to avoid telling Pat the worse things got. Finally, it was obvious she knew he was trying to avoid her question and, to say the least, she was very angry. Bob absolutely did not know how to handle the situation and he did not want to lie to her. Finally, he had to walk out the door and go on his trip. He was sick to his stomach when he did this. He could totally understand why Pat was angry. She had a right to be.

After Bob walked out of his house that morning, he knew he had made a mistake in not telling Pat the same thing he told his supervisor. After the encounter he and Pat had that morning Bob knew there was no way he could be a secret engineer for the government on this project without deceiving both his wife and supervisor. He had to work in deceit to save lives, which possibly could include Pat's.

Bob then drove to the airport near his city and boarded a plane and flew to Detroit. He rented a car and drove to the tool and die shop and quickly checked out the progress on the tooling they were building for him. All of their tooling work was progressing as Bob wanted, so he told them he would be back in about two weeks and walked out the door.

As Bob closed the door behind him, he had an odd feeling in his heart or mind. He was about to embark upon a journey in his life that he had never experienced. He was taking his first step in secrecy and deceit that would last for a few years to come. All kinds of thoughts were flashing through his mind as he walked to his rented car. One was, what if his supervisor made a phone call to the business he was just at and found he was there only a short time? He would think Bob would be back home that day, but Bob would not get back for two days. How could he ever explain that without letting him know about his secret job?

There was another thing that entered Bob's mind. He was going to be flying about 500 miles away from where he was to a city where the government officials wanted him. What if he had an accident there in the rented car and that information got back to his wife or supervisor? He would not be able to explain why he was there to either of them. With all of this in Bob's mind, he thought about saving thousands of soldier's lives and determined it was all worth the risk and he was going on with his assignment.

With these thoughts running through Bob's mind, he got into the car and drove back to the Detroit airport, turned in the rental car, and boarded the plane for the city where the government agents wanted him. The flight went very well and arrived right on time. Bob got the car the woman reserved for him and made a long drive through the city to the location the woman agent directed him to. He found the business and, without getting into details, took care of the engineering on the part they were making for the secret project. The company had no idea what they were making their part for and Bob made sure they did not know.

After Bob was satisfied with his engineering at that company he drove back to the airport and flew back to Detroit. He stayed there all night and early the next morning flew to another city and drove to a company that was doing work for the secret project. He spent a big part of the day there doing engineering work on their part. After that he flew back to Detroit and boarded another plane and flew to his home city and got back to his home at about 10 o'clock that evening.

While Bob was doing the engineering at the two companies on the secret project, he was able to put his full concentration on what he was doing. For most of the rest of the time Bob felt sick in his heart because of the way he had walked out on Pat. He even dreaded to return home because he feared she would demand to know where he had been. He knew he could not tell her and things could get worse. She might even think he had been with another woman. When Bob walked into his home late on the second evening after he left, he was shocked at Pat's reaction. She treated him as if he had been at work on a normal day. She did not ask one question about where he had been. Bob did not know how this had happened, but he was very happy it did.

After that trip, Bob knew he could never again walk out on Pat as he previously had. His life had changed and he had determined that his new way of life had to include deceit and he would do it without a feeling of guilt, but as the honorable thing to do. In his new way of living he had to keep up his communications with Pat and his supervisor as much as possible so they would not question his whereabouts. Since Bob could never stay overnight in a city where he traveled to on his secret job he would fly back to a city where a shop was building company tools for him and stay overnight there. From there he could call home or call his supervisor and they would think he had been in that city all day.

Bob started doing this and it seemed to be amazingly successful because his activities were never questioned and his supervisor, wife, and peers never had the slightest idea he was deceiving them. However, he had to be constantly on guard with his words when he was around people, including his peers, wife, and family. He had to make sure he did not slip up and say anything that would cause a question about his activities. It was very important not to mention being in a certain city or location that could cause someone to wonder or ask why he had been there. Also, it was constantly on Bob's mind of the possibility of something happening in a city he had to travel to that could reveal where he was on his secret job.

After three years, Bob's work on the secret project was completed and he was officially dismissed from his secret job. Even though he was relieved that he did not have to continue being deceitful about his activities he did not tell anyone, including his wife, all that had taken place. A few months later Bob and Pat attended a large function at a Bible college near where they lived and the speaker was a military general.

Much to Bob's shock, the general told in detail about the secret project and how effective it was to the military. Over and over he emphasized how many lives were saved as a result of the military having the secret devices. Bob knew he was right in every detail, but he became very angry because the general was telling the secret. He remembered how hard it had been for him to keep the secret and here this general was telling all about it. Little did the general know that a key player of the project was sitting in this group of people and the key player was not happy.

Right after the general finished speaking, Bob almost ran to the platform and shouted at the general, "Sir, I worked on that project and it is a very high secret and here you have told this large group of people all about it. Sir, what you did was wrong!" The general seemed shocked at Bob's strong attack. Being a general, he probably had never been accused of breaking a military secret and here this civilian man was boldly confronting him for doing it. The general very politely spoke back to Bob and said, "The project was declassified two weeks ago and it is no longer a secret." The general seemed to appreciate

Bob's strong attitude of keeping the secrecy and he seemed very pleased to have met a man who worked on the project. Bob did not apologize for attacking the general, but he was very happy to hear that the project was declassified.

The two men then looked each other in the eye for a few seconds. They did not even know each other, but they knew they both had been involved in something that was very important to their country. One man helped build the secret project and the other man was involved in its use. Both of the men had kept the secret for a long time and they parted company with a respect for each other.

For three years Bob wondered if he would ever be able to tell Pat what he had been doing. He also wondered how she would handle it if she found out he had been taking all of the trips and deceiving her. Possibly she would never trust him again. It could have a lasting negative effect on their marriage. If he told her he did it to protect her and to save thousands of lives, she might not even believe it. The story almost sounded phony to Bob and he had lived it. He could hardly blame Pat if she thought it was all a lie.

Now things were different. What a blessing it was for Pat to have heard the general tell about the project. He even bragged about its value to the military and how many lives were saved as a result. As they were walking to their car after the meeting, Bob thought, "It is time to tell Pat what I have been doing. Yes, there will never be a better time than right now." After they drove down the road a few miles, Bob said, "Pat, the general had an interesting talk this evening." Before Bob could say another word, Pat said, "Yes, it was very interesting to hear how that thing helped save so many lives."

It was difficult, but Bob said, "I have secretly been very involved in that project for the last three years. I had to keep the secret from everyone including you. You are the first one I have told about this. Pat, I even had to have a very high government secret clearance for the job. I did this work because of my love for America and to save thousands of soldier's lives." Bob hesitated a few seconds and then said, "Pat, I have been deceiving you about what I have been doing for three years. Many of my trips in the last three years have been to work on this project. I wanted so badly to tell you, but I just could not." Then he told Pat everything he had been doing and how he had deceived her many times.

After hearing Bob's story, Pat sat there in her seat looking angry and in shock. Bob deeply hoped she would understand, but he still did not know how she would take it. After about five minutes Pat said, "Bob, I am glad you did it. I totally understand why you did not tell me. I am happy about what you did for our country." Hearing this was like having a great weight lifted from Bob's shoulders. He was very joyful as he said "For the past three years I was hoping you would feel this way. I am glad it is over. It has been very difficult and I lived with a guilt feeling because I was deceiving you. Yes, I am glad it is over." After that, Bob and Pat never discussed his secrecy and deceit again. Also, Bob's children did not know their father had been a secret engineer for the government until Bob was in his eighties.

Bob's secret life was very difficult for him, and yet so important that the secret was kept in order to save lives. This was during war time and secrecy and deception during most wars has been a high priority. Being able to know an enemies' plans before they put them into action has been the goal of most armies in the world. For years armies had watchmen that they sent out or had on towers to see when an enemy was coming. They did this so that their side could be ready and know when and from what direction they were coming. We see from Ezekiel 3:17 that God had watchmen to warn the people of their sin.

Ezekiel 3:17 (NIV) ***"Son of man, <u>I have made you a watchman</u> for the people of Israel; so hear the word I speak and <u>give them warning from me</u>.***

Bob was involved in this, and the way they found out information on what the enemy was doing was a top secret, just like it has been through many wars of the past. When Bob signed the government document it was the same as if he volunteered to be in the military. He was heavily involved in the war even though he did not wear a uniform or carry a gun and no one knew it other than the government agents who contacted him and the woman agent who called him. Also, the company woman who gave him his plane tickets, car rentals, and travel expenses probably knew he was a secret engineer for the government, but she did not know what he was working on.

Bob hated his deceit, but it seemed strange that he did not feel convicted by the Holy Spirit that he was sinning or God's disapproval on what he was doing. His deception was not for himself, but for his country and fellow soldiers. Was this all in God's plan to save the lives of many American soldiers? It is impossible to answer this question, but Bob knows this, "If it was in God's plan to save these lives, it was very successful and I would do it again!!"

1977 Front- Bob, Pat, Tanya McCauley Back- Tony and Mike

Chapter 7
Give It All to Me

By the time Bob was 35 years old and Jim 33, both brothers had made a total commitment of their life to Jesus Christ and wanted His will in everything they did. God had lovingly dealt with each brother and brought them to the place that they wanted God's will in their lives more than they wanted life itself. They both had committed their life to the Lord as a living sacrifice according to Romans 12:1 and had a deep desire to live a holy life according to Hebrews 12:14.

Romans 12:1 (NIV) *Therefore, I urge you, brothers and sisters, in view of God's mercy, to offer your bodies as a living sacrifice, holy and pleasing to God, this is your true and proper worship.*

Hebrews 12:14 (NIV) *Make every effort to live in peace with everyone and to be holy; without holiness no one will see the Lord.*

God had plans for Bob and Jim, but His plans required that they live holy lives and also live a life of death to self. The brothers often discussed being a living sacrifice to God. This meant that their life was to be totally obedient to God in everything. They wanted to live as if they were dead to their desires and were living totally for what He wanted. It was also evident to them that God wanted everyone to live a holy life. This meant to reject sin in every form and to have nothing to do with it. The brothers' decision on these two points would stay with them the rest of their life, and it would have a major effect on how God used them in the years to come. When the brothers made the decision to live according to Romans 12:1 and Hebrews 12:14 their goal changed from getting wealth to being a living sacrifice for Jesus Christ.

They were quite wealthy at the time, and had been very successful in meeting the goals they had when they were in their teen years. As was said above, Jim and Mary were on their way to becoming millionaires and they owned a lot of very good farm land and had a lovely home. He was the largest pork producer in the area and had a job in skilled trades with General Motors. God had blessed Bob on his engineering job and he was a senior engineer for G.M. He and Pat also had two farms, a backhoe business, money in the bank, and G.M. stock. They too were quite wealthy at that time.

When they came to the place of wanting to be a holy living sacrifice to God, He started to direct them to quit their jobs, sell out, and follow Him, much like Jesus told the ruler in Luke 18:18-22.

Luke 18:18-22 (NIV)[18]*A certain ruler asked him, "Good teacher, what must I do to inherit eternal life?"* [19]*"Why do you call me good?" Jesus answered. "No one is good—except God alone.* [20]*You know the commandments: 'You shall not commit adultery, you shall not murder, you shall not steal, you shall not give false testimony, honor your father and mother.'"* [21]*"All these I have kept since I was a boy," he said.* [22]*When Jesus heard this, he said to him, "You still lack one thing. Sell everything you have and give to the poor, and you will have treasure in heaven. Then come, follow me."*

Jesus told the ruler to sell everything and give the money to the poor and follow Him. When the ruler heard this, he refused to do it and walked away sad. He was tested and failed. Are we ever tested in like manner today as the ruler was? The answer is, "Yes we are." Sometimes He wants people to do what Jesus told the ruler to do. Even Jesus was tested before he went into His ministry.

Matthew 4:1 (NIV) *Then Jesus was led by the Spirit into the wilderness to be __tempted__ by the devil.* (Note: The Greek word for tempted can also be used for tested)

Other Scriptures below on being tested:

Luke 8:13 (NIV) *Those on the rocky ground are the ones who receive the word with joy when they hear it, but they have no root. They believe for a while, but in the time of __testing__ they fall away.*

Acts 20:19 (NIV) *I served the Lord with great humility and with tears and in the midst of severe __testing__ by the plots of my Jewish opponents.*

James 1:3 (NIV) *because you know that the __testing__ of your faith produces perseverance.*

Hebrews 11:17 (NIV) *By faith Abraham, when God __tested__ him, offered Isaac as a sacrifice. He who had embraced the promises was about to sacrifice his one and only son,*

Nearly two thousand years have passed since the ruler was tested and today, he probably wishes with all of his heart that he had obeyed Jesus and followed Him. His money means nothing to him today and most likely he suffers in Hell for eternity. It is too late for him to reverse his decision. To have God's plans come about in his life required his obedience and he refused.

1 Peter 1:7 (KJV) *That the trial of your faith, being much more precious than of gold that perisheth, though it be tried with fire, might be found unto praise and honor and glory at the appearing of Jesus Christ:*

The brothers had committed their life as a living sacrifice to God according to Romans 12:1, but that was going to be tested. The results of the test would determine if they would fit into God's plans for their future.

In the mist of the brothers driving themselves hard to make a good life for their families and themselves, they both heard the Lord speak to them as Jesus did the ruler. The brothers then had to make a choice. They could obey God or they could do exactly what the ruler did. It had been easy for them to serve the Lord in the beginning of their commitment to Him because nothing much was required from them on their part. Now it was different.

Throughout the Bible we see how God gave men and women a free will to either obey or reject His will and commandments. Obedience to God is the key factor in determining if God's plans for a person will come about. In Exodus 19:3-6 we see how God said He carried the Israelites on the wings of eagles out of Egypt and how He would bless them if they obeyed Him.

Exodus 19:3–6 (NIV) *³Then Moses went up to God, and the LORD called to him from the mountain and said, "This is what you are to say to the descendants of Jacob and what you are to tell the people of Israel: ⁴'You yourselves have seen what I did to Egypt, and how I carried you on eagles' wings and brought you to myself. ⁵Now if you obey me fully and keep my covenant, then out of all nations you will be my treasured possession. Although the whole earth is mine, ⁶you will be for me a kingdom of priests and a holy nation.' These are the words you are to speak to the Israelites."*

In verse five we see the conditions for the blessings, "If you obey me fully and keep my covenant---. "Yes, God had good plans for the Israelites, but they refused to go into the Promised Land that God had for them. God counted this as sin and all of them over twenty, except

Caleb and Joshua, died in the wilderness and never saw the wonderful plans God had for them. The Israelite's disobedience became a great tragedy for them that they probably later greatly regretted.

Both brothers, at nearly the same time and totally separate from each other, fully decided to obey God and do exactly what He told them to do. They knew their decision would cost then nearly everything they loved very much and had worked so hard for, but they would do it anyway. Each brother, on their own, then started the process of selling out and quitting their jobs. The brothers had passed this one test, but there would be many more to come. We see in James chapter one that we will face many kinds of trials and tests.

James 1:2-3 (NIV) *²Consider it pure joy, my brothers and sisters, whenever you face trials of many kinds, ³ because you know that the testing of your faith produces perseverance.*

Little did the brothers know they would later face many more trials and tests as Satan did everything he could to cause them to give up and turn back from their original decision to obey God. These tests would include facing death, sickness, witch doctors trying to kill them, separation from their children, living in terrible conditions, and many others.

Bob prayed about when and how to turn in his resignation from his job. He wanted to do it in a way that was honorable, which would mean giving them time to find a replacement and for him to have time to train the new engineer. As a result, he resigned, but said he would not leave for four months and would train his replacement. When he resigned his supervisor asked why he was doing this. Bob told him about God's call upon his life and that he would be going to Africa as a missionary.

Bob's supervisor said he had heard of God's call upon a person's life and he believed it, but it had never happened to him. He went on to say he had planned to promote Bob to be the top engineer over one of their G.M. plants. This would have been a tremendous promotion and increase in salary for Bob and it would have put him in a high position with his company. This was another test and Bob, at the time, could have turned his back on God's plan for his life and accepted the position. Rather, Bob said, "Thank you for considering me for such a high position, but I cannot take it because I must go to Africa as God has called me to." The supervisor said, "I understand your position and I did not think you would change your mind and take the job."

After that the supervisor asked Bob if he knew of any person they could hire for his replacement and Bob recommended a man. They hired that man and Bob worked with him for the rest of his time at the company.

Bob's department had a special send off for him and everyone gave him their best wishes for his new journey in life and they gave him a very nice typewriter as a going away gift. Bob appreciated all of them very much and it was difficult for him to give them his "Good Bye" knowing he would never work with them again. He then took his personal items out of his desk, closed the drawer, picked up his new typewriter, and walked out the door.

As Bob walked towards his car thoughts of the last eighteen and a half years flashed through his mind. He was sad in some ways, but also happy that he had advanced with his company from a stock boy on an assembly line to senior engineer with his company. He knew God had blessed him in being able to do it. Also, Bob knew the company had treated him very good, but that time in his life was over and he was now able to walk out with honor and respect.

Jim and Mary had also made a vow to follow the Lord no matter where it took them. Then at about ten o'clock one cold winter night Jim went out to his hog lot to check the water fountains to make sure the heat lamps were still working okay so the water did not freeze. As Jim was walking through his barn lot, suddenly the brightest light he had ever seen appeared in the sky. When Jim looked up, he saw that it was a huge very bright triangle and he also saw many angels in the sky. He stopped walking and stood there looking up at the scene before him.

Jim was amazed at what he was seeing and also that the extremely bright light did not hurt his eyes. The scene stayed in the sky for several minutes and then a very large arrow or comet appeared in the sky and shot towards Africa. After that the sky turned dark with the many stars shining as they normally did.

Right after the sky went dark Jim thought about this and came to the conclusion that God was confirming to him that he was to sell out and go to Africa. Jim hurried on to check the hog's heat lamps and quickly went back inside their home and told Mary.

Mary believed every word Jim told her and they both agreed this was a confirmation that they were to sell out and go to Swaziland. They started the process of selling out right away, even though they knew it was a tremendous undertaking. Selling their pork operation alone was going to take a huge amount of time and work. They also had to sell their land, except where they lived, their farm equipment, grain, hay, and household furniture etc.

In their process of selling out Jim went to the bank they dealt with and told the owner he was selling out and going to Africa as a missionary. The bank owner was quite shocked and told Jim he was planning on asking him to be his bank manager in another town. He highly respected Jim and his ability to manage money and he wanted him to be in charge of one of his banks. This was an offer that would have made Jim a very respected man in the community and he would have received a very good salary. He knew beyond any doubt that he had a much higher offer and that was from the one who created all of the world. Jim sincerely thanked the bank owner for considering him for the job, but kindly told him he could not take it. The bank owner respected Jim for this and wished him the best in his new work.

Both brothers had been tested in nearly the same way when they made their first step in selling out and quitting their jobs to follow God's call upon their life. Bob had been tested in taking a job as the top engineer of a General Motors plant and Jim had been tested in taking a job as a bank manager. As was said above, Jesus was tested before He went into His ministry and the brothers were also.

What would have happened if the brothers had refused to obey God and leave their homes to serve God? Most certainly they would have missed His plans for their lives. Then, they could have missed God's plans for them to help other people, such as little Zenzele, who was dying alone in the remote area of Africa.

It was fifty years ago when the brothers obeyed the Lord so we can now look back a half of a century and see the results of their obedience. An interesting point we could ask the brothers would be, "Did your obedience have any effect on other people during the past fifty years?" Also, fifty years later we could ask the brothers how they now feel about their decision and would they do it again? We will do this later in the book, but from here on we will look at the results of the brothers' obedience.

Chapter 8
Baptism of The Holy Spirit

John the Baptist made a statement in Mark 1:8 that Jesus would baptize you with the Holy Spirit.

Mark 1:8 (NIV) *I baptize you with water, but he will baptize you with the Holy Spirit."*

Jesus made a statement in Acts 1:8 that you would receive power when the Holy Spirit comes on you.

Acts 1:8 (NIV) *But you will receive power when the Holy Spirit comes on you; and you will be my witnesses in Jerusalem, and in all Judea and Samaria, and to the ends of the earth."*

Luke told about the people being filled with the Holy Spirit on the day of Pentecost in Acts 2:4.

Acts 2:4 (NIV) *All of them were filled with the Holy Spirit and began to speak in other tongues as the Spirit enabled them.*

In Acts 2:17-18 Paul quoted Scripture telling how God would pour out His Spirit in the last days on His servants, which includes both sons and daughters and men and women. Then they would prophesy, see visions, and have dreams given to them by the Holy Spirit.

Acts 2:17 (NIV) *"'In the last days, God says, I will pour out my Spirit on all people. Your sons and daughters will prophesy, your young men will see visions, your old men will dream dreams.*

Acts 2:18 (NIV) *Even on my servants, both men and women, I will pour out my Spirit in those days, and they will prophesy.*

It is in God's plans that Christians be baptized in the Holy Spirit. This gives His servants a power to live in the Holy Spirit and be powerful witnesses for Him in everything they do. Miracles and deliverances will happen that will astonish the world and Satan's works will be destroyed. Demons will be cast out and thousands of people will be set free from the power Satan has over them.

In the book of Acts, we see that God's servants had a power to witness far beyond what they had on their own and He wants this for us today. He wants the book of Acts to continue in our lives. God's plans for

Bob and Jim included them serving Him with this power! When the brothers became Christians, they knew very little about the baptism of the Holy Spirit and the power that came with it because it was not taught in their church. However, God changed that before He took them deeper into what He wanted for their lives. When they both came to the place of totally dedicating their lives and everything they had to Him, He brought about the circumstances to give them the power they would need in being His witnesses.

One of Jim's friends invited him to go to a weekend of Lay Witnessing Meetings with him. This was to be a series of meetings at a church where men would give their testimonies of becoming a Christian and living for God. Jim agreed to go and on the given date the two drove to a neighboring state and attended the meetings. During one of the meetings a man talked about the baptism of the Holy Spirit and he gave his personal testimony of being filled with the Holy Spirit. He also gave scriptures to support what he was saying. Jim had never heard about this, but he believed what the man was saying. When the man finished talking he asked if anyone wanted to receive the baptism of the Holy Spirit and Jim immediately held up his hand. The man asked Jim to come forward.

When Jim got up front the man very softly laid his hands on him and asked the Lord to baptize him in the Holy Spirit. Immediately Jim felt the presence of the Holy Spirit come upon him in a way he had never experienced. Immediately he started to pray and praise God in a language he did not know. He did however know he had just received the baptism of the Holy Spirit and it was extremely wonderful and a very joyful experience. His love and desire for the Lord's will in his life intensified many times over. All Jim wanted at that time was to love and serve God with everything he had and possessed.

The first thing Jim did after returning home was to make the twelve mile drive through the country to his brother's farm house and tell him about the baptism of the Holy Spirit. When he got there he told Bob and Pat the details of what happened on the Lay Witnessing trip. Bob had never seen his brother so happy and excited about anything in his life. Jim was always in a hurry and after giving the details of his experience of the baptism of the Holy Spirit, he said, "I have to go." and he walked out the door.

Bob sat there thinking about how excited Jim was and that he had never seen him like this before. After thinking about this for a few minutes Bob got up, walked up the stairs, and went into a bed room that they only used for guests. He knelt down at a chair and simply said, "God, I would like to have what You gave Jim." Bob then opened his mouth to pray some more about this, but rather than the words coming out in English they came out in a language Bob did not know. He immediately felt an exuberant flow of joy as he spoke the words. It was a joy and love for God and His Son Jesus Christ that he had never experienced or knew was possible.

As Bob continued to speak in this new language he realized he did not understand the words, but he knew what he was saying. He was praising God in a way he had never done or heard anyone else do. The flow of words went on and on praising God for His greatness in many different areas, such as His creation of the universe and for His love that caused Him to send His Son to die for our sins. This praise went from one subject to another for about an hour and then it stopped and Bob heard Pat calling up the stairs that supper was ready

After supper Bob went back upstairs and into the same bedroom and knelt down again and started praising God. Bob knew the Holy Spirit was leading him because he was amazed at there being so many different areas in which he could praise God and His Son Jesus Christ. This praise went on for another three hours and then it stopped and he went back downstairs and got ready for bed. The next morning Bob found that he could start or stop praying in the Holy Spirit as he wished. He could and did easily go from praying in English or in the Holy Spirit and he was in full control of it.

The amazing thing was, neither of the brothers went to a Pentecostal Church or had friends who did. Their pastors and those in leadership thought this was only for the early church, so it never entered the brothers' minds that being baptized in the Holy Spirit was for today. Only after Jim heard the man at the lay witnessing meeting talk about the baptism of the Holy Spirit did either brother know Christians could have this power and blessing in the time they lived in.

After both brothers were baptized in the Holy Spirit the Lord started to teach them how to walk and live in the Holy Spirit. One very important thing was hearing the still small voice of the Holy Spirit. There would be times in the brothers' future when it would be critical that they heard the still small voice of the Holy Spirit. We see in 1 Kings 19:11-13 that Elijah heard it.

1 Kings 19:11-13 (KJV) *And he said, Go forth, and stand upon the mount before the LORD. And, behold, the LORD passed by, and a great and strong wind rent the mountains, and brake in pieces the rocks before the LORD; but the LORD was not in the wind: and after the wind an earthquake; but the LORD was not in the earthquake: ¹²And after the earthquake a fire; but the LORD was not in the fire: and after the fire a still small voice. ¹³And it was so, when Elijah heard it, that he wrapped his face in his mantle, and went out, and stood in the entering in of the cave. And, behold, there came a voice unto him, and said, What doest thou here, Elijah?*

God directed the brothers many times through the still small voice of the Holy Spirit. There were other times when Jim would have a very vivid dream that was so unusual that he wondered if the Holy Spirit had given it to him. He would tell Bob about it and, if it was of the Holy Spirit, He would give Bob the meaning of it. Always it was a personal direction for the brothers in what God wanted them to do. The brothers spent a lot of time praying together and the Holy Spirit used the spiritual gifts of tongues and interpretation, prophecy, knowledge, wisdom, healings, and power to cast out evil spirits in their ministry. For God's plans to come about in their lives, it was very important that they live and function in the power of the Holy Spirit.

Chapter 9
Jim Was Dying

While Jim and Mary were in the process of selling out, Jim woke up one morning with a terrible pain just below his ribs. The pain was so bad that he was delirious and felt like he had been shot in that area. Mary rushed him to the hospital and they put him in intensive care. After some tests they found that Jim had acute pancreatitis.

When the doctor told Mary and Jim, they remembered this was what Jim and Bob's mother died from. She only lived twenty-four hours after she was taken to the hospital in the same condition as Jim was in. The doctor did not give Mary or Jim any hope of him recovering. Back then there was little a doctor or hospital could do for this illness, so they had little hope that he would get well. Every hour the pain increased and nothing the doctors or nurses did seemed to help.

The pain became so bad that Jim felt like he was being burned up from the inside and that was close to what was happening. As he lay there in that hospital bed, he thought about what the doctor told them after they did the autopsy on his mother to see why she died. He said a person's pancreas makes an acid strong enough to help them digest food. Their mother's pancreas was making an acid so strong that it burnt through an artery in her stomach and she internally bled to death. Jim knew beyond any doubt that this was happening to him and he was not only in severe pain, but was becoming weaker as the hours passed.

As he was lying in the intensive care bed, he still knew God had called them to sell out and go to Africa. He also could vividly remember his dream of moving to Swaziland and preaching and also seeing the triangle in the sky. Jim still believed it was going to happen, but he could see no way for it to come about. He was lying in a hospital bed in extreme pain and the doctor was not giving him any hope of a recovery. Jim remembered watching his mother as she was having this exact type of pain shortly before she died.

What was happening to Jim and Mary and their call from God to sell out and follow Him? They had obeyed God in every way and had even started the process of selling out. Now Jim was dying. They knew they had not been disobedient in any way and yet they were suddenly faced with what seemed a sure death for Jim.

Jim's pain became so bad he could hardly pray, but he could hear Mary crying as she sat beside his bed. Mary was in terrible grief as she sat there watching her husband suffer so much pain. She knew Jim would want Bob there at that time, but he and Pat were 700 miles away at a mission headquarters in Pennsylvania called Worldwide Evangelization for Christ (WEC).

At about noon Mary made a long-distance phone call to the WEC Mission in Pennsylvania and talked to Bob. She was crying as she told him that Jim was in the hospital with the same thing that their mother died from. She also told Bob that the doctors were not giving Jim any hope of recovering. Bob was extremely shocked and told Mary he would come home and leave right away. He could hardly believe this was happening because he knew God had clearly called Jim and Mary to Africa and now it seemed Jim might not live through the day. It just did not add up and Bob was very confused. Regardless of this he needed to quickly get back to Indiana to be with them and it was a 700-mile drive to get there.

Bob told Pat and the mission staff about Jim's situation and they all prayed for him. Then Bob checked the airlines and bus station to see what was the quickest way to get home. He could not get an airline ticket right away, but he could get a bus that was leaving Philadelphia in about an hour and a half. It would go to Indianapolis, Indiana with only one stop along the way and get there nearly as quickly as if he drove himself. Bob took the bus and Mary picked him up in Indianapolis at 2:00 AM. Sunday morning.

They drove directly to the hospital where Jim was and got there at 3:00 AM and went right to his room. Bob was very alarmed when he saw how ill Jim was. Jim saw Mary and Bob come into the room and tried to talk to Bob, but Bob could not understand him because his voice was so weak. Bob leaned over him and put His ear about two inches from Jim's mouth. Jim asked Bob to take care of Mary and their children. Bob told him he would make sure they were well cared for.

Then he tried to give Bob more directions on what to do with their finances in helping Mary and their children, but his voice became so weak that Bob could not understand him. The one thing Bob knew however was that he wanted to make sure they were taken care of. After that Jim went to sleep. Mary and Bob stayed in the room with him for a while, but at 4:00 AM decided they needed a few hours' sleep themselves. Mary drove them to their home and they got about two hours sleep and then started making phone calls to Christian friends and pastors asking them to pray for Jim. At about 7:00 AM Mary called the hospital and they told her that Jim was still the same. It was Sunday morning and they both decided to each go to their own church and request prayer for Jim.

Both of their churches, as well as several other churches, had special prayer for Jim that Sunday morning. In addition to that many of the Christians they called were praying for Jim. After church Mary and Bob went to see Jim. They were expecting to see him nearly dead because that was how they left him just a few hours before. Instead he was sitting up on the side of the bed with a big grin on his face looking at them as they walked into his room. Bob is sure he and Mary had a startled look on their face as they saw Jim sitting there. It was almost unbelievable. Yes, they did ask many people and several churches to pray for him, but it startled them to see evidence of how God had answered all of the prayers that were sent up for Jim.

Bob and Mary walked on into the room and up to Jim's bed. He looked perfectly healthy with normal color in his face. A few hours before this he had a grayish color that looked like death moving in. Now he was totally back to his normal self, laughing and joking, but also thanking the Lord for his recovery. It was obvious that the Spirit of God had moved on Jim and healed him that morning as the churches and people were praying for him. Just a few hours before this he was so weak that he could hardly speak as he was trying to give Bob directions of what to do after his death. Now he was no longer talking about dying, but back to preparing to go to Africa.

Jim was very surprised at how good he was feeling. It took him a little time to realize that God had healed him. After talking to him a few minutes about how he felt, Mary and Bob told him that many people and churches had prayed for him that morning. Jim, Mary, and Bob all knew God had healed him as people were praying for him.

Jim believes God showed him that he would have died at that time in his life just like his mother did, but God healed him. Today he fully believes God gave him an extended life so Mary and he could obey His plans for their lives.

Not long after this Jim was taken out of intensive care. and put in a normal hospital room. He was in the hospital for a few more days and during that time he signed the papers to sell one of their farms. After he was released from the hospital and had his strength back, he and Mary continued on with their plans to sell all of their farm land except the 48.8-acre farm where they were living. The Lord had given them the word to keep the farm they were living on, but to sell the rest of their land before they went to Africa.

Finally, the day came when they finished selling and they were ready to leave their home in obedience to God's call to go to Africa. Jim and Mary still remember their final farewell to their friends on their farm. Their entire church came and they had an old time bon fire and a picnic. People were all sitting around on bales of straw singing, eating, talking, praying and crying.

By this time Bob and Pat and also Jim and Mary knew from God's direction for each of them that they were to go to Africa with a mission in Pennsylvania called Worldwide Evangelization for Christ (WEC). It was a large non-denominational faith mission with around 1,800 missionaries in about 70 countries. The United States headquarters was located on the north side of Philadelphia near a city called Fort Washington.

The next day Jim and Mary loaded up their pickup with some of their belongings and Mary drove the car with Belinda and Jim drove the truck with Mark and Debbie. They made the 700-mile drive to the WEC headquarters. Bob and Pat were already there and the brothers and their wives started their four months candidate program during the first week of September in 1971.

Was there any victory in Jim's illness for Satan? The answer is a clear, "No there was not." Satan tried to kill him or to discourage them so much that they would stop obeying God's call upon their lives and return to farming. This did not happen! However, God did let Jim and Mary see that Jim would have died at that time, but God healed him. If he would have died, his wealth would have meant nothing to him. He and Mary know that God extended Jim's life so they could serve Him in Africa. Through this experience, their dedication to obeying God became stronger and Satan's attack was defeated.

Jim and Mary were in the process of selling out as God had directed them before Jim became very ill. They were being obedient in every way they could. His sudden illness was not caused by disobedience any more than Job's crisis was caused by sin or disobedience. In Job 1:1 we see that Job was blameless and upright and in Job 2:3-7 we see that Satan told God that Job would curse Him if he (Satan) could afflict him. God had confidence in Job and allowed Satan to do it.

Job 1:1 (NIV) *In the land of Uz there lived a man whose name was Job. This man was blameless and upright; he feared God and shunned evil.*

Job 2:3-7 (NIV) *³Then the LORD said to Satan, "Have you considered my servant Job? There is no one on earth like him; he is blameless and upright, a man who fears God and shuns evil. And he still maintains his integrity, though you incited me against him to ruin him without any reason." ⁴"Skin for skin!" Satan replied. "A man will give all he has for his own life. ⁵But now stretch out your hand and strike his flesh and bones, and he will surely curse you to your face." ⁶The LORD said to Satan, "Very well, then, he is in your hands; but you must spare his life." ⁷So Satan went out from the presence of the LORD and afflicted Job with painful sores from the soles of his feet to the crown of his head.*

Satan then severely afflicted Job and yet he did not curse God.

Job 2:10 (NIV) *He replied, "You are talking like a foolish woman. Shall we accept good from God, and not trouble?" In all this, Job did not sin in what he said.*

Job was severely tested by Satan, but, through it all, he remained true to God. God was very proud of Job and He greatly blessed him after this. Jim and Mary were probably tested by Satan just as Job was and, like Job, they remained true to God through it all. Job's friends accused him of being in sin because of his troubles. This had to have been hurtful to Job and God made his friends later apologize to him for doing it. Bob and Jim suffered some also as a result of friends accusing them of being in sin when a crisis came in their lives.

I want to say this and make it very clear. If a Christian gets sick or has a crisis, it does not mean they are in sin or disobedient!

Chapter 10
Burnt their Bridges

There was an old saying, "They burnt their bridges behind them." This was originally a term and also an action used by different armies. Later it became a term used by civilians. It first meant that an army could not retreat because the bridges behind them were gone. It also meant that their enemies could not easily follow them because the bridges across the rivers were destroyed. This term had two meanings for the brothers. One was that they were totally committed to obeying and following God and they would not retreat. The second meaning was they could never go back to things as they were because they no longer existed. They had sold their land, quit their jobs, left their homes, and their old way of life was gone forever.

God's plans for the brothers included testing their obedience to give Him all of the material things they loved, owned, and had worked very hard for years to get. The brothers had to make a willful decision to obey God no matter if it cost them everything they loved and worked for. This test included making it impossible to return to their old way of life. Yes, their bridges were burnt behind them! This included the land they owned, which today would be worth millions. Bob and Jim were both planning to buy more land that would someday greatly increase in value making them worth even more.

Also, both brothers worked for General Motors and they knew that someday they would have a very good retirement from the company. On top of that they had given most of their funds to God's work so they had no income and very little money to live on. Were they sad and in grief about this? No, they were not! They had clearly heard God directing them to do this and their total desire was to advance in God's work and retreat was out of the question. In their minds it was impossible.

The Holy Spirit led the brothers to a mission called Worldwide Evangelization for Christ (WEC). It was a faith mission started by an Englishman named CT Studd. He was a top cricket player in England and became very famous in Europe. He accepted Jesus Christ as his Savior in 1880 when he was twenty years old. In 1883 he inherited a huge sum of money from his father. It would have been in the millions by today's standards. Also, in that same year he totally committed his life to serve Jesus Christ. After this he said, "If Jesus Christ be God and died for me, then no sacrifice is too large for me to make for Him."

CT believed God wanted him to do exactly as Jesus told the ruler in Luke 18:18-22 and give all of his wealth to God's work. He obeyed this and he was so wealthy that it took him about five days to give it all away. C.T. Studd had burnt his bridges behind him and God led him on in victory to win thousands to the Lord Jesus Christ in China, India, and Africa. Stud also believed that God would furnish all of his needs according to Philippians 4:19 and he did not have to ask for support. This became a way of life for Studd and God did supply all of his needs.

Philippians 4:19 (NIV) *And my God will meet all your needs according to the riches of his glory in Christ Jesus.*

Bob and Jim, and their wives, were told by the WEC mission staff that they were not allowed to ask for money or make their needs known to get support. They were also told that if God had called them to be missionaries, He would also provide for them. The brothers had never heard of this type of mission policy on funds, but it sounded good to them and they gladly accepted it.

As was said above, WEC had around 1,800 missionaries in about 70 different countries. They had mission headquarters in many different countries with the main one being near London, England. The United States headquarters was near Fort Washington, PA. which is on the north side of Philadelphia.

The mission headquarters was located on a hill called Camp Hill because George Washington and his troops camped there for a time. It was once the sixty-acre estate of a very wealthy family. The main building was an old stone three story house that looked much like an old castle. There were also three other building that were originally part of the estate. They were all located on a circle drive with a very tall rusty unused flag pole in the center of the circle.

WEC had the policy that new missionaries had to live at the mission headquarters for four months as candidates to become missionaries. During that time the candidates attended missionary related classes for four hours every morning and did physical work for four hours every afternoon. Every Friday afternoon they went into the streets and shopping centers witnessing to people about Jesus Christ. All of the candidates ate three meals a day together in a very large dining room. If a family was married with children, they each had their own table. The others could sit and eat where they pleased. Also, each married couple had their own room. If a couple had children, they were given a small apartment.

At the end of the four months the staff voted to either accept or reject the candidates to be missionaries with them. If a candidate was accepted, they could then go to the country where they felt God had called them. On Monday of the first week in September of 1971 the candidate program started with twenty-six candidates attending.

WEC had the policy that a person had to have at least one year of Bible school before they could to be missionaries with them. Most of the candidates were single young people just out of Bible school. There were only four married couples in the group, with the McCauleys being the oldest by far. All of the candidates, except the McCauleys, went directly from high school to Bible school and then to WEC Mission. As a result, they never had a normal job, nor did they have any building or mechanic skills.

Since Jim and Bob had been in the normal labor force for years, they acquired some skills in building, plumbing, electrical, welding, and mechanical work on cars, trucks, and farm equipment. Some of the candidates and staff had old cars that needed repairs and the brothers were able to repair nearly all of them at little or no cost to the owners. Also, there were different building projects that needed done and the brothers were able to lead others on doing them or did the work themselves. As a result the brothers' skills were greatly valued by the WEC staff and candidates.

Chapter 11
God Given Skills

God had plans for the brothers in Africa and they were on their way there. However, God is so multifaceted that He had plans for them to bless people and help in His ministry along the way. God even used His Son this way. Jesus' main goal in coming to earth and being born of a virgin was to be a sacrifice for the sins of the world. However, along the way He healed many people and blessed them in other ways. One was the time when He turned water into wine at the wedding. The host ran out of wine and Jesus helped him out. You probably have a job that God has blessed you with. This might be God's perfect plan for you, at least at this stage in your life. It is also God's plan for you to bless and help people with the skills He has given you.

Both Jim and Bob knew they had skills that most people did not have. But they also knew that the Holy Spirit could show them ways to do some jobs that no one including themselves knew how to do. As we read the Word of God, we see that this was also true so many years ago.

God had a plan for the Israelites to build a tabernacle in which they could worship Him while they were in the wilderness. The Lord knew they did not have the skills to build the tabernacle and the things he wanted in it so He gave special skills to a man named Bezalel.

*<u>Exodus 31:3-5</u> (NIV) **Then the LORD said to Moses, ² "See, I have chosen Bezalel son of Uri, the son of Hur, of the tribe of Judah, ³ and I have filled him with the Spirit of God, with wisdom, with understanding, with knowledge and with all kinds of skills— ⁴ to make artistic designs for work in gold, silver and bronze, ⁵ to cut and set stones, to work in wood, and to engage in all kinds of crafts.***

During the days of Bezalel people did not have the tools to work with gold, silver, bronze, stone, and wood as we have today, yet God gave Bezalel wisdom and knowledge on how to do it with the tools they had. Does God ever give people special skills today as He gave to Bezalel? Yes He does!

While the brothers were at the WEC mission headquarters God gave them special skills, wisdom, and knowledge far above what they normally had. It was like an advanced knowledge came to them on how to do something with the tools they had on hand at the time. Many times, this knowledge came to them right when they needed it and it was beyond what they would have thought about on their own.

The WEC staff were wanting to get some projects done, but there was a lack of funds to do them. Also, with the mission's policy of not making their needs known, they could not write to a church or tell people that they were short of money to do the projects. The staff fully believed God was going to somehow get the projects done even though they had no money. The staff did talk and pray about the projects and the brothers heard about them. After hearing the staff's conversation and prayers an idea came into Jim's mind on how to quickly get enough money to do one project. The idea was so unusual that it had to be God who gave it to him. Jim quickly told the WEC staff how he could get the money and it was right on the property the mission was built on. The staff were amazed and gave him permission to do it.

When the wealthy family, who originally built the estate, put electricity into their very large home and out buildings they ran very large copper wires placed inside of a steel pipe up from the road to a main electrical box on top of Camp Hill. The wires were very large to make sure they always had enough electrical amperage to run their estate. For years the wealthy family used the original wiring for their electricity. Years later the original wiring was outdated and the estate was totally rewired with new wiring. However, the original wires and pipe from the road to the mission main box were left in the ground. The large copper wires were about 300 yards long and buried about one foot deep alongside of the winding driveway.

The idea Jim believed God gave him was to remove all of the old unused wiring and sell it. The price of used copper per pound was very high at the time and there would be several hundred pounds of it just laying underground or in the buildings. Jim dug a few holes alongside of the driveway down to the pipe and cut it into with a hack saw. He pulled all of the old wiring out of the steel pipe and removed all of the old wiring that he could get to, from the buildings. After that he cut the wires into small strips and burnt the insulation off of them. Then he sold the copper and received a very large sum of money, which he gave to the staff to pay for one of the projects. The staff were very impressed how Jim came up with the money, but he gave God the credit for it.

Then there was another project that desperately needed to be done. There was a four-inch diameter steel water pipe that ran underground from the pump house to the water tower. The water pipe had been there since the original house was built and it was rusted out and leaking badly. This was costing the mission a lot of money, but the expense to hire a company to replace the four-inch pipe was to be in the thousands. They would have to buy the pipe and backhoe through the trees and roots of a very wooded area for about 600 feet. Then they would have to lay in the new pipe, hook it up, and bury it. It would not only be very costly, but it would probably kill several of the large trees. Also, the dug-up grounds would look bad for a long time.

When Jim heard about this God gave him a word of knowledge on how quickly to do it for a very low cost and no digging at all through the trees. Jim did some quick calculations and saw that it would easily work, so he immediately told Bob and the WEC staff. WEC had a very qualified man named Lavern Wenner, who was in charge of the mission's maintenance and building programs. Lavern and the WEC staff fully agreed with Jim's idea and gave him permission to do it.

Jim's calculations showed that the four-inch steel pipe was far larger that they needed to supply water to the mission. Also, the calculations showed that a three-inch pipe would give them more water than they would ever need. Jim's plan consisted of disconnecting the four-inch steel pipe at both ends. Then they would push a three-inch diameter plastic pipe through the four-inch diameter steel pipe and reconnect it at both ends.

After purchasing a long coil of three-inch diameter plastic water pipe, Lavern, Jim, and Bob did this work and it worked perfectly, with no water leaks at all. This took a short time and did not disturb the grounds or trees at all, plus it cost a small fraction of the original estimate. The mission had enough money to pay for the plastic pipe and fittings and thanked God for the idea He gave Jim on how to replace the leaking water line at such a low price.

There was also another very urgent project that was going to be very expensive and there was no money for it at the time. The main house was a large three-story building that was heated with steam heat. The very large old furnace had sprung a leak from the water jacket to the fire chamber. As a result, a mist of water was spraying onto the flame as the furnace was burning. This was causing major problems and the mission was faced with replacing the old furnace with a new one before cold weather came. The cost for a new steam furnace was going to be in the thousands and the cost to remove the old one and put in the new one would be extremely high.

Lavern told Bob about this problem a few days after he arrived at the mission. He took Bob to the furnace and turned the water on so he could see the leak. An idea suddenly came into Bob's mind and he told Lavern that he would like to see if he could fix it. Lavern agreed to let Bob see what he could do. The leak was clear to the back side of the combustion compartment, which meant that Bob would have to crawl into the furnace to fully check it out. Both men then made sure everything was properly shut off so that the furnace did not turn on while Bob was inside of it.

The door was just large enough that Bob could crawl through it to be able to see the leak. It was very tight, but Bob was able to get inside of the furnace and look closely at the hole. When he got very close to the hole, he could see that the cast iron had developed a very small hole from the water jacket to the inside of the furnace. The hole was no larger than a pin but it would let enough water spray onto the fire to cause the problems.

Bob believed he could drill a hole in the cast iron and tap it for a one quarter inch diameter brass plug and it would stop the leak. Then they would have time to test it before the cold weather came. The heating chamber was very tight for Bob and it was more difficult to crawl back out than it was to get in. He slowly tried to make every move count for getting out and he finally made it. Bob told Lavern that he felt he could fix the leak and how he planned to do it. Lavern agreed to let him try it.

Then Bob went to a hardware store and purchased a small right-angle electric drill, drill bits, pipe tap, and brass plug that he would need. After that he went back to the mission, crawled back into the furnace with the electric drill and the parts he purchased to plug the hole. With Lavern standing on the outside to assist Bob in anything he needed, Bob drilled, tapped and firmly screwed the brass plug in place. After that Lavern turned on the water to full pressure while Bob was looking through the open door to see if he saw any leakage. Bob was very happy that there was no sign of a leak or dampness around the plug. Then they fired up the furnace and let it get up to heat and there was still no sign of a leak. Lavern and the staff were very happy about this and thanked God for it.

For years the mission wanted to paint and repair the pulley of the rusted flag pole in the center of the circle drive. At one time they got an estimate to bring in a bucket truck that was large enough to lift a person to the top of the forty-foot-high pole so they could do the work. The estimate was about one thousand dollars and the mission staff felt they could not justify spending that much money on the pole.

When Jim and Bob first saw the pole, they thought it looked ugly and out of place compared to the rest of the buildings. They also thought it would look so nice if it was painted and had the American flag flying at the top. God gave them an idea on how they could repair the pulley and paint the pole with the tools they had on hand. As a result, the brothers asked if they could do the work themselves and the staff gave them permission to do it.

There were two twenty-foot ladders on the mission station. The brothers took one ladder and stood it on end and tied it tightly top and bottom to the pole. Then they took the second ladder and stood it against the pole and loosely tied the top rung to the pole so that the ladder could be lifted up and the top not fall away from the pole. Then they climbed the lower ladder lifting the top ladder up as they did. When they got to the top of the lower ladder, they tied the bottom of the top ladder to it. Both ladders were now end for end and tied securely to the pole so that the brothers could easily climb to the top and repair the pulley and put a rope through it.

They did this and painted the pole as they came down. All of this work only took about four hours and the flag pole was ready to use after the paint dried. The next day, with all of the staff present they raised a new American flag to the top and it immediately spread out and waved with the wind as the staff sang the National Anthem.

Again, God gave the brothers the idea of how to do something with the materials they had on hand and at nearly no cost to the mission. The only cost they had was for the paint, rope, and flag. However, there was something more major than fixing things and saving money that God had called the brothers to leave their old life to do. It was to save souls from an eternity in Hell.

God did give the brothers special skills, but there is a skill He gives every person who accepts Jesus Christ as their Savior and are Born-Again. It is the skill to win people to Jesus Christ! It takes no Bible school and actually little Bible knowledge. If a person knows enough to accept Christ as their Savior, they know enough to win someone else to Him. Many within Christianity have made this so complicated that few are doing it. Many believe you have to be someone special like a pastor to be a witness for Jesus Christ, but this is not so.

Jim had no Bible school when he first went to WEC mission yet God greatly used him there. As was said above, every Friday afternoon the candidates went into the streets and shopping centers to talk to people about the Lord Jesus Christ. One Friday afternoon Jim and another missionary, whom I will call Joe, went into a large shopping center near the mission to talk to people about the Lord. Before the two men left the mission headquarters, they prayed that God would lead them to the right people to talk to. When they got to the mall, they started walking through it trusting God to lead them to the right person. Jim saw a very dignified looking man dressed in a very nice suit and he felt he should talk to him. Jim and Joe then walked to the man in the suit and Jim asked him if he could talk to him about the Lord. The two men were pleased to hear him say that they could.

Jim gave the man some details about himself and the man told Jim he had retired from working for the CIA and had traveled to many countries in the world. He even gave many details of his travels and Jim was impressed with him. Then Jim gave him details about Jesus Christ and God's plan of Salvation. The retired CIA man listened closely and was very interested in what Jim was saying. Jim asked him if he wanted to accept Jesus Christ as his Savior and the man said, "Yes I do." Jim then led the man in the "Sinner's Prayer." After that Jim got the man's address and phone number and he also gave the man his.

The retired CIA man was so excited about his Christianity that he went to Bible school and then became a pastor. Later Jim went on to Africa and they never saw each other again, but became very close friends as they corresponded with each other. Even though Jim did not have one day in Bible school God used him to completely change the life and eternal destination of the retired CIA man.

Bob and another young man, whom I will call Allen, from New Zealand had never met until one Friday morning when a group of candidates were getting ready to go into the streets of Philadelphia witnessing for Christ. The candidate leader, Dwayne Olsen, assigned Bob and Allen to go together. They got in Bob's car and made a 40-minute drive to the center of the city and found a place to park. After that they started walking down the street trusting God to lead them to the right person.

After walking about two blocks they came to an open area near the center of the city that looked much like a small park. It had several park benches among some small trees surrounded by the very tall majestic buildings. Bob and Allen saw an elderly man dressed in a gray suit and white shirt with no tie. He was reading a newspaper and there was not one other person in the area. Bob felt they should talk to the man so he and Allen walked to him. Allen then asked the old man if they could talk to him. The man agreed and Allen started telling him about God and Jesus Christ.

The elderly man listened for a short time and then stopped Allen and said, "You boys are wasting your time on me. You see, I have committed the unpardonable sin against the Holy Ghost and can never be forgiven. I am now 84 years old and will soon die and be in Hell forever. You boys may as well go talk to someone else." Bob spoke up and said, "What did you do to sin against the Holy Ghost?" The old man answered and said, "I committed adultery and that is the sin against the Holy Ghost."

Very quickly Bob said, "That is not the sin against the Holy Ghost and God will forgive it." He started to pull a small Bible out of his pocket to show him that this sin could be forgiven, but before he did the old man pulled a Bible out of a top pocket of his suit jacket. Bob then asked the old man if he could use his Bible and the old man gave it to him. Bob used the Scriptures to show the old man how God would forgive the sin of adultery.

After hearing the Scriptures and Bob explain God's forgiveness the old man said, "You mean I can be forgiven for this sin?" Bob answered, "Yes you can." Almost instantly the old man dropped his face between his hands and started to pray and ask God to forgive him for his sins. He continued to pray and cry for several minutes as Bob and Allen stood there silently praying with him. Bob noticed that the cement below the old man's face became a puddle of tears from his crying. After a while the old man started to laugh and then he would cry for a bit and then laugh again. This time it was crying and laughing for joy because he knew God had forgiven him.

Bob and Allen did not say a word during that time and the old man stood to his feet and shook the two men's hands and hugged them. He thanked them over and over for telling him that he could be forgiven. Then he said something very startling, "Now I can go home and see my daughter. I have not seen her for eighteen years. Bob and Allen did not know what he meant by that, but they both felt it was best not to ask! After this they said good bye to the old man and never saw him again. Then they walked back to the car and made the 40-minute drive through the city back to the mission headquarters.

Bob and Allen were very happy about how God brought them together that day to lead the old man to Christ. It was like God had a plan to let the old man know he could be forgiven and He used them to do it even though they had never seen each other before that day. It was somewhat strange for Bob and Allen to know that Bob grew up 700 miles away from where the old man was sitting reading his newspaper and Allen grew up across the ocean thousands of miles away. It was obvious that God brought these three men together so one of them could be Born-Again and be in Heaven for eternity. Right after they got back to the mission headquarters Allen went on his way to follow God's direction for him and Bob did the same and they never saw or heard from each other again.

Winning these two men to Jesus Christ was the first fruits of the brothers' labor for the Lord after they left everything and followed the leading of the Holy Spirit to WEC mission. Yes, this was exciting and encouraging to them, but they had no way of knowing that they would be involved in winning thousands more to Jesus Christ in the years to follow.

Chapter 12
Holy Spirit Direction

Bob and Jim and their wives attended nearly all of the WEC staff prayer meetings. During every prayer meeting they prayed that God would send a pilot to Liberia, West Africa because their pilot had been killed in a jungle crash. They did not send out word to churches that they needed a pilot because they did not make their needs known. They were just praying that God would send them the right pilot. They had already bought a new Maule Rocket plane and it was in Liberia, but they needed a pilot to fly it. At the time a man named Bob Gilbert was flying the plane until WEC got a permanent pilot.

Bob McCauley would always pray with the staff that God would send them a pilot even though he was one. He loved to fly, but God had not directed him to be their pilot and he was not going to volunteer unless God spoke to him to do it. From the time Bob was a child he had a desire to be a pilot. He started flying when he was 18 years old and then he and his cousin, Gene, bought their first airplane, which was a 1939 Aeronca L3.1. Flying was the only hobby Bob had and through the years he had owned part interest in planes and had a lot of experience in rebuilding aircraft engines and air-frames.

When the mission staff heard about Bob's flying experience, they felt God had answered their prayer and sent them a pilot. The WEC staff then officially asked Bob to be their pilot. Bob wanted to say he would do it, but he did not agree to it. He said, "I love to fly and would be happy to do it, but God has not directed me to be your pilot and I don't want to agree to it because it might not be God's will for me."

Bob knew he had very good experience in flying and working on planes that would be needed in jungle flying. He had hundreds of hours doing work on aircraft engines and air-frames plus he had a lot of experience in flying in and out of very short farm fields. He even had a lot of experience in doing loops, stalls, spins, and slow flight etc. to give him a good feel for flying. The WEC staff seemed to feel for sure that Bob was to be their pilot, but he continued to refuse because God had not directed him to do it.

Near the end of the four months of candidate classes God woke Bob up from a sound sleep at 3:00 in the morning. He knew God was going to speak to him so he got out of bed and knelt down and said, "What is it

Lord?" The Holy Spirit then spoke to him in the still small voice and said, "Go to Liberia and preach My Word first and fly the plane second." Bob was thrilled with this word and the next morning he told the WEC staff about what had happened and they gladly agreed that he should be their pilot. God had given Bob the desire of his heart from the time he was a child and now he would be a missionary pilot flying in Africa.

Then God spoke to Jim in a similar way and told him that he and Mary were to put going to Swaziland on hold and go to Liberia first. However, they did not know what God wanted them to do in Liberia. Jim and Mary told the WEC staff about this and they were delighted. The director then wrote a letter to Wesley Bell, who was the field leader in Liberia, and told him that Bob and Pat and also Jim and Mary McCauley were coming to Liberia. Bob was a pilot and would replace their pilot who was killed. Pat was a licensed school teacher and she and Mary could teach in their mission schools.

The mission director also told Wesley about Bob and Jim's building and mechanical skills. Wesley was delighted because he was planning on starting a large building project and he desperately needed a good builder to lead it. After hearing about Jim coming to Liberia, Wesley felt God had answered his prayers and was sending Jim there to lead the project. This was God's plans for Jim, as well as for Wesley, so Jim and Mary were thrilled that God was going to use Jim's skills in Liberia.

WEC had the policy that every missionary had to have two semesters of Bible school before they became missionaries. Bob and Pat already had their Bible school before they came to WEC so they could go to Liberia right away; however, it would be six months before Jim and Mary could go to Liberia because they needed to finish their Bible school. This information was sent to Wesley and he agreed that if Jim and Mary arrived there in six months it would fit well into his plan.

Bob and Pat went on to Liberia, but they left Mike and Tony with family friends David and Mary Ann Long so they could finish their school year before they also came to Liberia. It was extremely difficult to leave their sons behind, but they knew they would see them shortly after the school year had ended. Jim and Mary continued living at the WEC headquarters and going to Bible school from there.

Chapter 13
God's Plan Foiled

Is it possible for one person's disobedience to foil God's plans for other people? We could say, "Is it possible for a group of disobedient people to cause God's plans for righteous people to not come about? As was said above, the brothers' grandparents were godly people. One day, when Jimmy was eight years old, he and his Grandma McCauley were standing under a large maple tree in the boys' front yard. Suddenly Grandma said, "Jimmy, when God judges a nation the righteous people also suffer." This statement was so out of context from what they were talking about that Jim remembers it clearly today. It was like Grandma McCauley was giving him a word of prophecy. We see from Ezekiel 21:1-4 that the righteous can suffer because of the wicked.

Ezekiel 21:1-4 **(NIV)** *The word of the LORD came to me: ²"Son of man, set your face against Jerusalem and preach against the sanctuary. Prophesy against the land of Israel ³and say to her: 'This is what the LORD says: I am against you. I will draw my sword from its sheath and cut off from you both the righteous and the wicked. ⁴Because I am going to cut off the righteous and the wicked, my sword will be unsheathed against everyone from south to north.*

We know from Jeremiah 29:11 that God had plans for all of Israel and they were good. However, God's plans for the righteous were foiled or did not come about because of the disobedience of many. The brothers were about to experience how one person's disobedience foiled God's plans for Jim and another couple.

When Bob and Pat arrived in Liberia they were looking forward to Jim and Mary joining them in six months after their Bible school was finished. The field leader, Wesley Bell, and his wife Molly were desperately needing Jim and Mary to be there at that time so Jim could lead their large building project. Molly wanted to teach the Liberian women how to sew and a large sum of money had been given to build a school and dorms for the students. Molly had already set a date to start the classes, so it was very important to get the work done before that. Also, several hand operated sewing machines had been given to use in the classes and they would be given to the women when they graduated. Molly felt that if the women could learn how to make clothes it would give them a way to make money to help support their families. The Liberian women were very excited about attending the classes on the given date and Molly was also excited about it.

Wesley was very busy working as the mission leader and he did not have time to spend every day leading the building project, which would take several months to build. As a result, he needed a man with building skills to be there full time leading the project. He and Molly had prayed about this and they believed Jim was that man so they desperately wanted him there in six months. Everything seemed to be in place for the school to get started on the planned date, so the Bells were feeling very good about it.

Shortly before Jim and Mary finished their two semesters of Bible school the director of WEC mission headquarters in America received a letter from a WEC missionary in Liberia. The director was somewhat shocked when he read it because it said that Jim had to get linguistics training before he came to Liberia and it also suggested that he get the training from a linguistics school in Canada. However, they were not requiring this of Mary.

The letter sounded like this was the decision of the entire WEC mission field in Liberia. Many of the home staff were confused because never before had a WEC missionary been required to have linguistics, but now they were requiring it. Even though they were confused, the director felt they had to require this of Jim before they allowed him to go to Liberia.

When Jim and Mary were informed of the linguistics requirement they were devastated. Jim knew he would not be involved in Bible translation because he was going to Liberia to head up the building project and to be in Liberia for only a short time before they went on to Swaziland. He and Mary were ultra-confused and talked to the WEC leadership in America about this, but they said that it was the request of the mission field in Liberia so they had to obey it.

The letter about Jim arrived at the WEC headquarters in America at about the same time Wesley and Molly received a very shocking letter. It was from a medical clinic in Ireland saying that Molly had cancer and needed to have medical treatment immediately. They were from Ireland and during their last visit back home Molly had a physical exam. They receive no word from the clinic that she had any problems so they returned to Liberia. However, the test revealed that Molly had cancer. Rather than calling her on the phone while they were still in Ireland, the clinic sent a letter to Liberia telling the results. Also, they put a surface mail stamp on the letter rather than an airmail stamp. The letter then went by ship to Liberia and this took many months.

After receiving the letter, Wesley and Molly immediately knew they had to get back to Ireland as quickly as possible for Molly's cancer treatment. Also, they feared that the cancer might have spread to other parts of her body because many months had passed and the letter said she should have immediate treatment.

Wesley had started the large building project thinking Jim and Mary would be there within a few days and Jim could take over the project. On the planned date, Jim and Mary did not arrive and there was no way to communicate with them to see what happened. Wesley and Molly decided to delay returning to Ireland until they got there. They waited three weeks and Jim and Mary never showed up so, Wesley had to hire a Liberian man to lead the workers and buy the materials. He also had to give the man all of the funds he had to build the project. Wesley did not feel good about this because he was concerned about the man's ability to lead the project and about his honesty in the way he used the money. However, he gave the money to the man and he and Molly flew back to Ireland.

After their Bible school was finished, Jim and Mary had to make a hard decision as what to do about the linguistic training. They could see no reason for the training, but also knew God wanted them to go to Liberia before they went to Swaziland. They finally decided that they had no choice, Jim had to go to Canada and get the training. They knew it would be very difficult, complicated, and expensive for their children to leave America and get one year of schooling in Canada. They finally decided that Jim would go to Canada by himself and leave Mary and the children in America. As bad as they hated being separated, Mary and the children would have to stay in America while Jim was in Canada. It would be the first separation of their family and would be very difficult for all of them.

Jim left his family and went to Toronto to start his training at about the same time Wesley and Molly left Liberia and flew to Ireland for Molly's treatment. This was an extremely difficult time for both families. Also, Jim and Mary were very confused as to why Wesley changed his mind and said that Jim had to have linguistics before he came to Liberia. In turn, Wesley and Molly were quite confused as to why Jim and Mary did not come to Liberia as planned. In addition to that, Wesley was still very concerned about the ability and character of the man he hired to lead the building project.

Both families endured many difficulties for the months to follow. Molly's treatments finally finished and she and Wesley returned to Liberia about six months before Jim finished his linguistics training. When they returned to the Flumpa Mission Station they quickly saw that the building project was far from finished and they also found that the money was all gone.

When Jim finally finished his time in Canada, he and Mary made plans to go to Liberia right away. They decided to leave their three children with some friends until they got settled in Liberia and then have them come. Leaving the children was not easy, but finally Jim and Mary were on a plane heading for Liberia.

It is obvious that the letter from Liberia foiled God's perfect plan for Jim to lead the building project when Wesley and Molly returned to Ireland for her cancer treatment. It further endangered Molly's life because of the delay in getting back to Ireland as soon as possible. In addition to that, Jim was totally honest and highly qualified and would have finished the building project with the funds that were given. It was also unfair to the people who gave the large sum of money because it was misused. God did not orchestrate the letter and it caused many problems that were not of Him.

Chapter 14
Africa and Snake Bite

When Bob, Pat, and Tanya stepped out of the plane sitting on the tarmac of Robert's Field in Liberia they instantly felt like they were breathing hot air that came from an oven. They walked down the stairs and onto the tarmac and it even felt hot. From there they walked, along with the other passengers into the terminal. Since English was the official language of the country, they were able to communicate and were quickly through customs with no difficulty.

The WEC Mission in Liberia was called Liberia Inland Mission, and their business agent was at the airport to get them. As he was driving them through the city, they got their first look at Monrovia. It looked almost exactly as they had expected, with some buildings looking very modern and well-kept and others looking run down. Nearly all of the houses were very close together and most looked to be poorly constructed and very rundown. The people however all looked very clean and quite colorfully dressed. After about one hour of driving they arrived at the mission headquarters in Monrovia, which was a large house located near the center of the city and also close to the American Embassy.

The house was in an upscale part of the city, but it looked fairly rundown, as did most of the other houses around it. The inside of the house was very clean and had several bedrooms with a fairly large kitchen and dining room. The staff of four ladies treated Bob, Pat, and Tanya as if they were family and were very happy to have them there. After showing Bob and Pat their room, they invited them to have their first meal in Liberia.

It consisted of a few things they had not had before. One was cassava, which is a root from a tree. It is used much like potatoes are used in America. Another was plantain, which looks like a large banana. They cut it into long strips and fry it. It looks much like bacon after it is fried, but has a sweet taste. The food was very good and the conversation was even better as the staff and Bob and Pat all got to know each other.

The next morning Bob and Pat started the process of checking into the government offices so they could live in the country. Bob also had to get his Liberian flying license, which required a physical examination.

This all went very well and after three days they had all of their permits to live there and Bob had his flying license. When Bob went to the Liberia Federal Aviation Administration and told them he wanted to get his flying license, he also showed them his United States commercial flying license. They looked it over and, without requiring a flight test, gave him his Liberia flying license. They did however require his physical examination, which he passed okay.

While Bob and Pat were in Monrovia they met, Bob Gilbert, the pilot who went to Liberia to fly the plane until the mission got a full-time pilot. He took Bob McCauley to the airport in Monrovia and showed him the plane. Bob was excited the first time he saw it because he knew that soon he would be flying it across the jungle nearly every day. The body of the plane was painted yellow and white and the wings were an unpainted aluminum. A missionary woman had painted the words "Wings of Service for Jesus" across each side of the cowling. Bob liked this inscription on the plane because that was what he wanted to use it for.

From Monrovia Bob, Pat, and Tanya went with the field leader, Wesley Bell, on a two-hundred-mile drive on a jungle road to Bahn mission where they would be living. The road was dirt and gravel, so it was very dusty and extremely rough. The drive gave them their first look at the thick jungle where the trees and vines were so close together that it looked impossible in some places to walk through. As they drove, they were able to see many villages with their mud houses covered with grass roofs. Each village had poorly dressed, barefoot children playing in the dirt or kicking a coconut around as a football. Then there were the women and girls cooking in big black pots, which were sitting on three rocks over a fire.

Each village had a few chickens running around, plus some jungle goats. The women were colorfully dressed and all wore a scarf on their head. Even though many of the children looked poor, all of them and the adults were very clean. It was a hot, hard drive, but after about five hours they arrived at Wesley's mission station, called Flumpa, which was located on the same road that led to Bahn mission.

They arrived at Flumpa around noon and ate a meal prepared by the missionary ladies. The food consisted of the same things that they had at the mission headquarters in Monrovia, but they also had Paw paw which is a fruit that looks like a muskmelon, but has an entirely different taste. Their main staple was rice with greens and gravy on it. After lunch Wesley took Bob out to see the Flumpa airstrip. When he first saw it, Bob wondered if anyone could land a plane on it because it was so hilly and rough. Later he would find out that it was the best airstrip that the mission had. When they arrived at Bahn mission late that evening, the missionaries had lined the path to their house with arches covered with jungle flowers. It was beautiful, and Bob and Pat knew that they had spent many hours making the arches with the flowers. Many African Christians were there to greet them; all standing on the sides of the path to the house, and each greeted them as they walked down the path and through the arches.

They treated Pat, Tanya, and Bob like royalty. Next the missionaries had a very delicious African meal for them and the food was exactly what they had at Flumpa Mission Station. That evening they were taken to their house. It was a very small two-bedroom house with a kitchen and living room built out of sun-dried mud blocks with a concrete floor. The house had a lot of termites in it that had eaten large portions of the ceiling.

The bedroom was filled with mosquitoes that came into the room by going through the roof vents and down through the holes in the ceiling. With so many mosquitoes in the room, sleeping under mosquito nets was a necessity. Like all of the missionary houses, their rooms had little lizards that walked around on the ceilings eating mosquitoes. No one paid much attention to them, and neither did Bob and Pat. However, Tanya watched them closely and they seemed to be an entertainment for her. Their first night included all of this plus the jungle sounds, as well as the Devil Society drums beating until the very early hours of the morning.

The missionaries at the station were Bill and Jean Kimbery from England and they had two beautiful little daughters. Bill was the station leader, and he and Jean were both teachers in the mission school. June Harper from Ireland was the mission nurse. Shirley Collins was a teacher in the mission school; she and her two children were from Canada. Shirley was the widow of the pilot who was killed in the plane crash. Pat was also going to be teaching in the mission school, and Bob was to be the pilot. Bob and Pat were now at their home in Africa, living with the people that they would be working with.

The next day Bill and Jean took Bob and Pat down the mission hill and across a small creek to Bahn Town. It was a very large village of 10,000 people and was made up of about half of the people from the Gio tribe and half of the Mandingo tribe. The village had about half a dozen stores run entirely by people from Lebanon. They sold food, shoes, clothing, some medicine, blankets, kerosene, paint, and some school supplies etc. There was an area in the center of the village where the Gio women sat on small stools or on the ground selling all kinds of food supplies that they had grown in their gardens.

It was a bartering culture and everything was sold after a time of bartering. When a person wanted to buy an item, they would always ask how much it was. The seller would usually ask a price that was about twice what they would sell it for. Then the buyer would offer a price that was much lower. After that they would bicker back and forth until they agreed on a price. No one got angry about it and it seemed that they all enjoyed the competition.

Bill and Jean introduced Bob and Pat to every store owner and many other people they knew. Every one they met were very friendly and seemed very happy to meet the new missionaries. They made Bob and Pat feel very welcome both on the mission station and in the town. This was all very interesting to them because they knew they would be working with all of these people in the years to come.

God had used many ways to get them there, which had included speaking to Bob with the still, small voice of the Holy Spirit and also through prophecy, tongues and interpretation, and what Bob calls inner visions. Bob had left his engineering job with General Motors and, as far as he knew at the time, he had lost his retirement income. On top of that, their family was now separated with their sons still back in America. With all of this in mind, they knew they were where God had called them. Also, they were in His plans for their lives and He was going to use them in a wonderful way right where they were at that time.

Something then happened shortly after Bob, Pat, and Tanya arrived at Bahn Mission Station that Satan tried to use to get them to return immediately back to the United States. Pat had started teaching in the mission school for the African children and Tanya was also attending the classes. Each day, during lunch break, Pat would walk on the path back to their little mission house to get lunch and Tanya would follow a

81

few steps behind her. The path was about four feet wide and had no grass growing on it. There were many deadly snakes in the jungle and the Africans kept the paths clean so a person could see and avoid being bitten if a snake was lying on the path.

Near Bob and Pat's house was a small tree with beautiful white blooms. It stood about thirty feet off of the path to their house and the area around it was covered with tall grass. One day, as Pat and Tanya were walking back to their house for lunch, Tanya decided to get one of the white blooms from the tree. She had been told to never leave the path when walking to avoid the deadly snakes, but when she saw the beautiful blooms she forgot about her warning and quickly left the path and ran towards the tree, looking up at the blooms as she did.

Pat did not see this because Tanya was behind her, but Bob was standing in the doorway of their house watching Pat and Tanya when he suddenly saw her leave the path and run towards the tree. Bob immediately knew the danger she was in, but before he could call out to stop her Tanya screamed and started to jump on one foot, holding the other foot up as she jumped. Instantly Bob knew she had been bitten by a snake! He ran to Tanya, looking down at the grass as he did in an effort to avoid the snake himself, but it was no longer there. He immediately picked Tanya up and looked at her foot. His fears were confirmed as he saw two fang marks in her foot about an inch and a half apart with blood slowly flowing out of them.

Pat also heard Tanya scream and turned around and saw Bob pick her up and she immediately knew it was probably a snake bite. Within seconds Bob carried Tanya to where Pat was standing; they immediately knew the danger Tanya was in! They knew she could die within a minute or two because some of the snakes were extremely deadly! Bob and Pat immediately started to pray as they carried Tanya into their little house. Bob quickly made a tourniquet out of a handkerchief and a stick and tightened it around her little leg about half way between her ankle and knee. They had a small kerosene refrigerator and Pat quickly got some ice cubes from it and wrapped them in a cloth and covered the snake bite with them. This all took place within a little over a minute after Tanya was bitten. Bob and Pat's goal was to slow down as much as possible the flow of the poison from Tanya's foot to her heart.

Bob said, "We must loosen this tourniquet every twenty minutes to get some fresh blood to her foot so she does not lose it." Tanya's foot started to swell up tremendously right after that. Then Bob told the mission nurse and other missionaries what had happened. They all came right away and felt that Bob and Pat did exactly the right thing and there was little they could do medically beyond that. They did however all pray and ask God to save Tanya's life. After that Bob and Pat closely watched the time for the next twenty-four hours and loosened the tourniquet every twenty minutes for two or three minutes. Then they felt it was best to leave it off so that they did not damage her foot or lower leg.

About twenty-four hours after Tanya was bitten Bob had an experience that greatly angered him. It was like Satan came to him and spoke in a voice that was nearly audible and said, "If you had not come to this place your daughter would not have been bitten by the snake!" The voice was so vivid and spoken in such a sarcastic way that Bob knew it was Satan trying to discourage him. Bob suddenly became ultra-angry at Satan because he knew he had probably caused the snake to bite his daughter. He knew the devil was trying to get him to regret his obedience to God and coming to Liberia. He immediately determined that he was not going to get discouraged and return to his home land, but was going to continue obeying God no matter what Satan threw at him! In anger, Bob snapped back at Satan and said, "Yes Satan, and if you had not sinned against God you would not be on your way to Hell!!" Immediately he knew Satan left him when he said that.

This event was so vivid and real to Bob that he has retained that anger to this day and remembers it fifty years later just as if it was yesterday.

During those first twenty-four hours Tanya was very ill and appeared to be partially unconscious. To say the least, Bob and Pat were very concerned about her condition and the possibility she might not live. They decided to take her to a mission hospital, which was a two-hour drive away. The hospital could do nothing more for Tanya so they took her to Flumpa Mission Station where Molly Bell was. She was an excellent nurse and felt that Bob and Pat did the right thing for Tanya in using the ice and tourniquet. Molly did however keep Tanya at her mission station where she could watch her for the next week and Bob and Pat stayed there also.

Tanya's foot swelled up an extreme amount and turned totally black. During the following week she did improve under Molly's care and then Bob and Pat took her back to their mission station. Tanya kept improving and after another month she was back to normal for which they all thanked God. Bob knew of many people who died from snake bites. In one year alone he knew of five people who died of snake bites so he and Pat were so thankful that their daughter lived through one.

This whole incident seemed to be another test for Bob and Pat and they did not give up and go home, but became even stronger in their dedication to obeying and serving God where He had called them.

Mike and Tony joined their parents and Tanya after their school year finished in Indiana. It was such a joy for Bob and Pat to have their family together and the boys seemed to enjoy it also. At one time Bob heard that the jungle is a special attraction to boys. The jungle has some great dangers in it, but it is also filled with adventures of many kinds for most boys and this was so for Mike and Tony. Also, they became close friends with Steve Collins, who was about Tony's age and the son of the pilot who was killed. The three boys had no fear of the jungle and loved exploring it in different ways.

Mike and Tony needed to continue their schooling even though they were 200 miles deep in the jungle. There were no schools they could go to there so Bob and Pat enrolled them in The American Correspondence School from Chicago. This meant that Mike could finish his high school and Tony could take all of his high school by correspondence. Now the boys would be able to live with them year-round and take their schooling right in their own home.

ob and daughter Tanya with the Mission Plane

Chapter 15
Two Bolts in The Wilderness

The day after Bob, Pat, and Tanya arrived at Bahn Mission Station, Bill Kimbery told Bob that they could no longer use their Volkswagen van because the engine had been torn out of it. He gave Bob the details about what happened. A large logging truck was coming around a curve on the wrong side of the road just as a missionary man, with his family, were coming around the same curve on the right side. To avoid a head on collision the missionary man swerved into the jungle. When he did this the van went over a tree stump, which tore the engine off of its mounts and did a lot of other damage.

The missionaries needed the van for the ministry, but they did not know if it could even be repaired. They had heard long before Bob got there that he was good in doing mechanic work and they hoped he could repair it. They had already looked at the damage and saw that the engine and everything attached to it had been torn out. They even questioned if their Volkswagen van could be repaired by anyone. However, God had said that He would meet all their needs according to the riches of His glory in Christ Jesus so they had already prayed about it before Bob got there.

Philippians 4:19 (NIV) *And my God will meet all your needs according to the riches of his glory in Christ Jesus.*

Bill took Bob to the van and Bob slowly started looking at every detail of the damage. The engine was mounted in the rear of the van. Bob could clearly see that the engine had been torn away from its mounts. The two large bolts that held the top of the engine in place had been stripped right out of the engine block. Also, everything that was connected to the engine was also torn out and badly bent. Even all of the gear shift linkage to the transmission was severely damaged. Bob had never worked on a Volkswagen before, but he believed God wanted him to repair this one. He felt he could possibly rebuild it. He would at least try to do it.

There was one major problem that Bob faced in making the repairs. He would have to tap the cast iron engine block with larger threads and that would require drilling the holes out to a larger diameter and tapping them for new threads. There were some very major problems in doing this. He did not have an electric drill to drill the holes out larger, nor did he have the proper size tap to put the threads in. In addition to that he did not have a tap wrench to hold the tap. He would also have to find two bolts with the exact diameter and threads per inch and length that he needed. This problem was complicated because of being back in the jungle two hundred miles with no hardware store where he could purchase the electric drill, bolts, drill bit, and tap for the threads, and a wrench to hold the tap.

For years Bob had the policy that when God gives you a job you start on it, doing everything you can and let Him furnish what you need when you need it! Even though Bob did not have the things he needed to complete the job he repaired everything he could find that was damaged around the engine area.

After finishing those repairs, he looked around the mission station for an old junk box. Usually there is a junk box someplace, and he found one. Bob dug around in the box, found an old drill bit and also an old 5/8-11 tap. He checked the drill bit size, and it was the exact size he needed for the 5/8-11 tap. This drill and tap size would work perfectly to repair the stripped-out holes in the engine block. Somehow, he was not really surprised. He just felt that God would provide, and He did. Bob also knew that all the equipment, cars, trucks etc., in Liberia used metric bolts, and the 5/8-11 tap was English, so the chances of finding two 5/8-11 bolts two and one-half inches long two hundred miles back in the jungle in Liberia would be nearly impossible.

While Bob was looking through the junk box, he found an old pair of vice grips. A thought came into his mind that he believed was of God. It was to use the vice grips to hold the drill bit since he did not have an electric drill. Bob had never done that before and he had never heard of anyone else doing it. He did know that God can show a person how to do jobs with the tools they have on hand if He chooses. He did this and was able to hold the drill bit with the vice grips and rotate it well enough to get each hole drilled out just as he needed.

Then he used the vice grips in place of a tap wrench and tapped each hole. This took several days, but it worked great. After Bob got the larger bolt holes tapped, he pried the engine up and in place under the van. He had it sitting on pieces of wood and located in the exact location so that the bolts would line up perfectly. After two months of work Bob was ready for the bolts. As he was still lying on his back after adjusting the engine block to the exact location that he needed to slide in the bolts, Bob said, "God, I am ready for the bolts now."

Immediately Bob heard the sound of a car or truck pulling up not far behind where he was laying on his back. He twisted his head around while still under the van and saw that it was an old, rusty, beat-up pickup truck. The driver was out of the truck and standing behind the van before Bob slid out. When Bob stood up, the man said, "Do you need those bolts now?" Bob was shocked when he heard this. How did he know to even ask him about the bolts? A person could hardly see under the van, let alone see that he needed two bolts. Bob said, "Yes, I do, but I need English and not metric, and they have to be 5/8-11 thread and two and one-half inches long." The man quickly answered, "I know, and I have them."

Again, Bob tried to tell him that they were English and not metric, but he insisted that he had them. He led Bob over to his pickup and pulled out an old, small tool box. It was completely filled with dirt. He dug down into the dirt and pulled out three bolts. Bob looked at them; they looked to be the right size, but he was not sure the thread was 5/8-11. Bob still thought they might be metric and would not work. The man seemed to be in a hurry. Bob wanted to pay him for them, but he would not take anything, and got in his truck and left.

Bob slid back under the van, put the first bolt in place, and rotated it to see if the thread would engage the threads he had tapped in the engine block. The bolt thread engaged the engine block threads as he hoped it would. He knew that if the bolt had a metric thread, it would lock up and not continue to turn into the English-threaded hole. Bob's heart was almost in his mouth as he slowly rotated the bolt. He was very happy as it continued to rotate all the way in. Then he did the same thing with the second bolt. They were perfect! The bolts had 5/8-11 threads and were two and one-half inches long, exactly as he needed. Bob already had a wrench lying under the van, and he tightened them up.

After this, Bob slid out from under the van and said out loud, "If God could furnish three (even one extra) 5/8-11 bolts two and one-half inches long at the exact time that I needed them, then He can truly furnish a table in the wilderness."

This happened nearly fifty years ago, and Bob has thought about it more than a thousand times since then. His question is always, "How did the man get those bolts and how did he happen to give them to me instantly when I needed them?" His conclusion is this, "I later found that the man was a Lebanese Trader in Bahn village. I don't remember doing this, but could I have told someone that I needed the special bolts and they told the man who gave them to me? I simply don't know, but I do know that exactly when I needed them God gave them to me! This timing had to have been of God!"

After Bob had the engine mounted in the van, he got into the driver's seat to start the motor and quickly discovered he could not move the gearshift lever. He got back under the van and started looking at the gearshift linkage to see what was wrong. It didn't take long to find that the A-frame between the front wheels was bent badly back into the gearshift linkage. Up to this point, Bob had only looked for damage in the back of the van around the engine area. It had not occurred to him to look at the A-frame. However, it was evident now that the very heavy piece of steel had been bent badly as the van went over the stump.

It was obvious there was no way they could use the gearshift without straightening the A-frame. Since the A-frame steel was very thick and strong, it would take close to one thousand pounds of pressure to straighten it. Bob certainly didn't have anything on the mission station to put that much pressure in the right location to do the job. He had no idea how he could straighten the steel so he knew God would have to give him knowledge on how to do it with the tools he had on hand.

Bob did what he always did in this kind of situation - he prayed and asked God for the knowledge on how to fix it. Almost instantly, the Lord spoke to him in His still, small voice and showed him how to get enough pressure in the right location to straighten the A-frame. It was so simple that Bob laughed out loud when the Lord showed him how easy it would be to do this job. He would never have thought of this on his own, but God gave him a word of knowledge just when he needed it. Without this it would have been impossible to do the job two hundred miles back in the jungle.

There was a very long log chain on the mission station. Bob did not know where it came from, but it was there when he arrived. There was a high hill leading up to the mission station houses from the road that led to the mission station. Near the top of the hill was a tree that was about three feet in diameter. Bob wrapped one end of the log chain

89

around the base of the tree and hooked it there. Then he had the schoolboys help him push the van up the hill to the tree. Next, he put pieces of wood behind the back wheels to keep the van from rolling backward down the hill. Then he hooked the other end of the log chain to the A-frame in the exact location where he needed the one thousand pounds of pressure to straighten it out.

Bob got in the van, and the boys removed the wooden pieces while he held his foot on the brake. After making sure the boys were out of the way, he braced himself securely, trying to make sure his head was not going to get snapped backward by the sudden stop. Then he quickly took his foot off the brake and the van rapidly rolled backward down the hill. When it came to the end of the chain hooked to the A-frame, the van stopped instantly. All the pressure to stop the van had put tremendous pressure on one point on the A-frame.

Bob got out of the van and looked at the A-frame. It was bent back to within about an inch of being perfect. He repeated the same process, but this time he only pushed the van up about ten feet and let it roll backward. This time the A-frame was bent back to the perfect position. The three-thousand-pound van rolling downhill had generated enough speed that it took about one thousand pounds to stop it instantly and this was what Bob needed to straighten the A-frame.

God once again showed Bob how to do the nearly impossible with the things he had on hand. Bob was absolutely amazed at God's ability in doing this. He knew it was not done from his abilities, but from God. What had seemed as impossible was taken care of within one hour as the result of a word of knowledge from the Lord. Years later he is still amazed at the great engineering ability of God. Bob never would have thought about this way to straighten the frame, but it came instantly after he prayed and asked God how to do it.

Tony, Mike, Pat, and Bob McCauley

Chapter 16
God Fed Bob's Family

God plans for an obedient person's life are always exciting, but sometimes He brings about events that we don't always understand. This can even happen when God is teaching us something. Bob and Pat went through one of these times not long after they arrived in Africa. God was going to let them experience His faithfulness. They had read about God feeding the children of Israel when they were in the wilderness with manna from Heaven and Jesus feeding the 5,000 with only five loaves of bread and two fish.

Exodus 16:4-5 (NIV) *[4] Then the LORD said to Moses, "I will rain down bread from heaven for you. The people are to go out each day and gather enough for that day. In this way I will test them and see whether they will follow my instructions. [5] On the sixth day they are to prepare what they bring in, and that is to be twice as much as they gather on the other days."*

Matthew 14:17-19 (NIV) *[17] "We have here only five loaves of bread and two fish," they answered. [18] "Bring them here to me," he said. [19] And he directed the people to sit down on the grass. Taking the five loaves and the two fish and looking up to heaven, he gave thanks and broke the loaves. Then he gave them to the disciples, and the disciples gave them to the people.*

Bob and Pat believed these stories in the Bible about God feeding His people, but they had never seen Him do it. However, He was going to show them He could do it for them personally. God had showed His faithfulness to Bob when He supplied the bolts exactly on time when he needed them. This time God was going to show His faithfulness in a different way.

A few months after Bob and Pat arrived in Liberia, West Africa, they ran out of money. They received no money from home, and within a short time they used what money they had on hand to purchase food. As was said above, they lived near a large village of about ten thousand people, called Bahn, where they bought most of their food. Women would sit on the ground or on a small stool near the center of the village with difference kinds of produce on a cloth in front of them. Their produce consisted of vegetables, fruits, rice, and there was a man in the village who sold meat. It usually was goat meat, but occasionally he had some deer hanging out in the open, covered with flies. They ate what the Africans ate, but it did take money to purchase it.

When Bob and Pat ran out of money, they had a little food on hand, but it was soon used up. It would have been easy for them to get discouraged because they were in the deep jungle with nothing to eat. At this point they could have said, "God is not meeting our needs for food and we are leaving this place as soon as possible." However, they did not do this, but continued to obey and trust God for their needs. Also, they didn't share their problem with anyone else due to the mission policy. However, they did go to God asking Him to provide their needs. They had seen their God provide for their needs before, but they wondered how He would provide food for them back in the jungle with no one knowing their need.

After they ate their last meal with the food they had on hand, they prayed and told the Lord they were out of food. Pat also told the Lord that they needed some meat, and she would like some deer meat and rice, etc. Well, before it was time to prepare the next meal, a little old lady, who looked very poor, showed up at their door with some rice rolled up in a piece of cloth. She said she felt that she should bring it to them. Then another old lady showed up with a piece of deer meat. Some more ladies brought some vegetables, and they had enough for a very good meal. They thanked God for the meal and prayed for the next one. Before the next meal needed to be prepared, more old ladies or men came with more food, and they had another good meal.

This was very good, but how long would it continue? Their funds came to Africa from America once a month. They felt that they would receive money when the transfer of funds came for the next month, but it did not come. This went on for four months. They had no money for all of this time and yet they did not write about it or tell anyone, including the other missionaries or the Africans. Every day for all of the four months, Africans came by with food. Many times, they looked very poor like they had very little themselves, but they gave food to Bob and Pat in their need. They were God's servants feeding Bob and Pat. They never missed a single meal. They always had a good balanced meal, and the food was very good.

Four months later Bob and Pat received money, and right after this the Africans stopped bringing food to their door. This happened exactly to the day when they received money to buy their own food. Never again did the Africans bring them food as they had. God used the Africans to spread a table before them in the wilderness. It was very humbling to accept food from people who looked so poor, but they knew that it was God who sent the African people to provide for their needs. Bob and Pat brought their needs to God in prayer, and He answered and provided. They learned a tremendous lesson: their God can provide for them in any situation! They praised Him and knew that He provided for them as they stepped out to obey Him. Praise His holy Name!

Chapter 17
Bush Flying Cost for Evangelism

About three months after Bob and Pat arrived in Liberia the flying was turned over to Bob and this allowed Bob Gilbert and his wife to go back to America. On his first takeoff, he was amazed at the power the Maule plane had with its large IO-360A engine. He had never flown a small plane with the acceleration it had or one that could get a large load off the ground as quickly as it could. It was a very good plane for flying in and out of the very short jungle airstrips. Also, the plane was able to carry about 1,000 pounds of weight, and this made it a very good cargo plane to fly supplies into the various missionary jungle airfields.

Bob's goal was to mainly use the plane for what he called "Medical Evangelism." Each mission station had nurses and a clinic where they treated thousands of African patients. Many times, a sick person would have to walk days to get medical help at the mission stations. Some of the far away villages had airstrips. If a medical person could go to those far away villages it would be a great help to the African people. If they had a set time when they would be there the sick people from the area could come on that day for medical help. This would be a much shorter walk for them compared to walking all the way to the Bahn Mission Station. Also, Bob or someone else could preach the Gospel to the people who came for aid.

Bob started doing this, but there was a major problem of paying for the cost to fly the plane to the villages. As a result, very few missionaries were using the mission plane for evangelism because of the cost. It was the mission's policy that if a missionary wanted to fly to a jungle village for evangelism or any other type of flying, they had to pay the cost per hour to fly the plane. The cost to fly the plane was determined by the amount of gasoline it took plus an estimated cost per hour for parts and maintenance on the plane. It is expensive to fly a plane anyplace, but it is especially expensive to fly in the jungle, due to the high cost of gasoline and parts for maintenance. The mission's policy was that every flight had to be paid for and the plane was not allowed to fly in the red.

It would take hours or even days to walk to some of the villages, but Bob could fly to the same village in one minute for each hour it took to walk. If it took ten hours to walk to the village, Bob could fly there in about ten minutes or less. He really felt badly about the cost of flying the plane, but there was nothing he could do about it.

Bob prayed about this problem, and the Holy Spirit spoke to him very clearly in His still, small voice, saying, "I will provide the money to pay for the cost of flying the airplane for evangelism. If the missionaries want to use the plane for evangelism, do not charge them. If they do want to pay, only allow them to pay for the gasoline and no more."

Bob knew what God said to him in His still, small voice, but he had one problem with what the Lord told him. Thinking of this problem, Bob prayed, "Lord, you know the mission has the policy that the cost to fly the airplane cannot operate in the red. I cannot fly the plane without having the money to pay for each flight. If I am hearing Your voice correctly, have someone send one hundred dollars to the mission plane for evangelism within two months, and I will put it in a special fund to use for evangelism."

Bob finished that prayer and dropped the issue at that time. He knew that the possibility for someone sending one hundred dollars to the mission plane within two months for evangelism was highly unlikely unless God did it. No one had ever sent a letter to the mission plane and the chances of this happening were almost zero. It just could not happen! However, Bob knew God could do it! Bob would honor WEC's policy and not tell anyone and this time it would include not telling Pat. It was between God and Bob.

During the next two months, Bob almost forgot about the prayer. One day he flew into Monrovia, the capital city, to get supplies and pick up the mail for the different mission stations. The business agent, a missionary from British Columbia, Canada, would put the mail for each mission station in a large plastic bag with the name of the mission station marked on each bag. It was Bob's job to get the mail to each station. The business agent said he had one letter that was addressed to the mission airplane.

Bob was standing about five feet away from him when he flipped the letter to Bob through the air and said jokingly, "Since the airplane cannot read, maybe the pilot can." It was his little joke toward Bob, suggesting he might not be able to read the letter either.

Bob looked at the envelope and it was from Denmark. He knew no one in Denmark, but he opened the envelope. It had a note in it that was handwritten in English, and it also contained a check. The note simply said, "To be used for evangelism with the mission airplane." Bob could read the note, but he was completely unable to read the check. From some markings on it, he thought it was in Danish marks, but he was not sure, nor did he know how much it was. Bob gave it back to the business agent and asked him how much it was. He quickly saw that the check was in Danish marks and figured out that it was for $100.03.

Bob suddenly remembered his prayer concerning the one hundred dollars and how the Holy Spirit had spoken to him in His still, small voice concerning the evangelism ministry. Bob knew the date of his prayer and quickly realized it was exactly two months before this that he prayed that someone would send one hundred dollars to the mission airplane for evangelism. He had told no one about the prayer, or how he felt God was leading him to fly the plane for evangelism, but here in his hand, exactly two months later, was the $100.

Bob was extremely surprised in a way, but in other ways he was not. He clearly had heard God's voice how the plane was to be used, and he knew God was going to bless the use of the plane. He asked the business agent to put the one hundred dollars in a special account and told him that he would use it only for evangelism with the airplane. This gave Bob a very small nest egg to start flying evangelism, but it was a start.

Bob flew back to his mission station and told the nurses about the one hundred dollars. They wanted to use the plane more for medical evangelism, but had not done it because of the lack of money. Now they felt they could do it more and were excited about it.

Not long after the initial $100 was sent to the airplane for evangelism Bob went up to the attic in their home to get something when he saw a cardboard box that he had not noticed before. He picked it up and it had a picture of a Coleman film strip projector on it. Bob opened it and there was a Coleman film strip projector that looked nearly new. Even the mantle lamp was in perfect condition. He had used Coleman lamps before, but he had never heard of a Coleman film strip projector. The box also contained many film strips with pictures of Jesus Christ and His teachings. Bob decided to test the projector so he put some

97

kerosene in it, pumped it up, and lit it. It burned well and the mantle was extremely bright. He put a film strip in it and it projected a perfect picture.

Bob knew he could take this projector to the villages and show film strips as he preached and taught about Jesus Christ. When he took nurses and went into the villages they always stayed overnight. Now he could use the projector and a film strip in his evening message. There was no doubt in Bob's mind that God had provided this projector for him and it was a tremendous success in teaching the Word of God in the villages.

A few days after the $100 came in, Bob and a nurse flew to a village called Sea-app-lee where he preached the Word of God, and then Bob became the nurse's aide as she treated the sick people. Bob was able to pay for that flight exactly as God had spoken to him through His still, small voice. This was the first flight of many through the next years of using the plane for evangelism. Everyone involved was very happy about this new financial policy for using the mission plane.

One hundred dollars does not last long flying a plane in the jungle. Bob knew this, but he was not concerned about it. He knew God had provided, and he knew He would continue to provide. God continued to supply the money to fly the plane for aviation medical evangelism and it was extremely amazing for Bob to see and experience this. After two years he started to wonder if God would send in more money if he flew into the villages to preach the Word and treat the sick people even more than he had been. Bob knew he was always very busy, but decided to put a major priority on his aviation medical evangelism ministry and to greatly increase the number of flights into the villages for it.

Bob knew God had been blessing this ministry and many were coming to Jesus Christ through it, and also many lives were being saved physically. He knew this ministry was part of God's plan for him at the time, but in the back of his mind was the thought, "Could I break the fund if I flew for aviation medical evangelism all I possibly could?" He made a firm decision to try to use up all of the money coming in for it.

Bob organized the nurses from the different mission stations and set dates and times to make the different flights. He started doing this and it was somewhat like continuing to work double overtime on a job with no let up. After doing this for a few months, he started to believe it was impossible to break the fund; that would only happen when God was through using the plane.

Bob was totally amazed at what happened. God seemed to respect his decision to make more flights for the medical evangelism ministry. As was said above, when he took nurses into the villages they stayed overnight, which gave them two days to treat the many sick people. Bob's decision to increase their medical ministry meant that he was preaching, eating, and spending more nights in the villages than all of the other forty-three missionaries put together. It was common for Bob to preach four or five times a day when they went to the villages and often people accepted Christ as their Savior after each message.

God blessed this and money came in for every flight. It came in from many countries of the world and from various other sources. At times Bob would receive special requests from business people who wanted flights back into the jungle villages. The mahogany trees in Liberia were in great demand at that time, and many logging people wanted to go into the deep jungle to locate the trees. The village strips were so short that the charter pilots would not take them, so they often asked Bob to take them because they knew he could fly into the short airstrips.

When this happened Bob would pray and the Lord would speak to his heart about how much to charge them. It was usually quite expensive, but when Bob told them the price, they always seemed more than willing to pay it. God led Bob to put the extra money into the evangelism fund. At times some of the nurses wanted to help out on a flight, but Bob only let them give enough for the gasoline.

After doing this type of ministry with the plane for about one year, Bob knew he could never use up the money because God kept sending it in. Yes, he gave up on trying to break the fund, but he continued doing the medical evangelism as he was because God was blessing. Bob kept a logbook of every one of his flights, and approximately 350 lives were saved from a physical death as a result of their medical evangelism. In addition, a vast number of people accepted Jesus Christ as their Savior, making a difference in their lives for eternity. Through this ministry, God was able to use Bob to make a tremendous difference in the lives of many people that lived in the deep jungle. Many lives were saved physically, and many souls were saved from hell.

Chapter 18
"The Plane will Crash"

The mission had a yearly conference for the Gio and Mano Christians at a mission station called Garply. About one thousand Christians from the area attended the week of meetings. Many had walked 25 to 30 miles through the jungle to get there. After the last service, Bob planned to fly as many as he could back to Bahn in an effort to help them get back to their villages as easily as possible.

The last meeting was on a Sunday afternoon, so as early as possible on Monday morning Bob took Pat, Tanya, Tony and one other person back to Bahn on his first flight out. They were going to prepare food for those who came to the mission station later that day. The flight from Garply to Bahn only took twelve minutes, but it was a very hard twenty-five-mile walk through the jungle. This was very difficult for women with children. Bob planned to fly back and forth all day carrying people from Garply to Bahn, so he had a heavy day of flying ahead of him.

That morning after they got into the plane, Bob turned the starter key, and it roared to life instantly. Bob taxied to the end of the airstrip, checked the engine, and it ran and sounded perfect; then he checked the controls and they checked okay also. Bob had his normal prayer for God's protection, and gave the engine the power and within seconds they were above the trees on a heading for Bahn. After about six minutes of their flight, Bob thought he heard a strange noise in the engine. It only lasted about one second, but it concerned him. He had spent hundreds of hours sitting behind that engine and he knew it's every sound. Bob looked his engine gauges over and everything looked okay, but he was still concerned about that strange sound.

Then, all of a sudden, Bob heard another sound like that of a twelve-gauge shotgun. Instantly, he heard a high-pitched screeching noise that sounded like the engine was being torn apart. Once again, he checked all the engine gauges over, and they still looked okay, but he knew something was being torn apart in the engine. He still had full power, but the sound was almost unbearable.

Pat heard the sound also, and she started to pray. Although Bob was praying too, he was also looking for trees in the jungle where he could have a controlled crash if it quit running. He knew it could not last long before the engine blew, so he had to be prepared to come down in the jungle. There were a lot of palm trees in the jungle that had very few leaves and very solid trunks. Bob had already planned that if he ever had to come down, he would try his best to avoid an area with a lot of palm trees because their solid trunks would tear a plane to pieces.

The tall trees with a lot of small branches would be the best to bring a plane down in, because the branches would help slow the plane before it hit the ground. Many of the missionary pilots had talked for a long time about how they planned to slow their plane down right above the tall trees in case they ever did have to crash-land. They hoped their wings would settle into the small limbs and take away most of their speed, which would ease their crash some. Their plan was trying to make the best out of a very bad situation.

If the engine completely quit running, it would be harder to pick out a softer place to bring it down. The Maule plane was a good short field plane with a lot of power, but when it was loaded, as they were, it had a terrible glide ratio. It would come down fast if it had no power. Bob quickly thought it over and decided to continue to fly as long as he could. They only had about five more minutes to get to their mission runway, and how Bob prayed and hoped it would keep running that long. The five minutes seemed like a very long time as he kept watching and picking out places with larger trees.

Bob did not know it at the time, but the front ball bearing in the generator had broken. The loud screeching noise was the gear on the front of the generator being torn up by the big ring gear, which also drives the camshaft and the magnetos. If one tooth on the ring gear broke, the engine would stop immediately and the plane would come down quickly. Bob also did not know it, but the front of the generator had a hole torn in it that was getting larger by the second. The hot engine oil was being dumped out of the hole in the front of the generator. It was spilling out into the engine compartment and along the sides of the plane. The villagers in one of the small villages that Bob passed over were telling each other that Mr. McCauley was pouring oil on them.

The screeching noise from the engine continued and the sound was terrible, but what was worse for Bob was knowing there was a good possibility that all of them could be dead or seriously injured within the next minute. He looked over at Pat and she seemed quite calm, even though she knew the same thing. Bob knew how serious their condition was, but he remained very calm and did not panic at all. He just kept flying and praying.

Back at Garply mission station, a line of Gio and Mano people were waiting for Bob to return and bring them to Bahn. He did not know it, but right then as he was flying, a demon-possessed woman was standing in front of the line, making fun of the people for standing there waiting for him to return. She kept saying to them, "The plane is going to crash, and all in it will be killed." She was laughing at the people as she said this. It was evident that the demons in her knew that Bob was going to have engine trouble, and they planned that the people in the plane would be killed as a result.

Bob did not know all the details of what was going on in the spirit world at the time, just as Job did not know all the details of what was happening to him, but he believes the demons had something to do with the bearing breaking, or else they would not have known about it. Bob is sure they wanted to kill them and stop what God was doing through them. However, God had different plans for all on board the plane and would only allow the demons to go to certain lengths when they attacked them. God agreed that they could cause the ball bearing to break. Of course, that was only Bob's guess, as he does not know the full story. He does know that the bearing broke and that the demon-possessed woman was making fun of the people for waiting for him to be back, and that she was telling them that they would be killed. She knew something was going to happen to the plane, and Bob believes she knew it as a result of her demon possession.

The loud screeching continued, but when Bob saw their runway at Bahn mission he felt better, but he knew he had to fly past the runway and then make a turn and get lined up on his final approach. He also would have to slow the engine down and slow down his airspeed. The worst part of this was knowing that if the engine quit during his approach when they were slowed down to land on the short runway, the plane would drop out from under them quickly and they would be killed. Bob planned to make his landing pattern as short as possible, but he also knew that he had only one chance to make it. He could not afford to miss his landing spot and have to make a go-around.

Landing on Bahn mission airstrip had its own peculiarities. A pilot could only land on Bahn runway from one direction because of a hill.

Most of the jungle airstrips were this way. There was a lower level of ground and then a hill and a higher level of ground. A pilot had to get the plane on the ground on the lower level and then let it roll up to the top level as he was applying the brakes to stop. There was also a very tall dead cottonwood tree about one hundred yards straight out from the end of the runway. These are the tallest trees in the jungle in Liberia, and they stand about one hundred feet above all the other trees. This tree was about twenty feet across at the base of the trunk. Bob found that the best way he could get around it was to come in on his approach at forty-five miles per hour and then make a slight cross control slip to his left, and then one back to his right, and then slow the plane down to about forty miles per hour in order to get stopped after getting the plane on the ground.

Bob lowered the plane to about thirty feet above the trees and made his turn so close to the end of the runway that he did not have to go around the tree. When he straightened it out, the engine was still running. He pulled the flaps right at the last second as he crossed the end of the runway, and then pulled the power all the way off, pulled back on the yoke, and they were on the ground. Bob immediately turned the engine off and they had just enough speed to roll up the hill to the second level. It worked out perfectly.

Bob got out of the plane and could hardly believe what he saw; the sides of the plane were dripping with hot engine oil. He opened the engine compartment, and the entire engine and everything in there was covered with hot oil - even the hot exhaust pipes were covered with oil. As Bob looked at the amount of oil on everything, he was amazed that it did not catch on fire. Bob and Pat knew that they all came very close to death that day. Again, their obedience to God's call for them to be there was tested and they refused to get discouraged, but rather praised God that they walked away from it with no harm.

The demon-possessed woman was correct when she said something was going to happen to the plane, but she was in error when she said they would crash and be killed. God had not allowed Satan to kill them that day, and they survived to win more people to Jesus Christ. As far as Bob knows, the demon-possessed woman never got delivered.

The Gio and Mano Christians had a good week of hearing the Word of God taught and preached, but getting home was quite a task for them.

Most were unable to catch a ride by car or truck, so they walked the twenty-five miles back to their villages.

Perhaps the devil wanted to hurt them as much as he wanted to kill Bob and his passengers. Bob does not know. Whatever it was, God was the winner as He always is for those who will serve Him with all of their heart.

Shortly after they arrived back at Bahn mission Bob started to examine the engine and found the front bearing of the generator had broken and had torn a large hole in the front of it. The oil in the engine was blowing out of that hole. Even though the front bearing was torn out, the generator was still rotating and tearing itself up and that was causing the loud high-pitched screeching noise. Bob removed the generator and closely examined the teeth on the ring gear that drives the generator gear and they were okay so he could continue using the engine, but they had to replace the generator.

Chapter 19
"Tower, Tower"

Bob learned in his early days of hearing and obeying the voice of the Holy Spirit that timing was critical. On two different occasions he heard the still small voice of the Holy Spirit direct him to talk to someone about the Lord. On both occasions he put off talking to them at the time, thinking he would do it the next day. The first was an older engineer and he died that night of a massive heart attack. The next were two young men and they stole an airplane and crashed it and were both killed that night. Bob was deeply crushed that he put off talking to these men because he believed they were not Christians and would be in hell for eternity. After that he made the vow to obey the still small voice of the Holy Spirit no matter where it took him in the world or how much it cost. Bob had no idea that immediately obeying the Holy Spirit would someday save his life.

One day during the rainy season a nurse asked Bob to fly to a village called River Cess and pick her up and fly her to a village called Botawea to treat the sick people there. Occasionally one of the small charter planes flew over River Cess Village and she asked Bob to fly very low over the village so she would know it was him and not some other plane. She asked Bob to fly to an airstrip that was about one mile north of the village. She would come to the airstrip on her motor scooter so he could take her to Botawea from there. River Cess Mission Station was about thirty miles from River Cess village, which was along the ocean, and Bob never had a reason to fly there so he was not familiar with that area.

His flight was very important because the people in Botawea were expecting the nurse to treat their sick that day, and from past experience Bob knew many of them would be very ill. Also, people from other villages would carry their ill for a day's walk or more to get medical treatment when they knew they were coming to Botawea to set up a clinic. Bob knew some people might be deathly ill and could not be properly treated by the nurse in the village so he would have to fly them to a mission hospital that was about one hundred miles away.

As Bob was making the hour and twenty-minute flight towards River Cess Village he could see in the distance thunderstorms in nearly every direction. He had been to Botawea several times and he knew it would be impossible for him to land the plane there if he could not see well due to rain. Botawea's very short, rough airstrip was tricky to land on because he needed to maneuver around some small trees and a hill before touching down. Landing there was like flying through an obstacle course and Bob had to be able to see well to do it.

Bob's flight to River Cess would take him right by Botawea, so he was watching the different storms and anxiously waited to see what the weather was like in that area. About forty-five minutes after he took off, he could see Botawea about two miles off to his left as he passed by. He was happy to see that the weather there was clear at that time. Bob did notice a storm front approaching the village from the south, so he knew he only had a short time to get the nurse there before the rain came.

As Bob got closer to River Cess Village, he saw rainfall over it. However, he could see that the airstrip north of the village about a mile was still clear. Now he faced a decision. He could avoid the rain, land at the airstrip, and wait out the storm, or he could fly through the rain and pass over the village to let the nurse know he had arrived. Then she would drive her motor scooter to the airstrip after seeing his plane over the village. Then he could fly her on to Botawea, and they should get there before the storm. Bob knew hundreds of sick people were waiting on the nurse and they would be extremely disappointed if she did not arrive, and some might even die. Therefore, in spite of the rain, he decided to fly over the village.

Bob knew there were no hills in the area to worry about so he felt comfortable with his decision, even though he was unfamiliar with the area around River Cess Village. He dropped down to about fifty feet above the trees and headed straight toward the village. He was flying about 130 miles per hour, at this low altitude, when he entered heavy rain. Immediately, he could see nothing out of his windshield, so he held his altitude by looking out the side windows. After about thirty seconds, Bob could see village huts and he proceeded to fly towards the village.

The raindrops were making extremely loud cracking sounds as they hit the front window. With the noise from the rain and the roar of Bob's engine, the noise level inside the cockpit was very loud. Despite this noise Bob suddenly heard a very still, small voice faintly whisper two words: "Tower, tower." Instantly, he realized this voice was the Holy Spirit.

Bob shouted to himself, "There is a tower in this town!" and immediately he yanked the control yoke all the way back and turned it fully to the right. He also pushed the right rudder pedal down at the same instant. This snapped the left wing and nose up in a split second, putting the plane in a steep right-hand climbing turn. Immediately Bob saw a huge tower flash by his left-wing tip and it missed the center of the tower by just a few feet and his wheels missed a large support cable by about two feet. The plane's wings were nearly parallel to the cable as Bob passed over it, otherwise his left wing probably would have hit the cable.

The shock of seeing the huge tower flash by his wing tip at 130 miles per hour and realizing how close the wheels came to the cable stunned Bob for a few seconds. He knew that he had just come extremely close to losing his life. If he had not reacted instantly, he would have hit the tower right in the center and died. Also, if he had not given the plane a very strong right bank and climb, he would have crashed into the support cables. If he had delayed one quarter of a second Bob would not be here to testify of God's deliverance. In addition to knowing how close he came to death, he also knew he was only alive because the Holy Spirit had spoken to him in His still, small voice.

Bob could not dwell on these thoughts however, because he was still flying a plane in a storm with almost no visibility out of his front windshield. Almost instantly he was well out over the ocean since the tower was located right at the edge of the water. He stopped his steep climb while he continued to make a right turn and flew over the water following the beach until he saw the little airstrip. By this time, he was out of the heavy rain.

Bob slowed the plane and landed on the airstrip outside the village, and the nurse arrived a few minutes later, just as planned. He quickly put her medicine and other supplies in the plane and set out for Botawea. They arrived a few minutes before the storm got there, so the nurse was there to treat the sick people just as planned. Bob never told the nurse how close he came to losing his life that day, but he has told this story to others many times for the glory of God. Bob still thanks God for saving his life and for the extra time He has given him to proclaim His Word to people who are lost and on their way to an eternity in hell unless they are born again through the blood of our loving Lord Jesus Christ.

Over forty years have passed since Bob heard the still small voice of the Holy Spirit say, "Tower Tower" and he is so glad he reacted instantly. Bob has asked himself many times since then, "What if I had delayed one second?" The answer is clearly this, "I would have died if I even delayed for a second. A second is so short, but it would have been long enough to have cost my life."

Today Bob wants to hear and instantly obey His voice just as he did that day. Perhaps you too need to hear God's voice to help you avoid a "tower" in your own life. However, you will never hear Him if you are not praying and living according to His Word. Obey Him at all cost and never compromise. Totally commit every area of your life to Him and ask Him to lead you in every way. Delight yourself in Him. Choose to please Him no matter where that choice takes you in this world or what it costs you. Study and believe His Word. As you do these things, you will hear His still, small voice and know His will for your life. And, as a result, you can have an eternal impact on the lives of others by helping them come to Jesus Christ and be Born-Again. God has plans for your life and they are good and they will only come about as you seek and obey Him in everything you do.

Chapter 20
Death and Back

As was stated earlier, before Bob and Pat arrived in Liberia, the mission's airplane crashed in the jungle and burnt. Their pilot (Don Collins), a missionary nurse, and an African young man were all killed in the crash. No one knows what caused the plane to go down. It was a terrible tragedy and a time of great sorrow for Don's wife and their two children, as well as for all the missionaries and the African Christians. Don was buried on the mission between the house he and Shirley and their children lived in and the airplane hangar. In their deep grief, Shirley and her children continued living at Bahn mission and were there when Bob and Pat arrived.

After Bob started flying the plane, he was away from their home on Bahn Mission Station about half of the time because of his flying. Every morning when Bob was at home, he walked right by Don's grave on his way to the hanger to get the plane ready to fly. He nearly always thought about Don laying in that grave and how hard it was for his wife and children. It was a daily reminder of how serious and dangerous flying in the jungle was. In many ways Bob's thoughts would flash on his own family and how he loved them. He also knew they loved him and how hard it would be for them if some day he could no longer be with them.

These thoughts made Bob want to spend as much time as he could with his family, but he knew he would always be away from them at least half of the time and there was no way he could stop it. Bob decided to try and be with his sons all he could by taking them with him when he had space in the plane. He would take one boy at a time and teach them how to fly by letting them take the controls of the plane and fly it towards their destination. Bob did this and it gave him quality time with his sons and they both learned how to fly very well, except for takeoff and landings, which Bob did not let them do because of the difficulty. The boys enjoyed their time with their dad and got to see a lot of the different mission stations and the country from the air.

Shirley Collins had a beautiful bronze plaque made for a marker on Don's grave and had asked Wesley and Bob to make a cement headstone at the head of Don's grave and mount the plaque in it. Early one morning Wesley Bell made the two-hour drive from Flumpa

Mission Station to Bahn mission. He and Bob spent the day making the form, digging the foundation, and mixing the concrete for the headstone. After the cement was poured into the form, they very carefully mounted the bronze marker on top of the wet cement.

Without saying anything to each other they stood there looking at the headstone in silent reverence for Don and his family. They could not help but think about Don and his family, the nurse, and the young man who had died in this tragedy, and all of the sorrow that it entailed. They were glad that they made the headstone, but it certainly was not a joyful thing to do.

After the two men finished their work on Don's grave, Wesley asked Bob if he would do some welding on his pickup truck before he made the two-hour drive back to his mission station. Wesley had made a metal topper to cover his truck bed that was about the size and height of a normal truck bed topper that you can purchase. He did a good job of making it, but the rough African roads had caused the metal frame to break in several places.

Bob had purchased a new portable Arco Welder / AC Generator from America and it was with them in Liberia. Bob told Wesley it would not take him long to weld the tubing, and he would be glad to do it. Wesley went to one of the mission houses to visit with the missionaries as Bob was getting ready to do the welding, so he was by himself during that time.

It was late in the afternoon, and Bob was in a hurry to get the welding done while he still had some daylight. He pulled the welder up behind the truck, plugged in the cables, got his mask in place, flipped the switch from AC generator to welder, and started the gasoline motor. A warning sign on the side of the machine said that the ground rod must be driven into the ground before being used as a welder. In Bob's haste, he did not drive the ground rod into the ground, and this proved to be a terrible error. The purpose of the ground rod was to prevent the possibility of the operator being electrocuted.

Bob welded most of the broken steel tubes very quickly while standing on the ground outside the truck, and after he finished welding all of those places, he carefully looked the topper over to see if there were any other places that he needed to weld. As he looked, he saw one

111

broken place on the frame that was located on the inside center top of the topper. He would have to get inside the truck bed to weld it.

Bob jumped up inside the bed with both cables. He hooked the ground cable on one side of the broken brace and got himself in place to weld it from the bottom side. He found that the topper was too high to weld while sitting down and too low to stand up. He would have to weld it in a crouched position. It was going to be an awkward position for welding, but he felt he could do it. Bob moved the tip of his welding rod close to the steel brace that he was going to weld, and then lowered his welding mask over his head.

At that instant, Bob lost his balance in this awkward position and stumbled backward. His reflexes then took over to keep from falling, and he grabbed the steel brace that he was getting ready to weld. In the process, he lost his hold on the welding rod holder, and as it fell, he grabbed the end where it held the welding rod. This all took place in probably less than a second, but it was a major error. Bob's left hand was holding the steel brace that was connected to the negative side of the welder, and his right hand was holding the positive side of the rod holder. This allowed the electricity from the welder to flow right across his chest.

The error of not driving the ground rod into the ground added to Bob's problem. He was the conductor between the positive and the negative sides of the strong electric power. The force of the electrical power was so strong that he felt like he had been hit with a ball bat swung at full force, nearly knocking him unconscious. The electrical current stuck Bob's left hand to the steel brace that he was going to weld, and his right hand stuck solid to the rod holder.

Immediately Bob started jerking badly as the electricity flowed through his body. He could hardly think, but knew that he had to get away. He tried to pull away, but could not do it. His left hand was stuck to the brace like a strong magnet. He had to get away! He leaned forward as much as he could, and very quickly threw his full weight backward. This broke the hold his left hand had on the steel tubing, causing him to fall out of the back of the truck and into a pile of sand.

Suddenly Bob realized he could not get a breath of air. His lungs were not working properly, and he struggled with all his might just to get a slight amount of air. The next breath, however, was harder than the first, and he realized that he was dying, but kept struggling with every effort to breathe. Bob knew he could not continue this very long before death would overtake him.

One or two minutes after Bob fell out of the truck, his two sons and Steve Collins, the son of the pilot who was killed, came out of the jungle on a path that went right by where he was lying. They saw Bob and asked, "What is wrong, Dad?" Bob replied as best he could, "I am hurt badly; go get Uncle Wesley." Bob knew they would also get their mother, and within seconds, Pat, their children, Wesley, and the mission nurse arrived, along with all of the African Bible school students.

They saw how badly Bob was hurt and all started to pray. Pat and their children were crying and praying. In a weak voice, Bob told their children that he was dying, and asked them to live for the Lord. At that time the African Bible students put their hands under Bob, lifted him above their heads, carried him to their house, and laid him down in their living room on the couch.

By this time Bob no longer had strength to keep fighting for breath, and he was becoming paralyzed. He knew that death was very close. He lost all feeling except a slight quiver around his heart area. Within a minute after he was placed on the couch, he was totally paralyzed. He could not even move a finger. He could still whisper very weakly, and Pat was kneeling over him with her ear right against his mouth to hear him say, "I love you and I am going." Pat was crying as she spoke back to Bob, "I love you too."

Bob wanted to die with his hands lifted and praising the Lord, and he managed to speak the words to her, "Lift my hands." She repeated his words to the others, and Michael lifted one hand and Wesley lifted the other. Right after they lifted Bob's hands, the presence of the Lord came on him like he had never experienced before. It was like his whole body was filled to the brim with God's presence. There was absolutely no fear whatsoever of death. Bob knew his body was going to die, but he would live a new life in God's kingdom. The real Bob McCauley was not going to die at all. What happened to his body at that time seemed insignificant. He was going on to heaven to be with his Lord Jesus, and this is what he wanted to do!

Not only did the Spirit of the Lord come upon him as he went through the process of dying, but also the most wonderful peace and joy that he had ever experienced came over him. It was so wonderful that Bob does not have words to express it. He lay there and thought, "All my life I have wondered how it would be to die and it is the most wonderful thing I have ever experienced." He totally lost all desire to stay in this world and wanted to go on to be with Jesus.

Then he felt his spirit exiting his body. It seemed like it came from about his heart area to his head and slowly went out. Also, there was not one instant when Bob could not think. It was like he was still alive through the process of dying. He entered no state of darkness or a time of not knowing what was happening. He knew everything that was happening, but had no control over it. The real Bob McCauley did not die!

Instantly after this, Bob saw, at about a 45-degree angle above him, a being dressed in a pure white robe waiting for him. He was standing in midair looking at Bob, who knew beyond any doubt that he was waiting to take him on to Heaven. With joy, Bob wanted desperately to go on and be with him. His desire to stay in this world was completely gone and he was looking forward to Heaven. At the same time, he knew God had called him to Africa and the work He called him to do was unfinished. The obligation to finish what God called him to do overcame his desire to go on to Heaven.

Somehow Bob knew he did not have to speak to Him with his mouth, but with his mind. He said to Him, "Jesus, I am ready to meet You, but people are going to hell, and I pray that You will give me a little longer to preach." At the time Bob called Him Jesus, but now he wonders if this could have been an angel and not the Lord Himself. Jesus, or the angel, spoke back to him and said, "I will give you a little longer."

Instantly Bob's spirit was back in his body and he could no longer see the Lord, and he could breathe again. He started to shout with a loud voice, "O death, where is thy sting, O grave, where is thy victory. I have come to the edge of death and looked in and saw nothing but glory in Jesus Christ." Bob then shouted, "I am going to live; stand me on my feet!"

Bob has thought about this thousands of times since it happened. He knows today that there is no fear in death for the person who dies as a

Christian living for God. The actual act of dying can be the best part of living! The struggle for life up to that time can be very difficult, as it was for Bob when he struggled to breath and became paralyzed.

When Bob died there were many people in the room with him and also many on the outside of the house who could not get in due to the room being so full. Nearly all of them were African Christians. Most of them could see Bob's struggle to breath and hear the nurse tell the field leader how bad his heart rate was. What they could not see was the joy of the Lord that came upon him about one minute before he actually died.

Bob never understood John 11:26 until he had the death experience.

John 11:26 (KJV) *And whosoever liveth and believeth in me shall never die. Believest thou this?*

For years Bob wondered about this verse because he thought, "We do die." Now, from experiencing death, he fully understands the meaning of the verse. During his death process there was never one second that he was not alive. Even while his spirit was leaving his body he could still think. He knew what was happening! The real Bob was still alive! The real Bob is his spirit and soul and it did not die, not even for a split second! From experience, Bob clearly sees this today and wants every Christian to see this wonderful joy that we all have in the fact that if we are Born-Again and are living for Jesus Christ when we die, our real self, which is our spirit and soul, does not die!

Seldom can a person testify what it was like to die. Bob can and wants to. Not for his glory, but to encourage every believer in Jesus Christ that there is no sting in death for the one who dies in Him.

1 Corinthians 15:55 (KJV) *O death, where is thy sting? O grave, where is thy victory?*

God's plan for all people is found in John 3:16. Note that He uses the word, "Whosoever" to show that it is for every person and each person has a free will in obeying God in His plan for their salvation.

John 3:16 (KJV) *For God so loved the world, that he gave his only begotten Son, that whosoever believeth in him should not perish, but have everlasting life.*

Again, I will quote John 11:26, which gives the results of John 3:16.

<u>John 11:26</u> (KJV) *And <u>whosoever</u> liveth and believeth in me shall never die. Believest thou this?*

Today, 47 years later, Bob knows God had plans for his life that were not fulfilled at the time of his death experience. Even yet to this day they are not. During the days and years that followed Bob's death experience God used him to bring many to Him in America and other countries.

Chapter 21
A Beautiful Day Turned Ugly

Nearly every person has faced a crisis of some kind, or they know of someone who has. Some might be so serious they could even take their life, such as cancer or being seriously hurt in an accident. Many times, life can be going very good and we are suddenly faced with some tragic event that we did not see coming. Sometimes it is so serious that we see no way to recover from it.

Bob had a similar event happen to him while he was flying in Africa and it seemed impossible to get out of. It was ultra-serious, because if God did not intervene, Bob and his son Tony would die that day! Below is the story.

One day Bob and his son Tony took off for a flight from Flumpa Mission Station to deliver a fifty-five-gallon barrel of kerosene to River Cess Mission Station. River Cess mission was in an area of the jungle where there were no roads, so all their supplies had to be delivered by plane. Bob and Tony were sitting in the front seats of the plane, and right behind them was the barrel of kerosene lying on its side in a cradle made just for this purpose. The plane was loaded to its maximum weight limit, but Bob knew they would still be able to get the weight off the ground due to the nine-hundred-foot-long airstrip at Flumpa.

When Bob got up to his altitude, he looked around to see if there were any storms in the area. There was not one cloud in the sky, which was very unusual for Liberia. All he could see was pure blue sky and the canopy of jungle trees below them. The day was beautiful! Bob told Tony that it was the best weather he had flown in since coming to Liberia. It looked like an easy day of flying.

Tony and Bob settled in for the hour and fifteen-minute flight and engaged in some great father/son conversation. Since they were not pushed for time that day, Bob adjusted the engine controls to a conservative setting to save gas. This meant the flight would take about ten minutes longer, but Bob was not concerned about the extra time because the weather was so good. He had no idea that in less than one hour he was going to regret his decision to save gas. Taking this extra ten minutes was going to cause a critical problem that he did not know was coming.

About thirty minutes after they took off, the weather changed drastically. A jungle storm had formed very quickly, and they were encountering very high winds with strong turbulence that caused the plane to rock about radically. Bob thought about turning around to get out of the turbulence, but when he looked behind them, he saw they were surrounded by black storm fronts.

He looked for an opening in the storm fronts that he could fly through, but saw that they were right in the center of a massive jungle storm that had formed all around them. He knew from the storm's nearly black color that the winds were so violent they could tear the plane apart. Bob scanned the area again and he saw there was no way out, and the fronts were closing in on them quickly. Bob had no other option; he had to get the plane on the ground right away.

One of their mission stations was about ten miles in front of them when Bob made the decision to get on the ground quickly. The weather was still clear there, but their five hundred-foot-long runway was too short and hilly to land on with the weight they had in the plane. About twenty miles beyond them was a rubber plantation, and they had a runway that he could land on if he could get there in time. If Bob did land there, Tony and he would have to wait for the storm to pass, which could take the rest of the day and most of the night. Bob knew his radio would not transmit far enough on the ground to call Pat and tell her they were on the ground waiting for the storm to stop.

Bob also knew Pat and the others would be very concerned if they did not hear from them. They would most likely think they had crashed somewhere in the jungle. Bob was hoping he could call someone and tell them they would be landing at the rubber plantation, and that they were going to be okay. Then they could use their radios to let the rest of the missionaries know this information so no one would have to worry through the night needlessly.

Many thoughts were flashing through Bob's mind as he was thinking about letting Pat and the other missionaries know he and Tony were going to be okay. He knew that every jungle pilot's wife was quite concerned or worried that their husband might be killed as Don Collins and some other missionary pilots were. Bob's desire to avoid this caused him to make another serious mistake that was going to endanger their lives.

Pat was teaching school at that time, and Bob knew she would not be near the radio if he called her. He also knew of no other mission station that would have their radio on and be able to hear their radio call. The mission station that was about ten miles in front of them normally did not leave their radio on because they did not have a generator to charge their battery. As a result, they only used their radio for fifteen minutes twice each day when all of our mission stations communicated at 8:00 am. and 5:00 pm. Bob's plan was to circle their station, rock his wings back and forth, and yell out the window to tell them to turn on their radio so he could call them and let them know that he was going to land at the rubber plantation. He was hoping they would realize that something was wrong and turn their radio on.

When they got to the mission station, Bob circled it at a very low altitude, rocking the plane's wings back and forth as he had planned. The man at the station came outside the house when he heard them and looked up in their direction. Bob slowed the plane down as much as he could, cut the power on the engine to eliminate the noise and yelled, "Radio, radio, radio." Bob circled three times, hoping he would know that he would not waste time on a flight doing this unless it was very serious. The man liked to joke around and he must have thought Bob was doing this for fun. He started running in circles in the center of the mission station yard waving his arms up and down as if he was mocking Bob for rocking the wings of the plane.

Bob was very disappointed because he went to his friend with a serious problem and he made a joke out of it. All he had to do was run back in his house and turn the radio on to talk to him, but he did not do it. In Bob's mind he was kicking himself for wasting precious time to do this, but there was nothing he could do but try and save their lives.

Bob flew on to the rubber plantation and when he got there, the weather was about a quarter of a mile away from the runway. However, Bob felt he had time to land before it hit them. The rubber plantation runway was level on the north end, but it had about a one hundred-foot-high incline on the south end. He would have to land the plane from the north and get it on the ground in the level area, and then let it roll up the hill as he stopped. There was no way a person could land coming in from the south due to the hill. Bob was flying very low when he reached the rubber plantation, so all he had to do was line the plane up with the runway, slow it down, and bring it in.

Bob slowed the plane down to about fifty miles an hour and lined it up with the dirt and gravel runway to make their landing. Everything was going well as they were coming in, but suddenly, as they were right above the trees at the end of the runway, they were hit with a very strong cross tailwind of about fifty miles per hour coming from their right rear side. The plane instantly lost most of its lift because the wind was coming at the wings from the back side. Instantly Bob knew they were in big trouble!

The right rear tailwind caused them to lose altitude quickly, and it pushed the plane to their left over the tops of the trees and the plane started dropping its altitude fast. Instantly Bob pushed the throttle in and the big IO-360A engine responded right away. He slowly raised the plane's flaps back to the fifteen-degree setting in an effort to get more flying speed. Bob's thoughts were totally on instant survival and not on the storm. To survive, he had to stop the plane from dropping any more, make a go-around, and try landing again. The heavy load they were carrying in the plane was making everything even worse.

Bob was able to keep the plane flying and out of the trees, but he was having a hard time getting it to climb due to the strong cross tailwind. He had to get the plane up enough to clear the hill, or else they would slam right into the side of it. Bob was holding enough back pressure on the control yoke to keep them in the air, but not so much as to cause the plane to stall.

They were climbing slightly and gained just enough altitude to clear the hill. That was a relief to Bob, but right after they cleared the hill, he saw a horrible sight in front of them. Someone had put a large electric power cable across the south end of the runway. It was about thirty feet high and they were headed right for it. Due to some small trees beyond the cable, Bob did not have enough space to go under it, and the plane was not climbing enough to clear it! The strong tail wind was hindering them from getting enough air going by their wings to make it climb! They were going to hit the cable, and that meant sure death for Tony and Bob!

Instantly in desperation, Bob had to try to gain a few feet of altitude. He reached down and grabbed the flap lever. With his eyes glued on the cable, he waited until the last second before they hit it and yanked the flap lever up, which snapped the flaps fully down in the landing position. This instantly gave the wings a tremendous amount of additional lift, and the Maule plane rose almost instantly up about ten feet, which was just enough to clear the cable. The negative side of this maneuver was that the extra drag from the lowered flaps instantly reduced their airspeed. Bob had traded air speed, which he desperately needed, for a few feet of altitude.

As a result of losing the airspeed, the plane's wings lost lift, and they started to lose altitude instantly after they cleared the cable. Bob quickly pushed the nose of the plane slightly down in an effort to gain some flying speed. The trouble was, he could only let the plane come down about twenty feet before they hit the small trees below them. The twenty-foot drop did give him a little more air speed, but he had to level it off right above the small trees and bushes beyond the electric cable.

Bob was still holding the flap lever and slowly pulling the flaps up in an effort to gain some flying speed. To make matters worse, they still had that strong cross tailwind. They were flying right on a stall now at about forty miles per hour, which was dangerously close to the wings losing all of their lift. If this happened, the nose would instantly drop and they would crash. There would be almost no chance that Bob and Tony would survive this.

Bob was losing the battle to gain some altitude and they were only a few feet above a very rocky ground with small trees when they came to the crest of the hill and the terrain dropped off at about a forty-five-degree angle. Just as they passed over the crest Bob pushed the nose of the plane down and followed the decline down the hill, staying just a few feet above the trees to let his airspeed build back up. The airspeed did increase and when they got about half way down the hill they were flying at about 120 miles per hour.

There was no doubt that God had delivered them from what would have been sure death. Bob was thankful for that, but they still had to get the plane on the ground quickly. He made a quick circle back to the north end of the runway. As Bob made the circle, he was evaluating what he could do to land under the very adverse conditions. They still had the strong cross tailwind to contend with and he knew his ground speed would be at least forty miles per hour above his indicated airspeed. He also knew he needed to increase his landing air speed in order to control the plane in the strong cross tail wind. This meant that their ground speed would be about 100 miles per hour, which would make it difficult to get stopped before they came to the end of the runway.

Bob was going to count on rolling up the hill to give them extra help in stopping. He knew that the narrow runway had tall trees on both sides and also had tall trees on the north end. The trees would help cut the cross tailwind down, so there would be little wind below the tree level. On the first approach they were hit by the strong wind when they were above the trees, so this time Bob wanted to have a high-flying speed above the trees and slow the plane down when they were below the trees.

This time Bob lined the Maule up on the runway and held it at about seventy miles per hour as he lowered it into the grove of trees. He could feel the strong tailwind as they flew, but at seventy miles per hour he had good control of the plane this time. Bob was watching the trees closely in anticipation of the coming wind changes, and almost instantly as they got below the tops of the trees, he could feel the cross tailwind drop off quickly.

Now he wanted to use the extra weight of the fifty-five gallons of fuel in the barrel behind them to quickly lose the 100 mile per hour ground speed. He instantly cut the power, pulled full flaps, and lifted the nose as much as he could. Bob wanted to keep the extra weight in the air as long as possible with no engine power so that the airspeed and ground speed would drop off quickly. This worked and within seconds they were on the ground, but still at a higher than normal ground speed. As the plane rolled up the hill with Bob pushing hard on the brakes the ground speed slowed enough that they were able to stop by the time they came to the end of the runway.

Bob taxied the plane to an area where they could wait out the storm, and then he shut off the engine. Within seconds the heavy rain hit the plane so hard that that the noise level inside the cockpit was unbelievable. Tony and his dad sat there listening to this as they thanked the Lord for His blessing in getting them down safely. God had truly saved their lives!

Bob and Tony knew people would be wondering where they were because they were expecting them to be at River Cess Mission Station, and they were sitting on the ground at the rubber plantation. Bob tried calling them on his radio, but they did not respond, so there was nothing they could do to let Pat and others know they were okay.

As Tony and Bob sat in the plane waiting for the storm to stop, Bob's thoughts were on how close they came to being killed and wondering why it all happened. Questions came into his mind, and he was looking for answers that only he could give. His son came close to dying that day and Tony knew it. Bob seriously asked himself the question, "Why did I waste time trying to let Pat and the other missionaries know where we were going to land? I should not have circled the mission station trying to get them on the radio. This caused about a two-minute delay in getting to the rubber plantation. If I had arrived at the runway two minutes sooner, the violent cross tailwind would not have hit us because we would have been on the ground when it came." Bob clearly saw that this mistake nearly cost Tony and him their lives.

Bob also knew his decision to save gas was a mistake because if they had arrived ten minutes earlier, they would have been on the ground before the strong cross tail wind came. He knew he made this decision because the weather was so good when they took off, but it was wrong and was a factor in them nearly dying that day.

Bob had another question, "Why would anyone put a power cable thirty feet above the ground at the end of a runway? They should have known better than to do this! We almost died because of that cable!"

Bob shook his head as he thought about his friend running around in a circle waving his arms up and down. His personality of making jokes out of everything he could showed up when Bob desperately needed him.

Also, Bob thought about the wind change in direction and speed that he did not expect or plan for. The wind direction was okay as he started his landing descent, but it drastically changed at the worst possible moment when he slowed down to 50 miles per hour air speed during his landing approach.

As Bob evaluated the day, he remembered how he told Tony that it was the best weather he had flown in since coming to Liberia and that it looked like an easy day of flying. At the time he did not know that within one hour they would be facing a bad weather crisis that would seem nearly impossible to get out of and his flying skills would be tested in a way like they had never been before. During that time Bob did everything he possibly could to keep them alive, but he was 100 percent convinced that God alone got them out of it.

Bob also knew he was where God had called him. He was flying in these conditions because of the call of God. God had spoken to Bob in the still, small voice of the Holy Spirit and told him to go to Liberia and preach His Word first and fly the plane second. He was doing exactly that, and even though it contained dangers, he was where God told him to go and doing what He told him to do. Bob knew this, and there was never one moment when he doubted his call to be flying in Liberia, even in the face of danger and possible death.

Other mission pilots were facing these same conditions daily. Occasionally they would see each other and talk about this among themselves. One of the pilots told Bob that every day before he got in his plane the thought came to him, "Is this the day I get killed?" That pilot knew he was where God had called him, but he also knew the dangers involved. Bob had three close pilot friends who were in jungle crashes, but lived through them. One even crashed upside down and survived. All of the pilots knew that some of their friends, who were very good pilots, had been killed; yet God had delivered Bob from similar situations, but had allowed others to be killed.

Why were some killed and others were not? None of the pilots, including Bob, knew the answer. However, Bob did know one thing. His life was in God's hands, and even if he was killed, he still won because he would be in heaven for eternity. As a result of knowing this, he was not going to be flying in fear, but in victory, because God had called him there! As Bob and Tony sat there with these thoughts running through Bob's mind, he had answered his own questions and was totally at peace with his conclusion and answers.

Tony and Bob sat in silence for a little while as their minds went through the events that had just taken place, and then they started to talk, enjoying their conversation as father and son as they waited for the rain to stop. From Bob's past experience, the weather looked like one of the jungle storms that could last for two or three days. Tony could see this also, so they both knew they might have to sleep in the plane for the night. At least they were safe on the ground. There were no people at all from the rubber plantation at the runway, so it was just Tony and Bob. Since they enjoyed each other's company, the time went quickly as they sat there conversing as the heavy jungle rain pounded down on the plane.

When it came time for all of the mission stations to get on the air at 5:00 pm., they heard the missionaries at River Cess call the other mission stations and tell them that Bob and Tony did not arrive. They were all wondering where they were and if they had crashed. Pat was on the radio with them, and Bob and Tony could tell that she was concerned about both her husband and son. Since their mission had a pilot who was killed in a crash in the jungle there was always a concern that it could happen again. As their mission stations were talking, Bob tried to call them, but his plane radio signal was just not strong enough for them to hear him. When the plane was in the air, the radio signal could travel quite far, but when it was sitting on the ground, the signal would only travel about forty miles in most cases. Bob and Tony wanted to tell them they were okay, but there was no way to do it.

Not long after their mission stations started talking about where they were, the Baptist mission stations also got on the air and entered into the conversation. They had two planes, and Bob could hear them say that they would start looking for Bob and Tony as soon as the storm cleared. From the conversations, Bob could tell that the storm was very widespread across Liberia. The Baptist mission stations reported that it was starting to show signs of letting up, so they were going to start looking for them as soon as it did. Bob could hear his Baptist friend, Abe Guenter, say to the other mission stations, "Bob knows the area well and knows where the landing strips are, so I believe he is somewhere waiting out the storm, but we will look for him anyway."

Abe was right; Bob was only about forty-five miles through the jungle from his mission station. Bob could hear his call clearly, and he decided to try to call him on his radio again. Abe heard Bob and called back, asking where he was. Bob told him that he was at the rubber plantation waiting out the storm. Abe knew Bob's exact location and relayed the message to the rest of the mission stations, and they called off the search. Pat and all the other missionaries were very happy to hear that Tony and Bob were safe on the ground.

About an hour after the radio call, the wind died down and the weather began to clear. By 6:00 pm. it looked safe to fly again, and Bob decided to continue their flight to River Cess since they were only about twenty-five minutes from their destination. After their preflight checks, Bob and Tony were on their way, and within twenty minutes they could see River Cess Mission Station. They had a seven hundred-foot, level landing strip so they could to get the heavy load down and stopped.

It was late in the day when Tony and Bob climbed out of the plane at the end of the runway. They would be spending the night there. Tony liked the idea of staying at River Cess mission overnight because he had a friend there named Gordy Hodgson. That evening Bob had a good time visiting with Cecil and Margaret Hodgson, Marion and Ella Peterson, and Elizabeth Bauman, and Tony enjoyed his time with Gordy. The next day Bob and Tony continued on their way for more jungle flying. After Bob had flown in the jungle about a thousand hours, he came up with a saying to describe it. It was, "Each day of jungle flying is a happening" and this day would probably fit into the same category.

Many times, our days just don't go the way we expect, or would like for them to. They start out beautiful and turn ugly. Some days we are disappointed. Bob was disappointed in the person that put the large cable thirty feet in the air right at the end of the runway.

If our day seems to go sour, does it mean we are out of God's will? No, of course not! It can be a time when we see the wonderful work of the Lord as He helps us get through some very serious situations as God did for Tony and Bob. It can also be a time of testing to see if we will go on with God regardless of the difficult time. During the difficult times, it is important that we know beyond any doubt that we are living for the Lord and doing what He wants us to do. Then, no matter how ugly the day gets, we know God is with us as we pass through it! Even when we face a death situation, He is with us and we have nothing to fear.

Bob faced death many times. The times have included not only possible death from flying, but also possible death from terrorists as he was preaching in their area. Then there was the time he actually died. He also faced the possibility of prison because of where he was preaching. Through all these times, God was with Bob and spoke to him in His still, small voice, giving him peace and comfort in the midst of difficult situations. The following verse almost brings tears to his eyes as he reads it and knows how close God is and has been when he faced near-death situations.

<u>**Psalms 23:4**</u> (NIV) *Yea, though I walk through the valley of the shadow of death, I will fear no evil: for thou art with me; thy rod and thy staff they comfort me.*

Chapter 22
Jim and Mary in Africa

About a year and a half after Jim and Mary left their farm home in Indiana their big plane landed in Liberia, West Africa. They were finally in Africa where God had called them. With a little excitement they got up out of their seats and made their way to the front of the airplane and stepped to the top of the stairs that led down to the tarmac. They looked around and could see that they were in Africa. The vegetation, trees, and all of the people were exactly like the pictures they saw many times of Africa. The exciting thing to them was in knowing they were there because of God's call upon their lives and were happy that they had obeyed Him.

As they walked out of their plane and down the stairs and onto the tarmac, little did they know that they would be in Africa for most of the next twenty-five years. They were still somewhat confused as to why God had redirected them to go to Liberia before they went to Swaziland. They knew He had a plan for them to be there, but they had no idea what it was. They did know however that it was to be good and they were going to fit into it the best they could. Both of them kept this in the back of their mind and focused on what He had for them in Liberia.

They had no problem getting through customs and they got a taxi to go to the mission house in Monrovia. When Jim and Mary arrived, they were greeted by four missionary ladies who lived there. They were very happy to see them and treated them to their first Liberian meal. The food was exactly the same as they served Bob and Pat when they arrived, and Jim and Mary really enjoyed it.

After their meal the WEC business agent took Jim and Mary to the different government offices where they received their official documents to remain in the country. This gave them an opportunity to see the city and it was just about what they expected it to be. The streets and houses were generally rundown compared to any city in America. There was a large area of the city where people lived in houses that were in a deplorable condition. Jim and Mary felt sorry for the people who lived there. It took them two days to get through all of the business of living in Liberia.

Bob flew to Monrovia on Jim and Mary's second day in Liberia. It was their first time to see him in over a year and it was a special occasion for the two brothers to meet now in Africa. On the third day the business agent took a missionary man named Dave Carson, a nurse from River Cess mission, and Jim and Mary to the local airport where they got their first look at the plane Bob flew. It was a white and yellow trimmed in green Maule Rocket that looked very good, but Jim could tell that it had flown through a lot of very heavy rain because the paint on the leading edges of the nose and other areas had been eroded off.

They all loaded their baggage in the plane, then got in and buckled their seat belts. Bob got in and said a prayer for a safe flight. The engine started right away with a loud roar and Jim could tell that it was very powerful. They waved goodbye to the business agent and Bob taxied out to the runway as he talked on his radio to the tower. When they got to the end of the runway, he did a check of the engine and controls and gave it full power and they were off of the ground in seconds. As they climbed out Jim and Mary got their first look at the city of Monrovia below them.

Bob turned the plane toward River Cess Mission Station and within three minutes they were over the thickest group of trees Mary and Jim had ever seen. They were getting their first vivid view of the jungle and how dense it was and they enjoyed it very much. However, Jim was surprised at how loud the roar of the engine was. It was so loud that it was very difficult to hear what someone was saying and this made conversation very difficult.

There was a very heavy overcast about 100 feet above them as they flew. It looked like they were seeing the bottom side of very heavy fog. Bob said this was common while flying in the jungle and that was why most of his flights were only about 250 feet above the trees. He said that it was very dangerous for him to get in the fog and he told Jim that before he came to Liberia, the mission board decided to purchase this plane with no instruments in it for flying in bad weather. Their reasoning was this. They wanted to keep their pilot safe and they felt the way to do it was to buy a plane with no bad weather instruments in it. Then the pilot would not get into weather where he could not see.

Bob said that their decision to buy a plane without the needed instruments in it actually increased the possibility of a pilot and his crew getting killed due to bad weather. He said that there was no way a jungle pilot could fly in a country that had the worst weather in the world and not get into some storms where he could not see. Bob also said that he had been trapped in bad weather where he could not see many times and it was very difficult flying on just the old basic instruments. It was obvious that he felt their reasoning was very wrong and put him in more danger every time he flew.

As a result of them flying this low Jim and Mary could easily see the villages with their huts made with mud walls and grass roofs below them. Many people in the villages would look up at the plane as they flew over and sometimes someone would wave at them. If they did, Bob would wave the wings of the plane back at them. Jim and Mary saw very few roads along the way, but they did see some large rivers. Jim did notice that Bob was watching his compass very closely as if he were doing all he could to make sure they were on a direct course to their destination. Bob had no radio signals to rely on for direction and Jim could see that it would be very easy to get lost flying over the jungle because there are very few land marks out there. The jungle all looks about the same from the air.

About one hour after they took off Bob said they were about there. Jim and Mary got their first look at a mission station below them with a few houses and a very short air strip. Bob said, "That is River Cess Mission Station." He slowed the plane down and got it lined up with the air strip. The strip looked short to Jim and he wondered how Bob could land on it. He started slowing the plane down more and more and raising the nose higher. Jim could no longer see over the nose, but Bob was looking off to the side of it. They were getting closer and closer to the trees and when they were over the last tree the wheels touched the ground with a rumble and they were on the ground. The plane quickly came to a stop near the end of the air strip and Bob shut the engine off.

Everyone got out of the plane and Jim and Mary were delightfully greeted by many Africans and a missionary couple named Cecil and Margaret Hodgson and also their three teenager children. They all were very excited to have them on their mission station. Another missionary nurse and also two missionary teachers lived there, but they were busy so they did not come to the plane. Many Africans came to greet Jim and Mary and shake their hands. They had a special handshake that snapped each other's thumbs. It was strange to Mary and Jim, but the

Africans delighted in showing them how to do it. Soon this was common to them and they did it with everyone they shook hands with.

Cecil and Margaret's home was only about fifty yards from the end of the air strip so they walked to it. It was Jim and Mary's first time to be deep in the jungle and they both looked around at it as they walked. The trees and vines were so thick that it would be nearly impossible to walk through it. Then they came to Cecil and Margaret's house. The walls were made with sun dried mud blocks and it had a metal roof. The outside walls had been white washed, which made them a very bright white. The house looked very well constructed and was neat and very clean around the outside.

They went inside and it was neat and clean with a cement floor and the inside walls were plastered and painted white with a few pictures hanging on them. The furniture was very clean and it all looked homey. Jim and Mary saw a table set for them. It was noon when they got there and Margaret had a very good meal already prepared for them. Jim and Mary had their first visit with the missionaries during the meal and then got back in the plane. Once again Bob started the engine and checked it and the controls and they took off. When they were just above the trees Bob banked to the left and headed for his mission station. For the next hour and fifteen minutes they had another very good view at the dense jungle below them.

After about one hour and fifteen minutes they flew over a large village called Bahn. Bob's mission station was on a small hill about one quarter of a mile from Bahn. As they flew over it, they could see the three missionary houses, the grade school, boarding school dormitory for the Liberian children, Bible school and small houses for the students. Jim could see that the landing strip was much shorter than the one at River Cess. It was on two levels connected by a fairly steep hill. Bob slowed the plane down and got it lined up with the runway. As they were coming in, they were just a few feet above the trees and flying very slow.

Jim could see that Bob was very focused on what he was doing to land the plane. About two seconds after they passed over the last tree, they were rolling on the lower part of the air strip and then quickly up the hill and onto the upper level. Bob stopped the plane in front of a very rough looking building that he called the hanger. It looked to Jim more like a roof held up by some poles than it did a hanger.

By the time they got out of the plane Pat, Mike, Tony, and Tanya were there to meet Jim and Mary along with many grade school and Bible school students. The students acted like Jim and Mary were their best friends and they had never met them before. Jim and Mary really felt at home and they could tell the Africans all loved them even though they had just met. Dave Carson, one of the other passengers, left right away and got a Liberian jungle taxi to go to his mission station called Saclapia, which was about a two-hour drive away. It was the only mission station that did not have an airstrip.

They walked up a little hill towards Bob and Pat's house. On their way there they saw Don Collins' grave. It was somewhat of a sad moment for them as they stood there a short time and looked at it.

Pat had a good evening meal for Jim and Mary and the brothers and their wives had their first visit for over a year. They were once again in the same location and were happy about it because they knew it was in God's plan for all of them be in Liberia, West Africa.

Chapter 23
Desperately Needed Sooner

After getting a good night's sleep and a good breakfast, Bob went to the mission Bible school and taught the first morning class and Pat went to teach at their mission school. When Bob was at his mission station, he always taught the first class, but many times he was flying in some other part of Liberia and he could not do that.

As was said earlier, Wesley Bell was the field leader of the WEC Mission in Liberia. He was also the one who planned for Jim and Mary to be there a year before this to lead the building program for Molly's new sewing class for the women. Bob told Jim and Mary that he planned to fly them to Flumpa Mission Station to meet Wesley and Molly Bell because they liked to meet every new missionary as soon as they could. Jim and Mary also wanted to meet them as soon as possible. Bob told them that it was usually around 10:00 in the morning before the fog rose enough to fly so they had a few hours to just relax. He also told them that it was a two-hour drive over some very rough roads to get to Flumpa, but it was only a twelve-minute flight to get there.

At about 11:00 that morning Mary and Jim got in the plane and Bob flew them to Flumpa Mission Station. From the air Jim and Mary saw the Flumpa mission houses below them and a very hilly air strip. It looked so hilly that Jim wondered if Bob could land on it, but he did it with no problem at all.

Wesley and Molly and their children were there to meet Jim and Mary and they were very happy they were there. Their home was about 100 yards away from the air strip and they all slowly made the walk towards their home, talking as they did. Molly already had lunch waiting so they went on into the house and sat down at the table. She served nearly the same Liberian food that they had in Monrovia, River Cess, and at Bahn and it was delicious. Jim and Mary enjoyed it very much, but they especially enjoyed their fellowship with Wesley and Molly.

As they were eating their conversation at first centered around their families and lives back in their own countries. Later in their conversation Wesley ask Jim why they did not come there as they had originally said they would. He went on to say that he and Molly had to go back to Ireland and he desperately needed Jim and Mary to be there to run the mission station and to lead the work on a building project while they were gone. He also said that it cost him a lot of money when Jim and Mary did not come.

Jim quickly saw that Wesley was very upset at Mary and him because they did not come to Liberia as they had originally planned. Jim was also very disturbed because he believed they were delayed because Wesley told the leadership in America that he had to have linguistics in Toronto before they came.

When Jim heard Wesley's question as to why they did not come to Liberia as planned he was shocked and very confused. Jim told Wesley that they were delayed because he told WEC in America that he had to have linguistics in Toronto before they came. Wesley was shocked at this and said, "I did not request that." It was then that Mary and Jim realized that this word did not come from Wesley, who was the WEC field leader in Liberia, but from an individual who wrote the letter. Wesley and Molly were also very shocked that the missionary in Liberia had taken it upon themselves to write the letter when they had no authority to do so.

The two families, who had been upset with each other for about a year, were suddenly faced with a startling revelation. For all of this time Wesley and Molly believed Jim and Mary decided to delay coming as planned and Jim and Mary thought it was the Bells who required Jim to go to the school in Canada before they came.

The results of the letter had put an unnecessary burden upon Wesley and Molly, as well as on Mary and Jim and their children. It cost Mary and Jim a lot of money and Wesley and Molly lost a lot of money because of it. Also, it cost a delay in getting Molly's cancer treatment. In addition to that the man that Wesley hired and gave the money to was dishonest and much of the money disappeared and he did not get the project done.

God's plans can be foiled by people when they make decisions without fully seeking God in prayer until they know what He wants. What God wants always fits into His plans for our life.

Through Jim's twenty-five years of being a missionary in Africa there was never a time when he needed linguistics. God knew his skills and

He wanted Jim there to use them. This was His plan for Jim and not to waste time and money getting the linguistics training.

It was later found that a very strong-willed person, who always wanted their way for what the mission did, wrote the letter saying that Jim needed linguistics before he came to Liberia. It was an offense against Mary and Jim and also against the Bell's. It was also an offense against God's perfect plan concerning Jim heading up Wesley's building program.

During Jim and Mary's delay Wesley and Molly returned to Ireland and Molly was treated for her cancer and they returned before Jim and Mary got there. As a result, Wesley no longer needed them to come to Flumpa mission, but he needed someone with Jim's skills to go to Saclapia Mission Station. An older couple needed to go back to their home in Ireland for a year of rest and Wesley wanted Jim and Mary to replace them while they were gone. After hearing this from Wesley, Jim and Mary agreed to go to Saclapia Mission Station and spend some time with Dave and Maud Carson. After that Bob flew Jim and Mary back to Bahn mission where they got some rest and had a good evening meal with Bob and Pat.

Chapter 24
Saclapia Mission Station

The next day after breakfast the brothers and their wives got in the car and headed down the mission hill and drove through Bahn village. After they got through the village Bob headed down a road through the jungle towards their destination. The road was very rough and was mostly dirt with a very small amount of gravel on it. They saw miles of thick jungle trees and vines. Jim had heard that a man could only walk about one quarter of a mile in a day through the jungle if they did not have a machete to cut the vines. They also said that the man's clothes would be about torn off of him by the end of the day due to the massive jungle growth.

As Jim looked at the Jungle, he felt that the things he heard about how difficult it was to walk through it were true. He could see that in many places a person would have to crawl on their stomach to get through some areas because the vines were so thick. Jim had also heard that if a person came down in a plane crash and lived, they had almost zero chance of living even for a few days in the jungle due to the snakes, insects, and other things out there to take their life. Jim knew Bob had to think about this since he was flying over the jungle every day.

While Bob was driving, Jim thought about the many people who lived in the jungle and had never heard about Jesus Christ. He knew they had a soul and God loved them so much that He sent His only son to die for their sins. Jim also thought about how God had called Mary and him out of a life of living in luxury and sent them to Africa so that these people could hear about His Son, believe on Him, repent and accept Him as their Savior. Jim was determined to let this be his main goal while they were in Africa.

They drove by many villages and the little children would hear the sound of the car coming and watch them as we passed by. They seemed excited to see them and Jim would wave at them and they would smile and wave back at him. He felt sorry for them because most of their tummies were bloated out severely, which is a sign that they were malnourished and filled with worms. In addition, their belly buttons were almost always pushed out to about the size of an orange due to improper care in cutting their umbilical cords when they were born. Even with that, the children were lovable and Jim and Mary enjoyed seeing them as they drove by.

After two hours of driving they drove into the Saclapia Mission Station and Jim and Mary got their first look around at the place where they would be living for the next year. The main house, where Dave and Maud Carson and Betty Bush lived was built nearly the same as the main houses on River Cess, Flumpa and Bahn missions. Dave, Maud, and Betty were expecting Jim and Mary and came out to the car before they got out. Also, there were several grade school students and Liberian people who lived on the mission and they came to meet them. They were all happy to see Jim and Mary and told them how glad they were that they were going to be living there. Mary and Jim appreciated the love they showed them and were happy that this would be their home for the next year.

After all of their greetings Maud and Betty said they had lunch prepared and it was time to eat. They had a very large table set up with many of the same Liberian foods that Jim and Mary had at the other mission stations. Their main staple was rice and cassava. There were no potatoes in Liberia because the soil was so high in iron that they would not grow. However, rice and cassava would grow and that was what the people ate along with other vegetables that grew there.

As they ate, their conversation soon centered around what Mary and Jim would be doing at the mission station while Dave and Maud went back to Ireland for a year. Betty would stay during that year so there would be three of them in the house. The details of all that they needed to know were almost overwhelming and that was why it was good to have this visit with the Carson's before they left.

Mary and Jim were surprised at how large their grade school was and how many boarding school students lived there. Jim quickly saw that it took a tremendous amount of work just to keep the buildings in repair and to keep the mission running smoothly. In addition to that, the mission had to plant cassava and vegetables every year for the boarding school children and missionaries to eat. After seeing all of the work it took to keep the mission going it became obvious to Jim and Mary why the Carsons had to delay going home until they got there.

Jim and Mary could also see that living in the jungle for five years takes a tremendous toll on a person's body and they needed to get away and have a time of rest. Most of this is because of Jungle diseases that most people get who live there. Even the average life span of the Liberians was only thirty-four years. At one time the Liberian people called their country, "White Man's Grave" because nearly all of the early missionaries died of jungle diseases not long after they arrived. Dave and Maud both looked very tired and there was no doubt in Jim and Mary's minds that they were in need of a long rest away from the jungle.

Dave was a soft-spoken man who was easy to like and he did his best to show Jim what he needed to know to run the station. He also told Jim that for years the local commissioner had been trying to take a large section of the mission station away from the missionaries. When the missionaries first came to Liberia the government gave them 250 acres of land in different areas with the agreement that they would build schools and educate their children and build hospitals and clinics and treat their sick people. The land was also for a place to grow food for the missionaries. The commissioner wanted part of that land for himself and he was constantly coming up with some way to get it. Dave knew he would see that Jim was a new person and he would try to get the land from him.

Maud and Betty showed Mary many things she would need to know to live on the mission station. After being there for about five- or six-hours Mary and Jim had a good understanding of what was required to run the mission station.

Jim and Mary fully believed it was in God's plan for them to be there for the year when the Carsons were gone. This was true, but there was something far greater that God had planned for them and they had no idea what it was or how great it would turn out.

After that, they got back in Bob's car and made the two-hour drive back to Bahn mission.

Chapter 25

Hogs and Swamp Rice

At 8:00 every morning the mission stations had a fifteen-minute segment of time when they communicated with each other on their two-way radios. A few days after Jim and Mary visited Saclapia Mission Station they received word by the radio that Dave and Maud were ready to leave their mission station and make the five-hour drive to Monrovia. They would stay in Monrovia a few days and then fly to Ireland. When the day came Bob drove Jim and Mary to Saclapia Mission Station and they moved into Dave and Maud's house. The next day Mary and Jim started to do all that was necessary to keep the mission running. They both were extremely busy, but they kept everything running normally. Working with Betty Bush was a blessing and they grew to appreciate her very much.

Shortly after Jim and Mary went to Saclapia Mission Station their three children finished their school year in Indiana. Jess and June Horner helped them make all of the necessary arrangements to fly to Liberia. Jim and Mary made the trip to Monrovia and were there when the children got off of the plane. It was a very special day for the children and their parents to be together. They were a family again, but this time living deep in the jungle. All of the sights and people were different to the children, but they were also excited to be in their new home. Not long after this they started doing their schooling by correspondence.

One of the first things Jim learned in Liberia was that it was very difficult for the Liberians to get enough meat to eat. The jungle was very thick, which made it nearly impossible for large animals to live there. There were some small deer, but they were nearly impossible to find. Also, there were very few monkeys left because the people had eaten nearly all of them. As a result, the people were nearly starving for good protein. Jim felt the Lord gave him an idea how he could help solve their problem.

Jim did some checking and found he could purchase a very good breed of hogs from a rubber plantation in Liberia. He made a pen for hogs on the mission station and then bought six of their forty-pound pigs. Then he asked Bob if he would fly to the rubber plantation and get the pigs and fly them back to him. The rubber plantation was about a forty-minute flight away so Bob took the back seat out of the plane and flew there and loaded the pigs in the back of the plane. He made the flight back to Bahn mission and Jim took the pigs to his mission station.

Jim also found that there was a company in the area where he could get rice browns. This company polished the outside of the rice off so that they could have white rice. They called the polished off part rice browns. Jim knew that almost all of the vitamins of the rice was in the part they polished off and they just threw the rice browns away. He felt he could probably get truckloads of them for free or at a very low cost. Jim strongly believed a hog would thrive on the rice browns.

America was also sending massive amounts of wheat to Liberia. The same company in Liberia was also polishing off the outside of the wheat so they could have white flour to make white bread. They called the part they polished off wheat browns and they had no use for them. Jim thought he could get it for free or for a very little cost. He knew it was also loaded with nutrients and felt that a hog would grow on it. Also, the jungle floor was loaded with things a hog could root for and eat. The jungle was full of a plant that looked like a fern. Jim thought they probably had very good nutrients in them and a person could gather all they needed if hogs would eat them. He also saw that people ate the leaves of the cassava trees so they must have some nutrients in them and they were very plentiful. Jim believed that if they were good for people, they would also be good for hogs.

Jim purchased an old pickup truck and used it to get a truck load of rice browns for free and started feeding them to the six pigs. They seemed to love them and gobbled them down. He also pulled some of the fern looking plants from the jungle and fed them to the pigs along with the rice browns. The pigs ate the fern like plants and gobbled them down just as they did the rice browns. Jim also tried feeding the pigs some of the leaves from the cassava trees and they ate them the same as they did the fern like plants.

Jim was very pleased to see that the pigs seemed to love eating the things he gave them and they quickly grew into hogs large enough to eat. Several Liberian Christian men watched Jim through the process of feeding the pigs and they were excited to see how well the pigs grew on what he gave them and that it cost him nothing. This greatly encouraged the Liberians because they knew they could do the same thing and this was Jim's goal in doing it.

When Jim purchased the pigs, he purposely bought five female pigs and one male pig. He did not give away any of the hogs when they were large enough to eat, but let the sows each have a litter of pigs. Soon he had about fifty pigs to give to the Christians so they could produce their own pork to eat. The process worked out beautifully and the Christians seemed to really appreciate the fact that they could have sufficient meat for their families at almost no cost except for their labor.

This whole process was no doubt in God's plan to give the Liberian Christians a way to have protein for their family. Both the Christians and non-Christians saw that this knowledge came from a missionary. All of them knew and greatly appreciated this man from America giving them a new way to feed their family. Within a short time, Jim was very popular with the Liberian people in the area and it greatly helped them listen to his preaching about Jesus Christ.

God, in His plan, had taken an obedient hog farmer from Indiana and used him to teach the Liberian Christians how they could raise hogs in Liberia and have a sufficient supply of meat to feed their families and also to sell. What did this take to bring God's plan about? It was obedience to God's call upon Jim and Mary's life to sell out in America and follow him!

As Jim continued to work at running the mission station God showed him another way to help the Christians supply food for themselves. Rice was their main food and they ate it every day. In fact, they loved their rice, but it required a tremendous amount of labor every year to produce it. The married Liberian men would each cut down about an acre of jungle every two years for their family farm. They started this in December, which was the beginning of the dry season. There was normally no rain for three months. During that time the trees and vines that were cut down dried out. At the end of the dry season they would set fire to the dried foliage and it would almost explode into a huge ball of fire.

After that the women would use short handled hoes to loosen up the soil between the trees and sticks that did not burn. Then they would scatter rice seed over the soil and let the early rains put enough soil over the seeds so they would grow. It was then a constant battle to stop birds and small animals from destroying the growing rice. After the growing season had ended, they harvested the rice with a small knife

141

cutting off one head at a time. The whole process was very labor intensive.

The soil in Liberia is so full of iron that they could only have a good crop of rice for one year. During the second year the rice was very poor and they would have no rice if they tried to plant it three years in the same place. Jim saw how each family seemed to run out of rice every year and then they would go through what they called hunger time. That usually lasted about two months and it was a very difficult time for the families.

Jim felt God wanted him to help them improve on how they grew their rice. He knew swamp rice produced four times as much rice per acre as dry land rice and that the many swamps in Liberia could be converted into rice paddies. It was Jim's opinion that there were enough swamps in Liberia to produce rice for the whole population. It would take a lot of work to make the paddies, but it would not be much more than it was already taking them to plant their dry land rice. After the first year of making the paddies, they could grow rice in the same paddy year after year. Jim knew that in China they grew rice in the same paddies for generations.

Jim heard that some Chinese were in Liberia on some project for the government so he asked them to tell him how to grow swamp rice. They were very helpful and explained in detail how to do it. Jim understood exactly what they were saying and he was not only a hog farmer, but also a grain farmer, and that helped him understand the process.

Jim knew the best way to teach the Liberians how to grow swamp rice was to do it exactly as he did in teaching them how to raise hogs. He would do it himself, but get the boarding school students to work with him through the whole process. This would show the men that even a child could do it. Jim would not have to tell the Liberian men that he was going to teach them how to grow swamp rice because they watched almost everything he did to maintain the mission station. He would simply do it and they would learn.

Also, Jim would personally do all of the physical work with the students helping him. He would not ask them to do anything he would not do himself. When it came to getting into the swamp and getting very muddy Jim would do it along with his helpers. This would be a good lesson for the Liberian Christian men who would be watching him. They would see that the missionary man was willing get in the swamp and get very muddy and then they would be willing to do it also. Jim's goal as a missionary was to teach them by example. As he was working, he would also be talking to those around him about the Word of God and His Son Jesus Christ. This would show that a person can and should represent Jesus Christ in all they do, even when they are working.

Jim started raising the swamp rice in addition to all of the other projects he had to do to maintain and run the mission station. To say the least Jim was very busy, but it was also like the Spirit of the Lord was guiding him daily and giving him strength in all he did. The swamp rice did extremely well and Jim had a very large harvest at the end of the growing season. The Liberians were absolutely amazed at how much rice came from the rice paddy. The president of all their churches in Liberia also came to Jim's mission to see what he was doing to grow the swamp rice. One day after Jim's rice was nearly full grown the church president pointed at a small area of the swamp rice and said, "That small area has enough rice in it to feed a family for one year." Shortly after that the church president personally made a rice paddy in a swamp behind his house. Even though he was president of all the churches he got into the swamp just as Jim had and made the paddy. Then he planted his swamp rice just as he watched Jim do and he had a very good harvest from it.

Many of the government people were also watching Jim's progress in growing the swamp rice and they were amazed at how well it did. Also, many missionaries were amazed. One Liberian man came to Jim and said, "Mr. McCauley, you have helped us save face, thank you." What did he mean? The fact that Jim, being a white missionary, got into the muddy swamp himself and planted the swamp rice showed every man there that it was not beneath them to do the same. This meant to them that it was not shameful to get into a swamp and get very muddy working.

The whole process helped many people see a better way of growing rice in Liberia. This also helped many leaders in the area appreciate what the missionaries were doing. Jim was the first person to grow swamp rice in that area of Liberia and possibly the first in the country. Today swamp rice is grown all over Liberia and is their main farm

143

crop. Jim was very pleased at how well the government leaders appreciated what he did. Many of them could see an extreme value in their people learning this new method of raising rice.

Jim knew God had used his talents to bring glory to His name in that area of Liberia. God had used him to teach the people how to raise hogs and this was a talent that he had before he came to Liberia. Then, because Jim was a successful farmer, he was always looking for a better way to produce grain on the land he had. Rice is a grain and God blessed Jim to find a better way to grow it in Liberia, and to teach it to their people.

All of this was not because Jim was so smart, but rather that God can use some one as common as he was to further His kingdom if they are willing to obey Him in everything they do. He also believes that teaching the Liberians how to raise hogs and grow swamp rice was fully in the plan God had for him back when he saw the large triangle and angels in Indiana. He saw the value of physically working to help these people and it helped his testimony for Jesus Christ in the whole area.

As was said earlier, Dave Carson warned Jim that the local commissioner was always trying to get a section of the mission's 250 acres for himself. One day Jim received word from some of the Christians that the commissioner was planning on putting a road through the mission's property. They said he was going to call it a short cut across a bend in the local road. Then some men showed up and marked where the road was to go through the mission. Also, Jim saw that they moved a large bulldozer to Saclapia Village.

Jim remembered Dave's warning that the commissioner might try something to get a large part of the mission for himself and he knew this was his plan to do it. He would claim the land on the other side of the road was his. Since the commissioner had not spoken to Jim about this, he knew he planned to do it without his permission and it was obvious he was going to do it right away.

God gave an idea to Jim how to stop the bulldozer from even starting to cut the road. He reminded Jim of a national law in Liberia that no one could cut down fruit trees, which included coffee and cocoa trees. There was a place nearby where he get all the coffee and cocoa seedlings he wanted, so he got 500 of them right away. In one day, Jim and the school boys planted them in the area where the road was going to go. Then he went to the commissioner and told him they had planted the 500 seedlings in that area and he immediately stopped his plans to make the road. After that, Jim had no problems with him.

By the time the swamp rice harvest was over Jim could see that their year of being the mission station leader at Saclapia was coming to a close. In a few weeks the Carsons would be back and Jim wondered what God was going to do with them after that.

Chapter 26
Build a Bible School

God is so fantastic that He can and does many things at the same time with people. He may send a person to do a job for Him, but has plans to use that person to do other things as he goes. God's main plan for His Son, Jesus Christ, was, no doubt, to die on the cross and rise again as a sacrifice for our sins. But when we look at Jesus' life, we see that He did many other valuable things on His way to the cross. Just to name a few, He taught the Word of God, He gave us an example on how we should live, He healed many people, He cast out demons and set men free, along with many other things.

Jim knew that God's plan for him to come to Liberia was to lead the building project at Flumpa mission, but that plan was foiled. He also knew that God planned for him and Mary to take the Carson's place when they returned to Ireland for a rest. Neither Jim nor Bob, had any idea that God's main plan for him in Liberia had not even started yet. It was a major plan of God to use both brothers' skills in a very important building project.

During the latter part of Jim and Mary's time at Saclapia mission station, Jim heard that the missionary women on a mission station in the Bassa tribal area were praying that God would send a man there to build a Bible school. He also heard that the women had wanted a Bible school there for years, but they knew they did not have the skills to build it and there was opposition from some missionaries against building it. Not long after Jim heard this God gave him a message in a dream that he knew was of God. The message was that God had called another man to build the Bible school, but he had refused to do it. God was now telling Jim to build it and this was why He directed Mary and him to go to Liberia before they went to Swaziland. In the dream God also warned Jim that if he did not build the Bible school it would never be built.

Now the question Jim had about why God sent them to Liberia before they went to Swaziland was very clear to him. Jim also had a feeling that God would send them on to Swaziland shortly after they finished the Bible school at the Bassa Mission Station. God's warning to Jim that if he did not build the Bible school it would never be built was a strong driving force within him to get it built no matter how much effort it took. Jim told Wesley about this direction from God and requested permission to move to the Bassa mission after the Carsons returned. Wesley presented this request to the mission board.

For many years, the mission had a Bible school at Bahn Mission Station. Bahn was in the heart of the Gio tribal area. The students were all from the Mano and Gio tribes. These two tribes were located side by side in the jungle, and most of the Gio and Mano people could speak and understand both languages. The mission also had a large work in the Bassa tribal area, but it was about a hundred miles away through the jungle, and they had a totally different language. The Bassa could not understand the Mano or Gio, and the Mano and Gio could not understand the Bassa.

Years before Jim and Mary came to Liberia, some Bassa students attended the Bahn Bible School, but it was very difficult for them. Each weekend the Bible school students were required to go into the villages and preach the Gospel. Since the Bassa could not speak the language, it was impossible to preach in the villages to the Gio or Mano people, and it was too far away for them to go to the Bassa villages. In addition to the language problem, many of the non-Christian Gio and Mano people treated the Bassa students very harshly. This made living in the Gio and Mano area very difficult for the Bassa students. As a result, no Bassa students attended the Bible school after the first group tried it.

When the field leader and the mission board talked about Mary and Jim moving to the Bassa Mission Station to build the Bible school, major problems arose. Two missionary women felt strongly that they should not have two Bible schools because they felt it would split the church. One of the women was the one who wrote the letter saying Jim was to get linguistics before he came to Liberia. Others felt that it would not hurt the church at all, and that they should have a Bassa Bible School in their own area. Then the students could go out every weekend, teaching and preaching in the Bassa villages in their own language. Also, the Bible school would produce many Bassa evangelists and pastors who had Bible school training.

There was a lot of discussion on whether or not to allow Jim to build the Bible school. It seemed to Jim and also to Bob that the decision should be made on what God was saying, and they felt He was saying to build it. What no one knew at the time, but God did, was that in a few years nearly all of the Christians in the Bahn area - men, women, and children - would be lined up and shot on the mission station where the Bahn Bible School was located. Then, a few days after this tragic event, the missionaries there would also be shot. This would be the end of the Bahn Bible School and it would never start again.

The discussion concerning building a Bible school in the Bassa area continued with several difficult and lengthy meetings. Those who were opposing building the second Bible school in the Bassa area were doing it on their own logic, which was that the Bahn Bible school was all they needed. However, God could see that the Bahn Bible school would be destroyed and most of the Christians, teachers, and missionaries would soon be dead. Those who believed God wanted the Bassa Bible school were hearing God. His will prevailed, and the final decision was that Jim could build the Bible school if they called it an Agriculture Bible School, and if raising hogs and growing swamp rice was part of the curriculum. Jim and Mary agreed to this and made plans and preparations to move to the Bassa Mission Station. Jim planned to take half of his hogs there with them and leave the rest with the Christians in Saclapia so they could start raising their own hogs.

It is very important when we are making a decision for ourselves or for other people that we are in deep prayer and hear God give us His plan.

Chapter 27

The Sow's Plane Ride

This chapter could be called, "Bob's Big Mess Up" or "Bob's Foolish Error." We could call it a lot of things, none of which would be complementary to Bob, so we will just leave it as "The Sow's Plane Ride." Any way you look at it, this has to be one of Bob's biggest errors and how God got them out of it.

Jim had one sow that was nearly ready to have pigs and she was a very prime animal. He planned to use her pigs to get the Bassa started on a new venture of raising hogs, but he was quite concerned about getting her safely to the Bassa Mission Station because it was a rough 300-mile drive in his truck to get her there. Jim knew there was a good possibility that all of the shaking around in his pickup would cause her to lose her pigs. Jim began to wonder if flying her there might be a better option, so he asked Bob if he could fly a 400-pound sow to the Bassa station in the plane and Bob said he could do it.

Bob said he could remove the back seat from the plane and use the empty area for the sow to stand in. Jim told Bob they would need to build a crate out of very heavy boards in order to secure her. Bob said he had some boards at his mission station and he could make the crate that same evening. Jim thought that would be great and told him to make it twenty inches wide and five feet long. He wanted to make it as small as possible to keep the sow from having room to move around. The brothers agreed that they would meet at the Flumpa mission air strip the next morning at 10:00. Flumpa was about an hour drive from Saclapia and that would give Jim time to load the sow in his pickup truck and get there at 10:00.

The following morning Jim arrived at the Flumpa mission air strip at 10:00 and Bob had just landed his plane there a few minutes before. Jim walked to the plane and opened the side double doors to see the crate Bob had made. He was shocked to see that Bob had made the crate nearly four feet wide and six feet long. Jim ask him why he made it that big and he said he thought it would be easier on the sow if she had plenty of room. Jim told Bob that he wanted it as small as possible because he did not want the sow to have room to move around.

Bob now understood the importance of the crate being built the size Jim had requested; however, he also knew it would take a whole extra day for him to get back to his mission station and build a new one. The sow was very close to having her pigs, and they both wanted to get her to the Bassa mission before she started having them. If they waited the extra day, it would require that Jim drive the sow back to Saclapia and then back the next day on the rough roads, which would definitely be a risk to her and her pigs.

Bob suggested that they put the sow in the plane and start the engine to see how the sow reacted to the loud noise. If she seemed calm, then they would take off and if she remained calm, they would go on with their flight. If she seemed excited in any way they would turn around and land. Jim agreed to the plan.

The brothers unloaded the sow from the pickup and drove her up a ramp that Jim brought along for loading her into the plane. The sow walked up the ramp and turned with her head facing the back of the seat just like this was a normal everyday occurrence for her. It sure was a funny-looking sight, a four hundred-pound sow standing in the back of the plane in a crate with her head directly behind the front seats. The brothers looked at her for a bit and even took a picture of her standing there. She was as calm as could be! Bob had made a large door on the side of the crate for the sow to go through; they closed and secured it, and got ready for takeoff.

Bob started the engine, and it roared to life with its very loud noise level. The brothers were watching the sow to see how she reacted, and to their delight she did not act as if the noise bothered her at all. Jim felt confident that things were going well. Bob taxied to the end of the mission runway and turned around, and still the sow did not move or react. Things looked good and they took off. The sow acted like an old pro at flying. She was just standing there motionless with her nose right behind the seats. She was not excited at all.

Bob and Jim continued to watch the sow for any reaction that would lead them to feel they needed to turn around. After about fifteen minutes of flying, they were starting to relax and feel more confident that she would stay calm. It was a very clear day, making it easy for Bob to see his landmarks along the way. The flight was smooth, and the dense jungle looked like a green carpet about five hundred feet below them. They were still about an hour from their destination, so Bob and Jim began having light conversation.

Their smooth, relaxing flight suddenly came to an abrupt halt at about the halfway mark of their trip. The sow suddenly became very violent, ramming as hard as she could against the sides, front, and rear of the crate. Jim and Bob could hear the boards cracking as she hit them with her four hundred pounds. She tried to jump over the top of the crate hitting the top or the cockpit as she did. They were at what some call the point of no return when this happened. It meant that they were just as far from their takeoff point as they were from their destination. It was useless to turn around, so they continued on their flight. They were in the worst possible location for this to happen.

The boards were made of a very strong wood from the jungle, but the brothers could hear them cracking every time she rammed them. She continued ramming the front and back of the crate and also throwing her full weight against both sides. Her four hundred pounds were like a heavy battering ram hitting the crate. It was like the demons themselves were causing her to do this. Today both brothers believe that is exactly what happened. Somehow Bob and Jim had to stop her.

Jim unbuckled his seat belt and turned around with his knees in the seat, and grabbed the sow by her ears. She was trying to turn around, and they were afraid if she did get turned around, she might bust out the back of the crate and lunge to the rear of the plane. If she did, the weight and balance of the plane would be off and Bob would not be able to control the plane, causing them to crash. Jim was holding her ears with all his strength, but she was fighting him with all her strength. She was extremely strong, and Jim was already getting tired, but he had to stop her from turning around. Jim could not relax for one second or they would lose the battle with her and it would cost them their lives.

The brothers realized they might have to actually kill the sow in order to survive. The question was how to accomplish it. Bob had a flare gun in his survival kit, but if Jim shot her with it, there was a good possibility it would set the plane on fire. That was out of the question. Jim knew Bob had a hunting knife in his survival kit that they might use to kill the sow, but if they didn't accomplish it on their first try, she would become even more violent. Both plans were too dangerous. If they were to survive, God would have to do it and give Jim the strength to stop the sow from causing them to crash.

Jim kept fighting to keep the sow from turning around, but after only about ten minutes of holding on to her, he was becoming extremely tired and sweat was pouring off of his face. The sow seemed just as strong after ten minutes of wrestling with Jim as she was in the beginning. Bob was fighting to keep the plane under control because it was rocking in every direction as the sow threw her 400 pounds of weight around.

After the first fifteen minutes Jim was so tired his hands and arms were almost numb and he knew he still had over 20 more minutes of this. He was desperately praying as he was fighting with the sow. If he gave up, they were both dead. God had to give him strength to continue holding her. Jim is sure that is what happened because somehow, he continued to have enough strength to keep her from turning around. Finally, Bob said, "I see the mission landing strip." Jim was so happy to hear that, but he now started to wonder if Bob could land the plane on the 600-foot strip with it rolling around like it was. The sow continued to violently fight Jim as Bob was coming in for the landing.

When Bob slowed the plane down to land the rocking became much worse because there was much less air going over the control surfaces. This reduced Bob's ability to keep the plane level, but there was nothing he could do about. He had no choice but to keep coming in for the landing and trying his best to keep the plane as level as possible. Jim knew Bob was struggling to keep the plane under control and he was trying his best to help his brother by holding the sow, but it was impossible to keep her from moving. Even with the violent rocking back and forth, Bob was able to control the plane enough to make a perfect landing. When the plane's wheels touched down on the air strip Jim was still on his knees holding the sow, but he was shocked to see that she completely stopped jumping around even before Bob stopped the plane.

The brothers were so relieved to be on the ground at last and they thanked God for His protection. They wasted no time getting out, opening the side doors of the plane, and getting the sow out. Bob and Jim were amazed at how the sow became quiet and peaceful right after they landed. She calmly jumped out of the plane and onto the ground as if it were a normal thing, she did every day. Jim then drove the sow up the path from the airstrip toward the missionary houses and put her in a pen that he already prepared for her. He had made arrangements with a Bassa boy to care for the sow until he returned.

Bob and Jim got back in the plane and flew to Flumpa Mission Station. From there, Jim drove his truck back to Saclapia and Bob flew back to Bahn Mission. It had been quite a day for them, but they survived and the sow was at the Bassa Mission Station.

A few days later Bob flew Mary and their children, plus their personal items, to the Bassa Mission Station and they moved into their new home. Jim loaded half of his hogs in his old pickup and made the 300-mile drive to the Bassa station and left the other half at Saclapia Mission Station for the Christians.

Right after Jim and Mary moved to the Bassa mission station the sow had a very large liter of pigs. Many of the Liberian Christians and children came every day to see what Jim was doing with them. They had never seen a person raise pigs before so this was quite a novelty for them. They watched as Jim pulled vines from the jungle and got the rice browns to feed the larger pigs and sow and also how he cared for the newborn pigs. Their interest in the hogs was exactly the same as the Christians at Saclapia.

Jim was very pleased as they asked him questions and watched his every move in raising the pigs. He knew they were learning how to do it even though he was not giving them official classes. He was once again teaching by example. The Bassa people quickly learned how they could raise hogs and furnish their family with meat. Jim gave them pigs from the sow and other hogs he had and this gave the people a start on raising hogs themselves.

Chapter 28
God Could Repair It

Is it possible for God to get a very good vehicle for one of His servants who does not have the money to buy one? Is it also in God's plans for His servants to have the equipment they need to get His Word out? The answer to both questions is, "Yes, it is!" God is so amazing in His ability to meet our needs and it is exciting to see how He does it.

After Jim and Mary moved to the Bassa mission they saw that they had an open door to minister in the Firestone Rubber Plantation during the evenings when the workers were off work. However, it was about a forty-mile drive from their mission station to the plantation and their very old truck was in no condition to make many trips. They needed a very reliable vehicle to ministry there, but they did not have money to buy a better one. As they usually did when faced with a situation like this, they prayed and turned it over to God.

Jim heard that there was a fairly new used Toyota Land Cruiser for sale at a very low price, so he drove his old truck to see it. They were selling it at a fraction of the normal cost because the motor misfired badly and it had very little power. Jim saw that it was a four-wheel drive vehicle that looked good and had very few miles on it. He tried it out and immediately saw that something was very wrong with the motor. It badly misfired and would not be reliable at all for what they needed. In spite of this, Jim felt they should buy it anyway and the price was so cheap that they had the money to get it. Jim and Mary purchased the Land Cruiser and one of them drove the old truck back to their mission and the other drove the Toyota, with it misfiring and running on about half of its six cylinders, all the way home.

The Land Cruiser was originally purchased from a Toyota dealership in one of the larger cities in Liberia. Normally they have good mechanics, but they were unable to find the problem with this particular vehicle. The people decided to sell it at a very cheap price because of how badly it ran and they could not fix it. After Jim bought it, he asked Bob to look it over to see if he could fix it. Bob had never worked on a Toyota, but he agreed to give it a try. At first Bob thought it might be an ignition problem, so he checked out the ignition, and found it was working well. After that he decided to check the carburetor for problems. Bob was used to working on American-made engines, and the Toyota carburetor was different than any he had ever seen; however, he took the carburetor apart and examined every detail, but could find nothing wrong with it.

It looked like it should work fine, but when he put it back on the engine and started it up, it ran just the same as it had before he worked on it. Bob checked the compression, valve timing, spark timing, spark plugs, and spark plug wires. All of them looked perfect to him, so he decided to take the carburetor off again and look at it more closely. Again, he could see nothing wrong. Bob knew something was wrong to cause the engine to misfire so badly, but he just could not figure it out.

After exhausting everything he knew to do, Bob desperately prayed for knowledge to find the problem. He knew God had to show him what the problem was because he was like everyone else who had worked on the vehicle and could not find it. After that, as Bob was looking at the inside of the carburetor, a clear thought came to his mind. He knew it was the still, small voice of the Holy Spirit saying, "Look at the two jets in the very bottom of the carburetor." As Bob did this, another thought came to his mind that one of the jets was for high-speed driving and the other for low-speed driving. Bob looked very closely at the jets; one had a very small hole in it, and the other one had a hole in it that was about twice as large in diameter.

Suddenly it all became clear to Bob. The low-speed jet was mounted in the location of the carburetor that takes over when the vehicle is at high speed. The jets were reversed. He simply took out both jets and remounted them in their proper locations. Then Bob put the carburetor back together and remounted it back on the engine and reconnected the gas line, etc. When he started it, the engine ran perfectly.

Bob's guess was that someone in Japan had reversed the two jets accidentally, and no one had been able to find the problem. Whatever happened, Jim was able to purchase the nearly new Toyota at a very low price, and the whole thing certainly worked in his favor. He could never have purchased it at the normal price! Now it was running perfectly!

Was this in God's plan to get a very reliable vehicle for Jim and Mary with the small amount of money they had? It had to be because it greatly helped them in the ministry God had called them to do in the Bassa area. Was it in God's plan to show Bob what was wrong with the motor? It had to be because Bob would not have found the problem if the Holy Spirit had not showed it to him. Jim made trip after trip during the evenings and nights to the rubber plantation preaching the Gospel to the workers there. Hundreds heard the Word of God as a result and had a Born-Again experience of accepting Jesus Christ as their Savior. Yes, God can and does take care of our needs as He did for Jim and Mary.

Philippians 4:19 (NIV) *And my God will meet all your needs according to the riches of his glory in Christ Jesus.*

Chapter 29
Bible School & Plane Crash

When Bob was an engineer, he always had a plan on how to do design and build tools for his company. He also liked to have a backup plan if something caused them to be unable to do his first plan. The main goal was to always be able to produce quality parts as needed for production. God always has a perfect plan for every person's life and for what He wants them to do. Sadly, many times man does not do God's perfect plan. God can and often uses a backup plan to get a person where He wants them. Also, many times this causes some very difficult times for other people as well as for those who are involved in what God wants.

We can see this in the Bible story about Jonah. It was God's first or perfect plan for Jonah to go to Nineveh to preach against it.

Jonah 1:1-2 (NIV) *The word of the LORD came to Jonah son of Amittai: ² "Go to the great city of Nineveh and preach against it, because its wickedness has come up before me."*

We know from the story that Jonah did not want to go to Nineveh so he ran from God and got on a ship going to another location. God caused a storm to come upon that ship and all of those on it suffered. They finally realized Jonah was the cause of the storm and they threw him overboard and he ended up in the belly of a huge fish.

Jonah 1:17 (NIV) *Now the LORD provided a huge fish to swallow Jonah, and Jonah was in the belly of the fish three days and three nights.*

To say the least, we know that Jonah did not want to be in the belly of the big fish and when he repented the fish spit him out and he went to Nineveh. God got him where He wanted, but it would have been much easier for him and those on the ship if he had just gone there according to God's perfect plan.

Sometimes, in our lives God wants us to be in a certain place at a certain time and He has a perfect plan for this. However, it is possible for someone else to stop God's perfect plan from coming about. In that case it can cause difficulties for the person God wants in some location and it can cause problems for the people who stopped them from going there. An example of this is found in chapter 13 called "God's Plan

Foiled." God had a perfect plan for Jim and Mary to lead the building project when Wesley and Molly Bell returned to Ireland. Another person foiled God's plan and Jim and Mary, plus their children, and also Wesley and Molly and the building project suffered.

God wanted the Bassa Bible School built and He had a plan for Jim and Bob to do it. Bob knew the Lord spoke to him that he was to help Jim build it. God also spoke to him in His still, small voice, and told him to go to the mission board and request permission to go to the Bassa Mission Station for four months to help Jim build the Bible School. Bob did this and told them he would continue to do his regular flying, but from the Bassa station rather than from Bahn mission. He told them that in his spare time he would work with Jim on the building project.

After Bob presented his request, he felt the Lord wanted him to leave it in their hands and not push the idea. The mission board said he was needed more at the Bahn station when he wasn't flying so he could not help Jim build the Bible school. After they turned down his request, he prayed and said, "God, I did what You said and they turned it down, so it is up to You to do what You want." Bob was completely at peace with this and went on with his daily flying, but he had no idea how difficult things were about to get for him due to the mission board turning down his request.

A few days later, Bob flew from Monrovia to River Cess Mission Station to drop off some supplies. He planned to fly on to the Bassa station, which was about fifty miles north of River Cess mission. While he was still at River Cess mission he gave the missionaries his flight plan and approximate arrival time at the Bassa Mission Station. He tried to always let people know where he was going on his next flight. In case he did crash, the people would know in what direction to look for him. Right after unloading the supplies, Bob took off and headed for the Bassa station.

Shortly after he took off, he looked at his watch and realized he was running ahead of the arrival time he had given the missionaries at the Bassa station. The missionary ladies at the Bassa station had asked him to fly four one hundred-pound bags of rice from a village called Gaguya Town to their station. They wanted the rice for a scheduled conference that would be held within a week. Bob had not been able to fly the rice to them yet, but since he was ahead of schedule, this seemed like the perfect opportunity. Gaguya Town was only forty miles out of his way, so he decided to change his flight plan and take the forty-mile jog to pick up the rice. Even with the extra stop, he should get to the Bassa Mission Station near his estimated time of arrival. There was no one manning the radio at River Cess or the Bassa station, so he could not tell them about his change in plans.

He flew to Gaguya Town and landed. Bob loaded the rice and as he was attempting to take off, he went over a rough area that looked like it was caused from the erosion of water that had flowed across the runway. When the plane's wheels hit that area, the sudden shock was more than the tubes in the landing gears could take and they broke and the plane's underside dropped to the ground. This tore a hole in the plane's belly and bent the propeller.

Bob was very upset because he had bent up the airplane and could not fly it out of the air strip. He also realized he had broken his own policy of always making sure the mission stations knew where he was flying to next. No one would know he was forty miles off of his original course. If they tried looking for him with other mission planes, they would be looking in the wrong place.

His only hope was to get out a radio signal and tell people where he was and that he was okay. Otherwise his wife and children and the other missionaries would be very worried about him. They would probably believe he had been killed in a crash. As was said before, Bob's airplane radio that he used to talk to the mission stations while he was flying would hardly get out a radio signal when the plane was on the ground. He knew this was a major problem.

Bob began trying to call out on his radio, but he could not get an answer. He knew the missionaries at the Bassa station would be wondering what happened to him since he was not there. Even though he could not use his radio to get a call out, he did keep it on because it would receive a radio signal very well when the plane was on the ground. After about an hour and a half Bob heard the Bassa Mission Station calling the River Cess mission to see where he was. He could hear the missionary at River Cess say, "He left here two hours ago and it is only a twenty-minute flight to your station. He said he was on his way there. Something has to have happened."

After hearing their conversation, Bob knew they were very concerned about him, and he continued trying to call them, but to no avail. The only thing they knew to do at this point was to wait until their mission stations came on the air at their 5:00 pm. radio broadcast; they would tell the other stations that Bob had not arrived at the Bassa station. Then all of the WEC mission stations would decide what action to take. They tried to call Bob's wife, Pat, but could not get her because she was teaching at the mission school and would not be on the radio until 5:00 pm.

While Bob was waiting for all of the mission stations to get on their radios at 5:00 pm., he decided to evaluate the airplane condition some more. The first thing he was concerned about was getting the plane out of the deep jungle to a mission station where he could rebuild it. He thought about carrying it out, but quickly gave up on that idea. There was no way to hand-carry a plane through jungle paths and over rivers, etc. The plane would have to be flown out; there was no other way. It was too valuable to just leave there. He had to figure out a way to repair it right where it was, and then to fly it out.

Bob evaluated the plane's condition to determine what he had to do to fly it out of the village air strip and back to a mission station where he could properly repair it. He came to the conclusion that he needed to repair the landing gears, make a temporary repair to cover a hole in the bottom of the fuselage, and put the old propeller on the plane that was at the Bassa Mission Station. Bob also knew he had to lift the plane up about three feet to do the repairs. He needed help to lift the plane and he hoped he could get word to Jim and ask him come there and help him.

Bob desperately wanted to let his wife and the other missionaries know he was okay and where he was, but he could not figure how to get a radio signal to them. The Bassa station was the closest one to him; they were only forty miles away and could not hear his radio signal, so there was no way he could get a signal to the other stations that were farther away. His wife and family were one hundred miles away, so it would be nearly impossible to get a signal to them.

Finally, 5:00 pm. came and their mission stations started talking to each other over their two-way radios. Bob had his radio turned on and could hear them tell Pat that he was probably down in the jungle somewhere. They told her that he had left River Cess at 11:00 am. and that he should have been at the Bassa station by 11:20 am. but never arrived. Bob could hear Pat's reaction, and he knew this news had shaken her up. Although she was trying to stay strong, he could hear the sadness in her voice. He so wanted to tell her he was okay.

Each mission organization had a fifteen-minute allotted segment of time for their radio broadcast. The Baptist mission stations had their radio broadcast at 5:15 pm. right after WEC missions' fifteen minutes so they had their radios turned on during WEC Missions' broadcast. They could not help but overhear that Bob was down, so they entered in on the conversation with the WEC missionaries in an effort to help find him. They had two planes and wanted to start searching for him right away. As they talked to the WEC missionaries, Bob could hear them forming a search party for him. It was very strange for Bob to hear them tell his wife that he was down someplace and also to hear them talking about forming an airplane search party for him. Bob desperately wanted to tell them he was okay, but he could not do it.

Suddenly God, in His still, small voice, gave Bob an idea. The plane antenna was a wire that went from the top of the cockpit back to the tail and then out to one wing tip. As they were discussing the details of the search party, Bob grabbed a set of wire cutters from his toolbox, cut the wire off of the insulator at the wing tip, and slid it through the insulator on the tail. This gave him a straight wire that was about thirty feet long. He had a long rope in the plane and tied one end of it to one end of the wire and asked the tallest boy standing near him to pull the wire straight with the rope and hold it as high as he could. The radio signal would not be reduced as long as he was holding onto the wire with the rope, and he would not get shocked by the radio signal.

Bob also knew that the strongest radio signal goes out at a right angle from a straight wire antenna. He knew the direction to his mission station where Pat was, so he chose a location for the boy to stand while holding the rope. The antenna wire would then be perpendicular to the direction of Bahn mission station, which was about one hundred miles away. Since God had given Bob this plan, he felt the radio signal would go one hundred miles to where Pat was.

Bob then keyed his mike and called, "Bahn, this is Bob McCauley," but he received no reply. He could not get through because the missionaries kept talking and his signal could not override their more powerful signals. Bob kept trying hoping to find a break in their conversation. Finally, Pat called to everyone and said, "I think I hear something." She called out and said, "Bob, is that you? If it is, I think I can understand a yes or a no. Just answer me with a yes or a no. Is that you?" Bob answered, "Yes." Pat said, "I heard the yes. Are you okay?" Bob answered, "Yes." She then said, "Is the plane okay?" Bob answered, "No." He wanted to give her details, but she could not hear him well enough and neither could any of their other mission stations.

There was a Baptist mission station located about forty miles perpendicular to Bob's wire antenna, but in the opposite direction as Pat. Bob had a very close friend at that station, and he interrupted the conversation and said he could hear Bob clearly. The change in the antenna had worked. Bob could not talk clearly to Pat, but since his friend at the Baptist mission was also perpendicular to his wire antenna, but in the opposite direction, Bob could easily talk to him. It felt so good to Bob that he was able to talk to someone on his radio. Bob was able to tell his friend where he was and to give him details of his situation. Bob's friend then relayed the details on to the other mission stations.

After everyone was satisfied that Bob was fine, they started asking him what he needed them to do to help. Bob asked the Baptist pilot if he would fly his brother to him the following morning. He also asked him to have Jim bring enough food and water to last for three days, a shovel, a hoist, a heavy rope, a hammer, and an ax. Bob's friend then relayed this information on to Jim, who was on the radio at that time. He could not hear Bob, but he could hear his friend well. They both agreed to be there the next morning with the food and equipment.

Bob's Baptist friend completely understood his situation, as he and his father had both crashed a plane in the jungle. Bob's friend actually came in upside down in his plane and lived through it. His father crashed in the jungle as the result of a faulty fuel valve. He also had his Super Cub torn up as the result of a bull running in front of him as he was landing on a village airstrip. He lived through both crashes.

Shortly after the sun came up the Baptist pilot landed his super cub plane on the Bassa air strip. Jim was ready with the food and equipment and loaded them into the plane and then got in himself. The Baptist pilot was a very friendly young man and Jim really appreciated him. Jim could easily understand why he and Bob were close friends. The Baptist pilot took off and there was still some scattered patches of ground fog in the area, but he had no problem with them. After about 20 minutes of flying they could see the village air strip with Bob's plane sitting near one end. The Baptist pilot landed and taxied to Bob's plane. Jim and the pilot could easily see the broken landing gears and bent propeller. They both got out and unloaded the food and equipment. The Baptist pilot hardly looked at Bob's plane, but just said call me on the radio when you need me to come back for you. Bob said it might take three days because they had to lift the plane and take the landing gears off. After that Bob's friend got back in his plane and took off.

The first thing Jim did was to give Bob some food and water. Then they cut down three trees that were about six inches in diameter. They used those to build a support for the hoist. Then, using the hoist, they lifted the front of the plane off of the ground high enough to remove the landing gears and to make temporary repairs to cover the hole in the bottom side of the fuselage. They removed the bent and broken landing gears from the plane and evaluated what they needed to make the temporary repairs to the bottom side of the plane. To Bob's surprise, the work only took them about five hours instead of three days. The brothers were ready to fly out, so they called the Baptist pilot on the radio and asked him to come and get them. He was very surprised to hear from Bob and Jim so soon, but within a short time he arrived and flew the brothers and the broken landing gears to the Bassa Mission Station.

It was so good for Bob to get back to Jim's mission station, and he was able to use their radio to call Pat and their children and tell them personally about his accident at Gaguya Town. They were as happy to hear his voice as he was theirs. After that Bob took a much-needed bath. He was covered with insect bites, especially around his head and ears. Jim loaned him some clean clothes while his were being laundered. Mary made them a good supper and Bob enjoyed it very much. Later that evening Jim and Mary's family and Bob joined together for prayer, thanking God that Bob was out of the village and at Jim and Mary's home. Then they asked God to help them get the plane repaired so Bob could fly it out of the village.

The next day Bob and Jim took the landing gears to the Firestone Rubber Plantation and used their machine shop and welder to repair the gears. They called the Baptist pilot on the radio that evening and asked him to fly them back the next morning to Gaguya Town. He was glad to, and the following morning they headed back with the repaired landing gears, the old propeller, and sheet metal to make some temporary repairs to the bottom of the fuselage. The Baptist pilot left Bob and Jim there so he could go on about his flying. The brothers told him that they would call him when they were finished, but not to expect a call before the next day. Bob wanted him to come back to pick Jim up, because he wanted to fly the Maule out by himself for two reasons. First, he wanted the weight to be as light as possible because he had found a crack in a frame brace. Second, he didn't want to put Jim in any danger if something should go wrong.

The brothers began work on the plane right away. Jim started working on making temporary repairs to the hole in the fuselage, and Bob worked on mounting the propeller and the landing gears. By about three o'clock that afternoon they had the Maule sitting on the repaired landing gears. That was sure a good sight to them after seeing it lying broken on the ground just three days before this. The old propeller was mounted; Bob had checked it to see if it rotated without any wobble, and it was perfect. The flange was not bent at all. Jim had repaired the hole in the bottom side so it would not catch the wind while flying over one hundred miles per hour.

Bob started the plane and it fired to life with its normal roar. He checked the propeller again when the engine was running; it had no vibration at all and the propeller control was working perfectly. Next, he checked the controls to see if they were working correctly and was thrilled to find out they were. The plane was ready to fly.

Bob taxied the plane to the edge of the landing strip and shut it off. They called their pilot friend, and within a very short time they could hear his Super Cub flying in their direction. Within minutes he was landing back at Gaguya Town to get Jim. Bob climbed into his plane, started the engine again, did his preflight check, and it still checked out okay. While Bob was doing all of this, The Baptist pilot and Jim loaded the tools into the Super Cub and he did his preflight check. Now that they were both ready to go, Bob went ahead and gave his plane full power. With the light load, he was off the ground and flying in seconds with excellent control.

The Baptist pilot was flying a short distance behind Bob and to his left. Bob had decided to fly at ninety miles per hour instead of the normal speed of about 130, because he felt the slower speed would help keep excess pressure off the cracked frame. He also felt that it was only fair to him and his family that he fly the plane to the nearest mission station, which was where Mary and Jim lived. Bob reached the station in about fifteen minutes and was able to make a normal landing. He taxied the plane near the house where Jim and Mary lived and shut it off. Within seconds after Bob landed the Baptist pilot landed. They unloaded the tools, and their pilot friend flew back to his mission station.

Now they could restore the plane to be completely flight worthy. Bob had worked and rebuilt engines and air-frames for years when he flew as a hobby. He was confident that with his knowledge of airplane mechanics and with Jim's welding and tinsmith skills, they could rebuild the plane to its original condition. First Bob needed to order a new propeller, landing gears, and a new support brace to replace the one that was cracked. One strut was slightly bent, but they could repair it. Fortunately, Bob already had materials at Bahn mission to repair the hole in the fuselage. The brothers knew all this was going to take a lot of work, but they also knew God would be helping them all the way. Bob was so thankful and felt so blessed that the plane was repairable and sitting at Jim and Mary's mission station.

The next day Bob made the two-hour drive into Monrovia and reported the accident. Just as he had expected, the aviation authorities said that he had to have all the repairs made and the plane completely inspected before he could fly it again. However, once the repairs were made, he could fly it to Monrovia for the inspection. Since Bob could not make a temporary repair and fly it back to Bahn, it meant that he was going to be at Jim and Mary's mission station for a long time, and there was nothing he could do to change it. Bob would have to be separated from his family for an unknown length of time while the plane was being repaired. He always hated being separated from them, but there was no one else to repair the plane so he had to do it. Bob's family would have loved to come and be with him, but Pat had to stay in Bahn because of her teaching job at the Bible school and mission grade school.

Bob ordered the new landing gears, new support brace, and a new propeller. He also made the long trip to Bahn mission station by road and got the supplies he needed for the rest of the repairs. As soon as he returned with all the supplies, the brothers began to make the repairs on the strut and the fuselage. The strut was finished fairly quickly, but the fuselage was covered with fiberglass cloth, and it had to be completely dry when they worked with it. Then it started to rain almost daily. The rainy season had started and they simply could not do the fabric work to repair the hole in the fuselage unless it was completely dry.

When the first day of rain came, it kept the brothers from working on the plane, so they decided to start working on the Bible school. There was one large existing building on the mission station that was in the location where they wanted a dormitory. The building was made out of mud blocks with a tin roof. It was about forty feet long and twenty feet wide with no walls or rooms on the inside. It had only one door, which was in the front, and it needed to have a back door. After deciding where they wanted to put the back door, the brothers used Jim's hand wood saw and sawed a door opening in the mud blocks. This worked great, and they were on their way to building the Bible school that many had been praying for. God blessed from that time, and the work progressed wonderfully.

As the rain continued, Jim and Bob kept working on the Bible school. Besides putting in the door, they also made rooms by adding walls. This was a big job that took them a few weeks to complete, but they ended up with a very nice dorm for single students. The brothers also started making individual huts for those who had families. The African Christians were very good at making huts, so they did most of the work on these. Bob and Jim also changed another unused building into classrooms.

They worked on the plane when it was dry and the school buildings when it was raining. The new landing gears, propeller, and landing gear brace arrived at about the time they needed them. Bob and Jim mounted them on the plane. Also, Bob painted the damaged areas and some other places where the paint had eroded away from flying through the heavy rains. After that the plane looked like new. There was no sign of the crash and the brothers were happy about their work and thanked God that the plane was okay again. At about the same time the Bible school buildings, with all of the living quarters, were finished and they all looked wonderful. Then Bob flew the plane to Monrovia and the inspector checked their work out very well and signed the plane's log book, giving his permission for the plane to fly again.

After the inspector signed the log book, he handed it back to Bob. Bob was elated that the inspector not only signed the log book, but he also gave Bob a good complement on how good a job he did on the repairs. Bob looked at the log book and the inspector's statement and he noticed the date that he signed it. Bob well remembered the date he had the crash and he noticed it was exactly four months to the day later that the plane was ready to fly again.

Immediately Bob thought about how God had spoken to him in His still small voice saying he was to ask for permission to go to the Bassa Mission Station for four months to help Jim build the Bible school and that he would continue to fly out of that station. He was amazed that, even though the mission refused his request, God got him there anyway. What had looked like a major tragedy God used to get the Bible school built in His timing. Jim could not have accomplished the work by himself without Bob helping. God had a plan to get the Bible school built and He sent Jim there along with Bob to do it. The timing also was very important because immediately after it was finished the first classes started.

Bob also could not help but think how much easier it would have been if the mission had let him go to the Bassa station and help Jim in his spare time from his flying. The mission would have had the use of the plane all of those four months and it sure would have been easier for Bob and Jim.

Where was God's plan in building this Bible school when the brothers were living in very adverse conditions during their childhood? Was He there when the brothers' mother and father were fighting over the shotgun and Bob was nearly killed from the shotgun blast? Did He have the plan for the boys to build a Bible school when they endured all of their emotional pain as they witnessed all of the fighting between their parents day after day? What was God's plan for Jim when he was lying out in the field nearly dead after the motorcycle accident?

How could God possibly have a plan for the brothers to build a Bible school in Liberia West Africa after going through these difficult things? The answer to these questions is very simple. Before the brothers were born God had plans for them as He has plans for all people. There is another question with a very simple answer. Could anything have stopped God from using the brothers to build this Bible school? The answer is simply this, "If they had refused to sell their farms and quit their jobs etc. to follow God, they would have totally missed out on God's perfect plan for them." They would have been just like the rich ruler when he refused to obey Jesus' word to him." The brothers' obedience made it possible for God to use them in Liberia.

Please note: The Bible school was built over 45 years ago and it is still going on. Thousands upon thousands have heard God's Word as a result. There is no way of knowing how many have been saved from an eternity in hell.

Chapter 30
God Made a Tunnel in the Fog

After the Bible school was finished and the plane repaired and signed off as being okay to fly again, Bob flew back to Bahn Mission Station and was able to be with his family again. It felt so good to be back home after a very busy four months. He knew he was soon going to be flying nearly every day and would be away from home about half of the time, but he knew he could fly back to be with his family and this was very special to him.

Bob went back to his normal flying and took his family with him when he could. One day he was flying back from a town called Yekepa, which was located on the northern side of Liberia. Pat, Tanya and Tony were on board the plane with him. Before he took off that afternoon he looked up at the sky and it looked very good, so he did not expect any problems on his hour flight back to his mission station. However, he also knew from past experience that the jungle weather can always change quickly, so he had that in the back of his mind.

About fifty miles after they took off the weather in front of them changed for the worse. They started to get into rain and fog and Bob started to get concerned. As a result, he decided to turn back to the airstrip from where they took off. As he was making the 180-degree turn, Bob saw that the weather back toward Yekepa was completely closed in. It looked like a large jungle storm had developed in that area. There was no way he could see well enough to go back and land at that airstrip, and there were no other airstrips in the area he could get to. They had to go through the rain and fog and continue on a heading to their mission station.

Bob knew they were getting into trouble; he had to fly low enough to stay below the overcast, and yet high enough to miss the small hills. The worst thing he could do now was to go on top of the overcast because he would not be able to find their mission station or know where they were. To make matters worse, there were no radio signals in the area that they could use to locate themselves. The visibility kept getting worse, and Bob kept lowering the plane's altitude to stay below the overcast. Finally, he was flying just a few feet above the trees and making sharp turns to miss the hills. They were in big trouble!

169

Soon they came to an area where the fog was solid to the ground. Bob could see nothing ahead of them. He also knew they were flying below the tops of many of the large hills in the area. The only thing Bob could do was pray as he gave the engine full power to climb out as steep as it could in hopes of getting above any hills ahead of them. The Maule Rocket plane had a lot of power, so it had a very steep rate of climb, and soon they were above the hills. Bob could see nothing outside the plane except the gray fog, so he was flying completely on instruments.

What made this flight even worse was that the mission plane had only the very basic instruments. During this time Bob wished the plane had an artificial horizon in it to help him in this zero-visibility flying, but it did not have one. The question again flashed through his mind, as it had many times before, "Why did they decide to buy this plane with no instruments in it for flying in bad weather?" This made it extremely difficult for him to fly in weather where he could not see outside. Bob was watching the basic instruments closely and praying desperately as they were making the steep climb in an attempt to avoid the tall hills. When they reached an altitude that he knew was safely above the hills, Bob was relieved to be past that danger, but he was extremely concerned about the situation they were in.

They were in solid fog, and Bob knew that when they broke out on top of it, their chances of finding a hole that they could come down through would be almost zero. Even if they did find a hole down through the fog, he would not know their exact location. He would have to know it in order to get to an airstrip. The trees all look alike from the air, and it is extremely easy to get lost in bad weather. Bob was aware that if he missed the airstrip by even one quarter of a mile, he would most likely fly right by it and not see it at all.

They continued to climb, and soon broke out on top of the overcast. The sun was shining and it was beautiful; however, they could not enjoy it because of the seriousness of their situation. The fog below them looked like a level white sea; it was all they could see in every direction. There was no indication at all of an opening down through the fog. Bob decided to keep the plane on the same heading that he was on when they were going toward their mission station - just in case they did crash, someone would know what heading they had been on.

As Bob was trying to evaluate their possibilities, it occurred to him that not only did they just have about forty-five minutes of fuel left, but it would also be dark very soon. Both of these factors presented a huge problem, as the only airfield with lights was in Monrovia, the capital city, and that was still one- and one-half hours away. In addition to that dilemma was the knowledge that a heavy overcast fog can sometimes stay in an area for days, making the chances of finding a hole in the short time span they had a near impossibility.

If they ran out of gas or daylight, they would have to come down in the jungle and probably would be killed. If they did survive, it would be nearly impossible to live long enough to find their way out of the jungle. Bob knew that they probably could not survive even one night in the jungle with all the deadly snakes and animals that prowl in the night.

At this point, Bob was checking his watch closely as each desperate minute passed by with ever increasing speed. He asked Pat to pray, which she was already doing. She knew they were in trouble, but seemed relaxed as she prayed for the Lord's deliverance from their impossible situation. The time was quickly passing and soon Bob was aware there were only fifteen minutes before total darkness would set in. At this point Bob said to himself, "Bob, you just killed your family." His heart was heavy and his prayers became more desperate. If God did not make a way, there would be no way they could survive, and He only had fifteen minutes left to do it.

Suddenly Bob saw what looked like the possibility of a hole through the fog straight ahead of them about a mile away. Could it be true? Within thirty seconds they were there and it was a hole! It was very small and almost round. It was like looking down through a pipe, but it was a hole down through the fog! Bob made a circle around the hole and could hardly believe his eyes. He could see all the way down through the overcast to the one mountain in all of Liberia that he knew from the top.

The mountain had a very large flat rock on top that Bob recognized. Some of the pilots called this mountain Old Baldy because the huge flat rock on top of it prevented any trees from growing on it. Although Bob knew exactly where they were, he still had many questions spinning through his mind. Was the fog down to the ground around the base of Old Baldy? If they got down through the small hole, would they be able to fly to an airstrip from there? Despite the unanswered questions, Bob had no choice but to go down through the hole and see what awaited them there.

To get through the hole, Bob had to put the plane in a very tight spiral. This required dropping one wing nearly straight down and making sharp descending turns. Bob told the family to hold on. Then dropped the left wing nearly straight down and made rapid dropping rotations. As he made the very tight descending turns the centrifugal force on their bodies and on the plane was very high, but they endured it okay.

Bob leveled off right above the mountain and then started to fly around the base of the mountain. To his disappointment, he saw that the fog was all the way to the ground. He could not fly through that fog even though he knew exactly where they were. They were still in trouble! Bob continued making the circle until he came to an area that was on the three hundred-degree side of the mountain. Once again, Bob could hardly believe his eyes because there was a tunnel about the height of a telephone pole above the trees and about one hundred feet wide on an exact heading of 300 degrees.

Flumpa Mission Station was on a 300-degree heading away from Old Baldy. They also had an airstrip, and it was only a ten-minute flight away. Bob could hardly believe it! The tunnel through the fog was on a three hundred-degree heading away from Old Baldy! Bob made a sharp turn and brought the plane around to a 300-degree heading and flew down the tunnel. He could see nothing but fog on either side of them, but he could see enough directly in front of them to keep flying. It was as though the fog kept clearing only in the 300-degree direction they needed to get to Flumpa. As they kept looking around outside the plane, they could see that there was solid fog right above them, and the fog was to the ground only a few feet beyond the wing tips. Bob stopped looking at his instruments, but rather just followed the tunnel.

This was absolutely amazing! They were flying through a tunnel in the fog. This type of setting was impossible! The fog just does not react like this! It could not have happened naturally! Only God could do this! They were in the middle of something that only God could have made for them. He made a way where there seemed to be no way!

Bob continued to fly through the tunnel and suddenly he saw the end of the Flumpa airstrip. The tunnel had taken them to the very end of the airstrip where they could make a sharp right turn and land. Bob saw that about fifty feet beyond the end of the runway, the tunnel ended and the fog was again completely down to the ground. Bob made a sharp right turn at the end of the runway and landed. By the time they stopped their landing roll it was totally dark.

As they sat in the plane a few seconds before they got out, Bob thought about how dangerous it was to step out of the plane in total darkness because there could be a deadly snake on the ground that they could not see. But he quickly dismissed that thought knowing how God had just delivered them from sure death with hardly a second to spare. He could hardly get over the thought of how close it was and how God got them down alive. It was only God and Him alone! There was no doubt about this!

God taught Bob and Pat a valuable lesson that day. It was the fact that He is never too late and He can get something done even when it is totally impossible, as it was that day in saving their lives. God had this plan to teach Bob and Pat and it was a lesson they would never forget.

Chapter 31
A Needle in a Haystack

One of the biggest challenges a missionary pilot in Liberia had when Bob was flying there was jungle storms. Every pilot, no matter what mission they were with, faced this major obstacle. The only way a pilot could eliminate this problem was to stop flying during the rainy season, which lasted nine months out of the year. There was no weather forecast at that time and the weather, including the winds, could change so quickly that a pilot could get trapped in a situation that he could not get out of.

The pilots would occasionally see each other and often talk about this problem, but never seemed to have a solution to eliminate it. One missionary pilot always tried to encourage the other pilots to be safe in their flying. Sadly, he got in a jungle storm and was killed, along with three teenagers who came to Liberia on a short-term mission trip. Bob faced this danger so much that encountering jungle storms was a normal day of flying. There were times when he would have been killed if God had not delivered him. One such story is below.

About thirty-five doctors from an organization called the World Doctors came to Liberia once a year and stayed for about two weeks administering medical treatment to those in need. The mission pilots banded together during that time, flying the doctors to various villages and towns to treat the sick people. One day Bob was asked to fly to a town on the very southern tip of Liberia, pick up some of the World Doctors and fly them to another area. The flight to get them there would take about two hours and over some of the most remote jungle in all of Liberia.

Bob had never flown in this area before and that made this trip unique. The town was about 240 miles south of his mission station, and his flight navigation would be made strictly by visual and magnetic compass. The maps of the area were very poor, and there were no navigational radio beams in that part of the country. Approximately one hundred miles of Bob's flight would be over what is called "The High Jungle" or "The Three-Canopy Jungle." These titles were established because the tallest trees in this area are about 150 feet high with one hundred-foot-high trees just below them. And just below the one hundred- foot trees are fifty-foot trees with an abundance of vines

174

below them. At this point there is almost nothing growing on the jungle floor because of the lack of sunlight even during the brightest part of the day.

The two-hour flight there would use up about twenty gallons of gas, so Bob had to have both twenty-gallon wing tanks full. He also needed to carry about thirty gallons of gas in containers inside the cabin of the plane to use when he flew the doctors to their different locations. Most jungle pilots do not like to carry gas containers inside of their cabin due to the increased risk of fire and Bob was no exception to this. However, all of them had to do this occasionally because there were very few places in the country where they could get aviation fuel.

After getting the plane fueled up and doing his preflight check Bob took a little time to visit with his wife and family because he knew he would be gone for a few days and would miss them. By about ten o'clock the fog had lifted to about two hundred feet above the trees. Bob was ready to take off. After he had climbed above the trees, he banked the plane and turned to a heading of 190 degrees. His only way of knowing the wind direction and speed was to watch the small limbs and leaves on the trees along the way. This was not a very accurate way of navigating, but it was the best he had.

Within thirty minutes after takeoff, Bob was already in unfamiliar territory. About an hour after he took off, he was over the high jungle, which was so thick that there were hardly any villages in the area. It had probably been about fifty miles since he had seen his last village. In fact, all he had seen for some time were trees and more trees. Then all of a sudden, he saw a very small village. It really surprised him that a village would be in this location so far from civilization. As Bob got closer to the village, he saw a little field at the edge of the village. It was almost square and it looked to be about 300 feet long and about that wide.

As was said earlier, while Bob was still working at his job as a senior engineer for General Motors, he made a vow to obey the still small voice of the Holy Spirit no matter where it took him or how much it cost. God was about to give him another test and lesson to show him how valuable hearing the Holy Spirit was. Also as was said above, God can see the present, past, and future at the same time. God knew that in order to save Bob's life two years after this flight it was critical for him to hear the voice of the Holy Spirit now! This was part of

God's plan for Bob, but he would have to hear and obey the Holy Spirit at this moment for it to come about.

As Bob was looking at the little field, the Holy Spirit spoke to him in His still, small voice and said, "Study this field and remember it." Bob heard the Holy Spirit speak and he turned and made a circle around the village. He knew it was very critical for him to know the details of the field, but he did not know why. He stared at the little field and tried to memorize every detail as he circled around it. Bob knew that soccer was the main sports event in the country and many villages would chop the trees down and level the ground to make a soccer field. This field looked like a soccer field, but it was very short for landing a plane on. However, Bob saw that it was an opening in the jungle that he might be able to land on if he had an emergency. To do this, he saw that he would have to land coming in from the direction opposite of the village because the trees were shorter in that direction. After making the circle around the village, he put the plane back on the heading to his destination. He continued to think about what he had just seen even after he was long past it. In Bob's mind was the question, "Why did the Holy Spirit tell me to study this small field in this very remote area of the jungle?" He did not know the answer to this question, but he did remember every detail of the little field.

Bob continued on his same heading for another hour, and he came to the village along the ocean where the doctors were. He landed at the village airstrip, shut down his plane, and went to their location. For the next two days, he flew them to the villages that they wanted to go to in the area. After they treated the sick people in a village, Bob would fly them to the next place. He found the doctors to be very highly trained and qualified people who were using their profession to make a difference in other people's lives. He really enjoyed being around them and appreciated their dedication to helping the African people. After two days the doctors were finished with his services, and he was free to continue his normal flying. Bob had to fly to another destination in the country, so he did not fly over the same remote area that he had on his way there.

About two years later, Bob was on a flight back to his mission from the Bassa tribal area. When he took off on that flight, the weather seemed to be good, but when he got within one hundred miles of his mission station, the weather in front of him changed. There was a very black front coming in his direction from the north and east. Bob knew this type of storm contained high-speed winds along with up-and-down drafts that were capable of breaking up his plane if he would attempt to fly through it. There was no choice but to turn back, so he banked the plane and made an 180-degree turn. Once the turn was made, he was startled at what he saw. The storm had formed in large U shape, with him in the middle of it. It was as black to the west as it was to the east and north. Both the east and the west sides of the U extended as far south as Bob could see.

Sometimes a black front has some lighter gray spots in it which a pilot can fly through. The gray areas indicate very high, rough winds, but they are not usually strong enough to bring a plane down. However, in this situation there were no gray areas to be seen. This left Bob with only one option, and that was to fly in a southerly direction. He quickly banked his plane and flew south between the two black sides of the front.

The winds in the jungle storms are usually very violent with speeds up to eighty miles per hour or more. It is hard to control a plane in this type of turbulent winds, much less the up-and-down drafts and the complete darkness. Bob had experienced these types of storms before and had barely survived them. As he looked and evaluated his situation, he knew he was in serious trouble, and started to seriously pray for God's help because he was headed for the high jungle area.

Bob knew there were no places to land in the high jungle area except that small village that he had flown over about two years before. To find it again would be like trying to find a needle in a haystack. Bob was also coming in from a different direction than he had flown two years before when he had first seen it. If Bob missed the village by a quarter of a mile, he would never see it in the high jungle. It was like taking a one hundred-mile circle and trying to find a speck of a village in it. And then to add to the odds, the speck had to be found in the middle of a storm. At this point Bob saw the sides of the front coming closer together. Soon they would catch him, and he doubted the Maule could survive the turbulence. This was a time that God would have to deliver him, or he would soon be dead.

As Bob was flying, he could see the space between the black walls of the fronts getting narrower by the minute. After about forty minutes of flying between the fronts, he saw that he had to find the village quickly, because the black fronts were now only about one-half mile on either side of him. Soon Bob would be picking up the very violent winds and would not be able to land in them. Then, all of a sudden, Bob saw the village.

He was amazed, but had little time to even think about it. Both sides of the fronts now were less than one-quarter mile away from Bob, giving him only seconds to land before he would be in strong rain and wind, making it impossible to see well enough to land on this very short field. Even though Bob had to get the plane on the ground quickly, he also had to land at a very slow speed to be able to stop the plane. The field did appear to be about 300 feet square, but he did not have that much length to land on because the lowest trees at one end of the field were about fifty feet tall. He would have to be above those trees at the edge of the field and, at best, he would use up 100 feet to drop down after that. This meant he would have only about 200 feet to land on. He had to make a very good, low-speed landing with no bounce at all, or he would not get stopped in time, and he could destroy the plane and seriously hurt himself.

Bob passed over the village as he slowed his plane down. He had to cut his final approach very short to keep out of the front and strong rain. Bob slowed the Maule down to about an indicated forty miles per hour with full flaps and lowered his altitude to where he was just a few feet above the trees. He lined it up with the field coming in from the same direction that he had decided on two years earlier. He slowed it down as much as possible without stalling and started bringing the nose up very slowly, adding just enough power to keep the plane from dropping.

Soon Bob was flying very slow and right on the edge of the stall trimmer with a very high nose attitude and high-power setting. The plane was hanging on the engine power at the prop. The nose was so high that he could no longer see the field by looking over the nose of the plane. In order to see his landing spot, he had to look out the left side of the windshield and the left side of the engine cowling.

Bob was no longer watching his airspeed; he was flying by the feel of his control yoke. His eyes were glued on the field, waiting for that last second before he cut his engine power. He wanted the plane as slow as possible, and hanging on the prop enough, that when he cut the power it would instantly stop flying and not float at all. He also had his toes on top of the rudder pedals with the brakes partly locked. Just as Bob passed over the trees at the edge of the field, he pulled the throttle back enough that his plane quickly dropped about fifty feet and then he yanked it fully back, pulling the yoke back at the same time. The plane instantly stopped flying, settled to the ground, and rolled to a stop within about 150 feet.

At last Bob was safe on the ground. About ten seconds after he stopped the plane, the heavy rain hit. It was coming down so hard that he could hardly see outside. He just made it with no extra time! He sat there, knowing that God had delivered him from death again! He did it and He alone! He kept the storm back just long enough for Bob to get on the ground. To this day, Bob is still amazed at how he found the village. He knows that he did not find it on his own, but that his God led him to it. He saved Bob's life that day! Also, two years before this, the Holy Spirit spoke to him in His still, small voice telling him to look this landing strip over and remember it, which he did.

As Bob sat in the plane, he tried to call his wife on the radio, but he had little hope that the call would go that far, since his plane was sitting on the ground. However, this time the conditions must have been just right, because right after he called her, she answered. Bob was so glad to hear her voice, and she was just as happy to hear his. He told her he was okay and safely in a village. He gave her the approximate location of where he was and told her he would be there for the night. He could rest much easier, knowing that Pat and the others would not be worrying about him now that they knew he was safe on the ground.

As Bob was passing over the village, the thought entered his mind that he didn't even know what tribe this was or if they were even friendly, but at the time, this was not a concern, compared to getting on the ground. Bob sat in the plane for a few minutes, reflecting on how hard it was raining and how close he came to not making it.

About five minutes after Bob landed, the villagers came running through the rain toward the plane. They were all excited to see a plane sitting on their field. As they gathered, Bob got out and greeted them. They led him to the center of the village, which was about 150 yards away, and had him sit down on a stool under a grass roof held up by four poles. As he sat there, he noticed the rain had lightened. After giving him a seat, they all left, and Bob found himself sitting there alone for about an hour. Although he was wet and a little chilly, he was

179

thankful to be safe in the village. Bob knew he would be spending the night, but he had no idea of the surprise that the Lord had for him that evening.

About an hour later, a few men came walking toward him. The rain had nearly stopped by now, and he could also see a few people starting to come out of their huts. When the men got close to Bob, one of them spoke up in perfect English. He greeted Bob and Bob greeted him, and then the man said, "How do you like your chicken?" This was an unusual question for Bob, especially in this location. Bob answered, "I like it any way you cook it." He spoke back and said, "No, you see, I am the cook for the American Embassy in Monrovia, and I know Americans like chicken different ways. I will make you a meal this evening, and I will make the chicken any way you want it." He went on to tell Bob that this was his village, and he had returned here for a visit. The man gave Bob some different ways he could cook chicken, so Bob picked one. Then the men left, and in about an hour, they appeared again with a very lovely meal. It was simply delicious - maybe the best tasting meal Bob ever had.

After the meal, they showed Bob to a hut with a bed in it that he was to use. As usual, they gave Bob a bucket of hot water for a bath and showed him where the bathhouse was. Every village has a bathhouse, which is usually a small round hut with a layer of small stones covering the dirt floor. It is always refreshing after a hot day in the jungle to be able to get a hot bath before you go to bed.

Bob did not see the cook from the American Embassy again, but there was another man in the village who spoke some English. There were several Christians in the village, including this man. He became Bob's interpreter, and Bob spent the evening with him and others teaching the Word of God.

The next morning the villagers gave Bob breakfast and asked if he would pray for some of their sick people. He gladly prayed for them to be healed and he also had the opportunity to talk to each of them about the Lord. They all seemed very happy that he was there to minister to them. It was such a refreshing experience to be able to minister to these lovely people that lived in this very remote place. Not only had Bob ministered to them, but they had ministered to him, a complete stranger, dropping in on them as he had.

By about ten o'clock the weather cleared and, along with most of the villagers, Bob walked back out to the plane. He did a walk-around check of the plane, including checking the fuel in his wing tanks to make sure he had enough to get home. Bob thanked the villagers for their hospitality, climbed in, and did a preflight check. Everything checked out okay and the engine started immediately. After a few minutes it was warmed up enough for a takeoff.

The little field was too short in any one direction for a normal take off. When Bob landed the plane in the field the day before, he was not thinking about how he would later make a takeoff. He was only thinking about saving his life in the storm. God had blessed and he was able to land and get stopped without a crash. Now he needed God's help to fly out of the short field and be high enough to clear those fifty-foot-tall trees at the end of it.

The Maule was a good short field plane, but Bob was confident that the 300 feet field was not long enough to get off of the ground and clear the 50 to 60-foot-high trees if he did a normal takeoff. He had been praying about this and by the time he climbed into the plane God had already spoken to him in His still small voice, giving him a plan on how to do this. It would be a very unconventional takeoff, but it would work. Bob is always amazed at how God can make a way when there seems to be no way. He was doing it for him right at that time.

Bob would taxi the plane to one corner of the field and start his take off run along one end of the field. He could get about half of his needed take off speed along that end and then make a left ninety degree turn at that speed and get the rest of his needed speed heading along the other side. The main obstacle to Bob's plan was keeping the right wing of the plane from tipping into the ground as he made his left-hand turn. A plane has ailerons on each wing that are used to bank it to the left or right. When Bob made the left turn, he would use his ailerons to help lift his right wing. There would not be a lot of lift, but it should be enough to keep the right wing from tipping down into the ground. This type of takeoff run was not taught in the flight manuals, but he had confidence it would work.

Bob made his take off exactly as he had planned and it worked perfectly. Thank you Lord! Just as soon as he cleared the trees, he made a turn to a heading of ten degrees and headed toward Bahn. Bob had enough gas to get there, but not much extra. He leaned the engine out all he could without hurting it, then set the engine and prop control for a flight to use as little gas as possible. Bob's heading worked out almost perfectly, and within an hour and fifteen minutes he was back home safe and sound, ready for another day.

During those days of flying, Bob did not always tell his wife or children all the details of how close he came to not making it. They had enough worries about jungle flying without him adding to what they already knew. Usually he just acted like he had a normal day of being a jungle pilot, which in many cases it was.

God knew two years before this that Bob would be caught in this terrible storm. He had him circle and study the little soccer field and keep the details in his mind. He knew he would not have time to study the details when he only had seconds to land before the violent winds came. It was critical that Bob knew that there was a little field in that remote area that he might find before the storm hit him. Otherwise he would have tried to fly through the storm in an effort to get to a landing strip that he knew and probably would have been killed. Then it was critical that Bob heard the Holy Spirit tell him how to make that very unconventional take off run. A very simple question could be asked on this, "What saved Bob's life on that flight?" The answer is clearly, "It was God!"

Chapter 32
A Hole in The Wing

God's plans for our lives includes helping us in advance of when we need it. He helped Bob in advance by telling him to remember the small soccer field in the remote area of the jungle. He can also give us some material thing He knows we will need in the future. Our part to help God do this for us is to be sensitive to His voice when He speaks to us.

One day Bob purchased a small box of sheet metal screws to have on hand in case he needed them to make any repairs around the mission station. He planned to put the screws in the small tool shop in their mission airplane hangar. As he was walking to the hangar carrying the small box of screws, the still, small voice of the Holy Spirit spoke to him and said, "Put them in the airplane." Even though this seemed like a strange request, Bob recognized the voice of the Lord, opened the door of the plane, and put them in the small toolbox that he kept under his seat. Bob had no idea why the Lord had directed him to put them in the plane, but he obeyed.

A village named Nee-aa-ka Town was in the process of making a new village airstrip. Whenever a village was making a new airstrip, Bob liked to go and check their work to make sure they were doing it correctly. He did not want to cause them extra work, and this meant that it was important that they do it right the first time. Bob figured the airstrip was about done, so he decided to go and check things out.

The easiest way he could get there was to fly to Boya Town and walk for three hours to Nee-aa-ka Town. He did this and when he got there, he looked the strip over and saw that it was nearly ready to fly into, but it was about fifty feet short of what he needed to land and get stopped before he hit the tall trees at the end of the strip. The pastor and people of the village told Bob they had many ill people in the village, and they wanted him to fly back there right away with medical personnel to treat them. Bob could see that they were very sincere in their request, so he told them he would return in one week, but they had to extend the airstrip by fifty feet. Bob showed them how far to clear the bush and told them to level the ground the best they could.

There was one tree right in the center of the extension that Bob needed to have removed, but the people of the village asked him if they could leave that tree in place. Bob told them and the local pastor that the tree had to be removed because he had to have that extra length to get stopped. The first part of the strip was on a slight incline, but the extra length was downhill at a fairly steep decline. Bob would not be able to see this part of the strip when he landed because it was on the other side of the hill, but it would give him a few more feet to get stopped. The pastor promised Bob that he would see to it that the tree was removed.

One week later a nurse named Elizabeth Bowman from Switzerland and Bob got into the plane and put the medical supplies in the back. It was a very clear day outside so they expected no difficulties with weather, but they had their usual prayer for God's protection and blessings. Then Bob yelled, "Clear prop," and started the engine. After doing his preflight check, he gave the engine full power and they were off the ground and flying within seconds, headed toward Nee-aa-ka Town. This town would have been a very hard ten-hour walk from the mission station, but they were there in ten minutes.

Bob made a quick flight over the village and then flew back to the airstrip and started his approach for landing. He lined the plane up with the five hundred-foot strip, slowed it down to about fifty miles per hour, and pulled full flaps for his landing. He slowed down to about forty-five miles per hour, and then very slowly started to lower his flight speed to forty miles per hour. Bob controlled his descent with his engine power and was lined up well to make his first landing at this airstrip. Because the strip was so short, Bob would land with his brakes partly locked, but not enough to nose the plane over. He cut the power at the beginning of the strip, and they were on the ground. Bob pushed very hard on both brakes and they were quickly slowing down, but he would need the extra fifty feet to get completely stopped.

Within seconds they came over the crest of the hill. Bob was shocked at what he saw. The villagers had cut the bush back for the extra fifty feet, but they left the small tree right in the center of that area. Bob was going to hit it straight on with the nose and propeller of the plane! In a split-second Bob thought, "Save the propeller," which would also save the engine. Bob jammed the left rudder down and the plane reacted instantly, turning slightly to the left. The entire rotating propeller cleared the tree, but the right wing hit it very solid. The impact of the right wing hitting the tree made a loud crunching noise, and they stopped instantly.

Bob looked over at Elizabeth and said, "Are you okay?" He knew the sudden stop had shaken him some and he wondered if it might have hurt her. Elizabeth answered, "I am okay, but what about the plane?" He knew the plane had suffered a lot of damage, but did not want her to worry, so he told her that he would repair it and for her not to worry about it. By this time the villagers were all around the plane, and some of them were looking at the damaged wing. Bob told Elizabeth they needed to go ahead and get her started treating the sick people. They unloaded the medical supplies and carried them to the village, setting them in order on a few tables furnished by the villagers. Many ill people were already there to be treated, so Elizabeth started treating them right away.

After Bob helped Elizabeth get set up, he walked back to the plane. During his short walk, he thought about how the pastor had promised him they would remove the tree before he returned. Bob was quite upset with him for not removing it, but he determined not to embarrass him before the villagers. This would cause him to lose face in the village and would hurt his ministry.

Later Bob found out that some of the villagers did not want to remove the tree. It was very possible that the tree was used in devil worship. This was very common in the villages. Bob remembered that in one village there was a tree that was used in devil worship. Every time he saw the tree, he thought about how the Devil Society had taken a little girl, broke both her arms and legs, and dug a shallow hole, and put her alive in the hole. Then they covered her up, planted a tree over the top of her body, and made an offering of the child and the tree to the devil.

It was a horrible act, but in a Devil Society many terrible things take place. There was something special about the tree that Bob hit with the plane that caused some of the men not to want to cut it down. They were willing to cut the other trees down but not that one. Whatever it was, Bob determined to not show any anger at the pastor for the sake of the Gospel of Jesus Christ being preached in that village.

When Bob arrived back at the plane, there were about fifty African men, women, and children standing there looking at it. Bob was deeply hurt as he stood there for a short time looking at the beautiful plane sitting against the tree with a wing caved in. He tried not to show any emotions and he gently asked the men to help him push the plane away so he could look it over. A limb of the tree had gone right through the leading edge of the right wing in one place, and the trunk of the tree had smashed the leading edge of the wing back almost to the front spar in another place. Bob examined the damage and found that the gas tank and the spar had not been hurt at all. The rest of the plane was fine. He had saved the propeller by quickly jamming the left rudder down to miss the tree trunk with the prop.

Bob's big question then was, "How can I fly the plane out of the jungle airstrip with the damaged right wing? If I would try to fly it out as it is, the 120-mile-per-hour wind, blowing through the large hole, would probably rip the metal right off of the ribs in that area, and then I would be in real trouble, because that wing would probably no longer fly. I have to get the plane back to my mission station where I can repair it, and it would be nearly impossible to carry the plane out of the jungle. I have to fly it out, but how can I do it with that big hole in the wing?"

As Bob was thinking about this, the still, small voice of the Holy Spirit spoke to him and said, "You have the sheet metal screws in the plane." Then he remembered how the Lord had spoken to him a few days before this in His still, small voice telling him to put the screws in the plane and not in the hanger.

A plan started to form in Bob's mind. He needed a piece of sheet metal to make it work. The Africans called sheet metal zinc, so Bob asked the pastor if there was any zinc in the village that he could have. The pastor said there was a piece, and Bob asked him to bring the zinc and also a hammer. One of the African men ran to the village and within fifteen minutes he brought back a small hammer and piece of sheet metal that was about eighteen inches square. Bob looked it over and noticed that it had a painting of the devil on it. Every village had a Devil Society that worshiped Satan, and this was probably a painting they used in their devil worship. Bob did not like having a picture of the devil on it, but he saw that it was the perfect size he needed and it was the right thickness, so he decided to use it anyway.

Bob had a nail in his toolbox, and he took the piece of sheet metal, laid it down, and used the hammer and nail to punch about six holes along the four sides of it. Then he laid it down above the hole in the wing and bent and formed it to fit almost perfectly the curve of the leading edge. He held it in place with one hand and used it as a template to mark the location of the nail holes on the wing. Bob took the nail and hammer again and punched small holes in the sheet metal of the wing.

After that he took out the screws that he had in his toolbox and used them to screw the sheet metal over the hole in the wing. When Bob finished screwing it down, it looked very good. His repair would totally eliminate the problem of the hole in the wing even at 120 miles per hour. Also, the leading edge was so perfect that he would have excellent lift in that part of the wing.

Bob looked the area over of the wing that was smashed back nearly into the spar and did not see any holes. He knew there would be very little lift from that area of the wing because of the large dent, but he also knew there would be enough lift from the rest of the wing to get the plane off of the ground in time to clear the trees at the end of the strip if he flew out by himself. This meant he would not take Elizabeth out with him.

Elizabeth had originally wanted to be in Nee-aa-ka Town two days, and Bob had planned to leave her there and return for her. He still needed to get her back to the mission station, but he knew he could not have the Maule repaired in time to fly her out. Bob asked if she would mind if his friend with the Super Cub came and picked her up in two days, and of course she agreed. Bob knew the Piper Super Cub could easily land in the short airstrip. Bob also knew he would not be able to communicate with Elizabeth when he flew out, so he wanted to have a plan in place to get her out of the village before he left.

Bob got on his two-way radio and called his Baptist friend and asked him if he would fly Elizabeth out in two days and he agreed to do it. They set a time that Abe would get Elizabeth and Bob was free to go. All of the missionary pilots had a good working relationship with each other, even though they were with different mission organizations. Each of them had flown for the other missions and they knew where each other's airstrips were.

Bob got into the mission plane, checked out the controls, and started the engine. It fired up immediately and ran perfectly. Then he locked the brakes and gave it full power. Within two seconds the engine was putting out full rpm and full power. He pushed the yoke forward, raised the tail, and released the brakes. The plane shot forward at a tremendous acceleration, and within about four seconds he was flying. It came off the ground easily, even with the large dent in the wing.

187

Bob climbed to about 250 feet above the trees and took a heading of about 260 degrees, and within ten minutes he was over his mission station. Due to the damaged wing, He had to increase his landing speed about ten miles per hour, but other than that he had no problem landing. He taxied to a location on the strip where he could easily work on the wing, but out of the way enough that Abe could land with Elizabeth when she was finished with her medical work at Nee-aa-ka Town.

Shortly after Bob got back to his mission station, he started to repair the damaged wing. He had the needed supplies and equipment to make a professional repair to the wing and he knew exactly how to do it. Within three days the wing was repaired, and it was almost impossible to tell that it had ever been damaged. Elizabeth Bowman had a very busy two days treating the sick people at Nee-aa-ka Town, and then Abe flew her back to their mission station.

Bob has often thought about walking out to their mission hangar with the box of sheet metal screws in his hand and how the Lord spoke to him in His still, small voice, "Put them in the airplane." Bob heard Him speak and he obeyed, even though he had no idea that within a few days he would desperately need them to repair a damaged wing in Nee-aa-ka Town. As was said before, God can see the past, present, and future at the same time and He knew Bob would hit the tree and seriously damage the wing. God provided the materials to repair and fly the plane out of Nee-aa-ka Town even before the plane was damaged. He already knew Bob would need a piece of sheet metal to make the repair and He had it already there. He also knew he would need the screws to make the repair and He already had them in the plane.

Philippians 4:19 (NIV) **And *my God will meet all your needs according to the riches of his glory in Christ Jesus.***

God promises to meet our needs and He will do it!

Chapter 33
The Jungle Run

We have given examples of God meeting our needs in many things, but can He meet our needs when it comes to needing an abnormal amount of strength or endurance when we are so tired we can hardly go? Is it ever in His plan to do this to get us out of some kind of trouble? Yes it is! God's Word in Isaiah 40:29 tells us that He gives strength to the weary and power to the weak.

Isaiah 40:29 (NIV) *He gives* *strength to the weary* *and increases the* *power of the weak*.

Here is an example of how God did this for Bob.

Preaching in the villages nearly always meant walking through the jungle and rivers on very dangerous trails to get there. This took many hours of walking and usually a person was very tired when they got to the village.

Some villages would make an airstrip so the missionaries could fly there and preach the Word of God and treat their sick people. One of these villages was called Sea-ap-lee. One day a man from there walked to Bob's mission and told him they were making an airstrip. Bob knew the people did not know what was important in building one so he decided to walk to Sea-ap-lee right away and direct them on how to make the strip. He left his mission station early in the morning and walked at a very fast pace for about fifteen miles to Sea-ap-lee. His walk took him through some very difficult terrain and through one large river. It was a very hot day and, even though he walked as fast as he could, it took him about three and a half hours and he was tired by the time he got there.

He started supervising the people who were working on the airstrip. The work required to make the airstrip was immense. It meant taking an area in the jungle and cutting down the trees, removing the stumps, and leveling the ground enough to land a plane. As Bob was supervising the men, time got away from him and he ended up staying in Sea-ap-lee longer than he had intended. At about three o'clock in the afternoon, he realized that he needed to leave and walk back to his mission station. He had three and a half hours of daylight left and he thought he could make it back in that time. An old African man said

189

that it was too late in the day for him to get there before dark. He tried hard to convince Bob not to go, but he insisted on going.

Bob started walking back at about 3:00 and he found that he was very tired. The fifteen-mile walk at a very fast pace that morning and the work during the day had put its toll on his body. He was tired, but still thought he could make it. However, he had not counted on one fact that the old man knew. He was soon to find out what the old man meant when he said Bob could not make it before dark.

After Bob had walked for about one hour, he saw that the narrow path through the jungle was quickly getting dark. Bob was trying to walk at a good pace, but because he was tired, he was not walking as fast as he needed to. He was putting out as much effort as he had on his walk to Sea-ap-lee that morning, but he was not covering as much ground as he had earlier. On top of this, the sun was getting lower in the sky and the extremely tall trees that overhung the small path were filtering out its light. It was like he was walking in a tunnel through the jungle. The sunlight was just not getting down to where he was walking. Bob soon realized that it was going to be dark in the deep jungle much sooner than he thought.

Bob still had at least ten miles to go and probably more. He estimated that he only had about one or maybe one and a half hours of light left before it was totally dark. If he tried to return to Sea-ap-lee, he was so tired that he might not make it there before dark either. He knew he was too tired to speed up his walk and it would be totally dark long before he got back to the mission. This meant that he would spend the night alone in the jungle and he did not like doing this at all. He knew that it was very dangerous to spend a night alone in the jungle with all the poisonous snakes and wild animals. Also, the mosquitoes would make a night in the jungle very difficult. Bob knew his wife and the other missionaries at the mission station were expecting him to be home that evening. If he did not get home, they would think something had happened to him and they would be very worried. Bob did not want this.

Bob knew he was in trouble and had to trust God for his help. Bob prayed and said, "God help me." Then he heard the Holy Spirit speak to him in His still, small voice saying, "Run home at a very fast pace." During Bob's high school years, he was a sprinter. He won a lot of races and received several ribbons. Bob knew the Holy Spirit was telling him to run like he had during his high school days of running the dashes, but he knew he had been a short distance sprinter and not a long-distance runner. He had never been able to endure running ten or eleven miles at a very fast pace. Now he was more than fifteen years older and there was no way he could make a fast run that long. Bob knew he did not have the strength within him to do it, but he prayed, "God, give me strength." After saying this prayer, he started to run nearly as fast as he did during his days of running the dashes in school.

Bob knew he could not continue the pace very long, but he kept running. Then he realized he was not getting tired. It was amazing! Bob was able to hold the pace for a much longer time than he had the strength within himself to do it. He was shocked at his endurance! He should have started to feel exhausted, but he was not! He had set up a fast pace and was holding it! It felt so good. Even in his best days at running when he was younger, he was never able to keep up a fast pace like he was doing right then. It took effort on Bob's part, but as he put out the effort, God was giving him the strength he needed.

The shadows along the jungle path were getting darker as he ran. Bob had to watch his step very closely on the uneven path and still keep up his pace. The terrain was difficult with lots of steep hills as well as gullies and an occasional jungle stream that he had to run through or jump over. There were many jungle obstacles along the way such as exposed tree roots, huge rocks, fallen trees, and vines that he could easily get tangled up in, but he did not fall or even stumble on any of them, although some of them did slow him down.

As always when Bob was in the jungle, he was watching out for deadly snakes laying on or near the path or hanging from a tree or vine ready to bite any victim that passed by. On top of that, he was constantly watching for huge constrictor snakes that might drop on him from a tree. Some of them are very large and can kill a man by wrapping tightly around him until he could not breathe. With all of these obstacles, Bob was still able to keep up the pace.

Mile after mile passed, and shortly before dark Bob could see the outlaying huts of the local village of Bahn. He did not slow down, but ran on a path around the village toward his mission station, which was at the top of a steep hill. By the time Bob arrived at the base of the mission hill, it was dark. He could barely see well enough to follow the path, but not well enough to see what was on the ground. There were a lot of flat rocks on the path that led up to his mission station, and poisonous snakes liked to lie on them to warm themselves. During the daytime a person could see these snakes, but it was so dark by the time Bob got there that he could not see well enough to avoid them, so he just kept running. He knew that if he stepped on one of them, they could kill him within minutes after the strike.

Bob personally knew of five people who died in one year from bites from these snakes, but he kept running and trusting God to deliver him from being bitten. He knew God had given him strength to run, but he still was on edge as he took every step, knowing that he could come into contact with one of those deadly vipers. It was very dark by the time he got to the top of the hill, but within minutes he was home. Pat and Tanya were there waiting for him with their supper ready when he arrived. They had no idea what he had just gone through and greeted him as though it had been a perfectly normal day. It was good to be home, and Bob thanked God for His strength.

Bob's strength to run came after he started and continued to be with him as he ran. God was his Provider. He helped Bob to mount up with wings as an eagle and to run, and not be weary; and to walk, and not faint. That day Bob saw Isaiah 40:31 literally come true in his life.

Isaiah 40:31 (NIV) **but** *those who hope in the LORD will renew their strength. They will soar on wings like eagles; they will run and not grow weary, they will walk and not be faint.*

Chapter 34
Jim Changed Their Farming Methods

Right after the Bible school classes began it was time for Jim to start planting the swamp rice at the Bassa mission station. He already made plans to do this so he knew exactly what swamp he wanted to use and where he was going to start the seedlings. Jim planned to do it exactly as he had at the Saclapia Mission Station in the Geo and Mano area of Liberia. Now he was going to do it 100 miles away in the Bassa area. With some school boys helping him, he made a seed bed and sprinkled grains of rice over it and covered them lightly with soil. Every day the school boys would help him sprinkle water over the seed bed. From the very first day, some Christian men and Bible school students watched the process of planting the swamp rice. Word got around the area about this new way the missionary was planting rice and even some government officials became interested in it, just as they had at Saclapia.

The men especially watched as the boys and Jim got into the swamp and made a dike around about a half-acre area. There is no way a person can do this without getting mud all over themselves. He could see that the Bassa men were shocked to see a white man work in a muddy swamp. This was unheard of before and here they were seeing it. They had seen Jim dressed up in a white shirt and tie preaching the Gospel, and now he was looking so different covered in mud. This made them even more intent in watching what he was doing and the progress of the swamp rice.

Jim was sure they were asking each other why he was doing this. He wanted to show them that he cared so much for them that he was willing to humble himself and get muddy so they could learn a better way to plant and harvest rice. He also wanted them to believe he was willing to do this because of his Christian love for each of them. The process of growing the swamp rice continued for a few months and the people continued to observed Jim's every move. He knew they were learning and was very happy about it.

During that time Jim and Mary's children kept busy doing their correspondence schooling and helping out on the mission station. Belinda and Debbie worked as nurse's aides in the mission clinic nearly every day. The clinic nurses were very busy treating around 100 sick people and delivering one or two babies daily. Mary did many jobs on the mission plus cooking meals for her family. Mark liked to explore the area on his small motorcycle. Every day he would try out some trail or path that he had not been down to see where it went. Not only did Jim work with the swamp rice, but he also mentored some of the Bassa Christians and went to the villages preaching with them. He also went to the rubber plantation many evenings and preached the Gospel to the workers.

The months passed and the swamp rice matured very well and they harvested it. Many of the Bassa were astounded at how much rice the swamp rice produced. The whole program was a total success and the Bassa people learned how to raise swamp rice. The Bassa caught on quickly to growing it just as the Mano and Gio had. It became an asset to them that greatly improved their quality of life.

As was said above, raising swamp rice is the number one farm crop in Liberia today. Jim set an example of how the Liberians could easily raise much more rice by growing it in the swamps compared to growing it in the dry ground. No other white man got into the swamps like Jim did and he was probably the main person who caused the country to switch from dry land rice to swamp rice. The hog farmer from America changed the farming methods of the whole country of Liberia, which was both in growing rice and raising hogs.

We could ask the question, "How was Jim able to change the farming methods of a whole country and how did this start?" It started with God and His plan for the Liberian Christians, but Jim's obedience to God's call upon his life made it possible for God to use him to do this.

Back when Jim and Mary made the decision to be living sacrifices to God according to Romans 12:1 they were only thinking about farming their own land and making as much money as possible doing it. Never in their wildest dreams could they have thought that they would someday be involved in changing the farming methods of a nation. However, God's mind is so far above our minds that He could see this long before it happened. We could quote the title of this book, "God's Plans: Obedience and Results." It was in God's plans for Jim to do this and it took his obedience for it to come about. Then we see the results of his obedience.

Jim McCauley working in swamp rice field with students

Chapter 35
The Devil Society's Demand of Mark

Obeying God's exact direction is critical in what we do in His work. In Numbers 20:8 God told Moses to speak to the rock

Numbers 20:8 (NIV) *"Take the staff, and you and your brother Aaron gather the assembly together. Speak to that rock before their eyes and it will pour out its water. You will bring water out of the rock for the community so they and their livestock can drink."*

However, Moses did not speak to the rock, but struck it with his staff and his disobedience angered God so much that God did not allow him to go into the Promised land.

Numbers 20:11-12 (NIV) *11 Then Moses raised his arm and struck the rock twice with his staff. Water gushed out, and the community and their livestock drank. 12 But the LORD said to Moses and Aaron, "Because you did not trust in me enough to honor me as holy in the sight of the Israelites, you will not bring this community into the land I give them."*

Moses should have obeyed God exactly as He directed, but he didn't and it got him in trouble.

God gave Jim a direction on Christmas Eve and it was very important that he follow it exactly as it was given him. God had a plan for him that would open up a door of ministry that would last for the next twenty years and his exact obedience was essential for it to come about. He was even to be obedient when it would be extremely difficult.

On the first Christmas after the harvest of the swamp rice, Jim and Mary and their children, Belinda, Debbie, and Mark, went to the mission station at River Cess, where Bob and Pat with their two children, Tony and Tanya, had moved to. Their son, Mike, was back in America going to college. All of their children were excited to be with each other and Christmas Eve was a joyful time as they had their meal and exchanged a few presents.

Later that evening, Bob and Jim went out to the mission carpenter shop to have prayer. The shop had a small second floor, and they went up there for their prayer. The room was not very clean, and the floor was covered with dust from different building projects, but it was a place where they could go and not be disturbed. As they started to pray, Bob heard the still, small voice of the Holy Spirit tell him to lie face down on the floor to pray.

Jim was feeling that the Lord was leading him to leave Liberia on the fifteenth of March and go on to Swaziland, and he wanted Bob to pray with him concerning this. Right after Bob started to pray with his face to the floor, the Lord spoke to him again in His still, small voice and gave him a word for Jim. It was, "Set your face toward the south and follow me." Since Jim was already in Africa, Swaziland was south from Liberia. This was a confirmation to Jim that he was to do exactly as the Lord had directed him.

Jim also felt the Lord was saying that he was to leave Mary and the children in Liberia and Mary was to take care of all of the details of leaving the mission and disposing of their belongings. Jim knew all of this would take Mary about two or three weeks and after that she and the children were to return to America.

Jim felt strongly that the date to leave Liberia was very important, but he did not know why. Later they would find out just how important this date was. Jim received no other word on what to do or who to see when he got to Swaziland. He was just to go there on that date.

Right after the prayer and the words from the Lord, Jim said to Bob, "I will plan on going to Swaziland on March the fifteenth just as the Lord told us." The brothers knew that this word from God and the date were very important. God said, through the gifts of the Holy Spirit, that Jim was to go on the 15th of March. This did not mean on the 14th or the 16th, but on the 15th.

Jim was simply going to obey what the Lord said. He was not planning on going there to see if he liked it or if he found something that suited him. He was not going there to test or spy out the land to see if it was a desirable place to live. Jim was going there for one reason only, and that was because God had spoken to him in His still, small voice. He knew beyond any doubt that this was God's plan for Mary and him and he planned to follow it with all his heart.

After their families had their Christmas together, Bob flew Jim, Mary, and the children back to their mission station. Mary and Jim started preparing for him to go to Swaziland on March the fifteenth. They did not know it, but Satan was going to strongly oppose Jim from going on this date. A major problem was to come up that was going to make it very difficult for him to obey God.

The preparations to go to Swaziland seemed to be going well through January and February, but things suddenly changed around the first of March. One day Mark was riding his motorbike down a jungle trail when he saw a very small path that led off the main trail. He decided to leave the main trail and see what was down this small path. There were signs along the way that showed the local Bassa people that they were forbidden to travel down that path unless they were members of the Devil Society. Most of these signs consisted of branches broken from the trees in a certain way that were a warning to the Bassa, but not to Jim and Mary's seventeen-year-old son from America.

Mark headed down the path on his motorbike, and he came to an opening in the jungle. In the center of the opening was a building with a very large grass roof that was supported by wooden poles. The sides were open, and Mark could see many African men doing something in the building. He was curious as to what was going on, so he slowly road his motorbike up to the side of the building and looked inside. All of a sudden, the men started running toward him. They were shouting and very angry. His motor was still running, and he quickly put the bike in low gear, gave it gas, let out on the clutch, and got out of there before the men caught him. He headed back to the mission station as fast as he could.

That same day, Bob had been doing some flying in the Bassa area and was on his way back home. His flight took him right by Jim and Mary's mission station, and since it was getting late in the afternoon, Bob decided to stop at their station and spend the night with them. Very early the next morning they all heard a loud commotion outside and looked out the window and saw many angry men walking toward the house. The men were so loud that it alerted the whole mission station and everyone came out to see what was going on, including Bob and Jim.

The men were from the local Devil Society, and they were demanding that Jim hand Mark over to them immediately. They said that Mark had violated one of their most sacred devil worship rites. He had seen the "host," and if anyone, who was not a member of the Devil Society, saw the "host", they had to go through the devil rites within twenty-four hours. This meant that Mark would be forced to make vows to the devil, worship him, and make a sacrifice to him. The men would cut Mark and get some of his blood and sacrifice it to the devil. They also could cut off a finger or some skin, and sacrifice it to the devil. Mark was in serious trouble, and the missionaries knew it. What made it more serious was the fact that the Devil Society was a strong part of the law in the jungle.

Each Devil Society sacrifices a human being to the devil once a year. They call the person to be sacrificed a "host." (The details of how the Devil Society captured their "host" and what they did with them are so evil and gruesome that the author has chosen to leave them out of this story) The Devil Society was in the process of sacrificing a human to the devil when Mark rode his motorbike up to the large building. Because Mark had looked into the building, the Devil Society members felt he had seen the "host" that they were sacrificing, and because of their strong law Mark had to go through the devil rites and join the Devil Society within twenty-four hours. In their law, they were to make no exceptions to this regardless of who the person was-including Mark.

They started shouting and made demands to Jim that he had to give them Mark right then. Jim refused to turn Mark over to them and the Devil Society men threatened to take him by force. The missionary women tried to help, asking them to take the case to the local government commissioner. He was a man appointed by the government over the area of the Bassa Tribe where the mission and Devil Society were located. His position was much like a judge in one of our cities or counties, so his decision was final when he heard a case. The Devil Society men agreed to go to the commissioner, so they all walked about a mile to his office. He was there and agreed to hear their case right away.

The Devil Society and the missionaries talked to the commissioner for about two hours. During this time, the missionaries saw no evidence that he was going to stop the Devil Society from getting what they wanted.

All of the missionaries saw a part of the culture that was disgusting to them. They knew this was part of the Liberian culture, but it was so far from the culture of their countries that it was almost unbelievable to them. The missionaries were from three different countries, England,

Canada, and America. Their countries, and many others, are based on a Judaeo-Christian culture and their laws are based on the Bible and are almost the same when it comes to right and wrong. In their culture, if murder was confessed to in a hearing, the judge's focus would be on that.

The Devil Society men freely admitted to the commissioner that they were in the process of sacrificing a "host" to the devil. They did not once try to deny that. The commissioner knew beyond any doubt that they were getting ready to murder a human being or had already done it.

In the civilized world, the government official would have focused on the murder and not on the boy who saw it. The commissioner never once brought up the fact that a murder had taken place. This fact was never questioned, but the whole focus was on the boy as being the guilty one for seeing it. This would never have happened in the countries these missionaries came from, but it was happening right before their eyes. They saw firsthand in this court of law that murder was acceptable in this part of Africa if the victim was sacrificed to the devil. It was obvious that the commissioner saw Mark as being guilty, but he seemed to want to lessen his sentence.

It is the author's belief that his reason behind trying to protect Mark was based upon his fear that the missionaries would leave his area if he let the Devil Society have Mark. The Bassa people in the commissioner's area had no schools, no clinics, no hospitals, and no place to treat their many lepers, but the missionaries did. Just one mile from his office the mission had a large clinic where they treated all of the sick people in his area, an airplane flight service where their very ill people could be flown to one of the three missionary hospitals in the country, a very large leper colony where the many lepers from his area were housed, fed, and treated. They also had a large school for the Bassa children and it was the only one in his area. Then in addition to that they had a Bible school and had taught his people how to raise swamp rice and hogs.

The commissioner knew missionaries would refuse to worship the devil and Mark would also. He also knew beyond any doubt that the Devil Society would kill Mark right away if he refused to worship the devil. There is no doubt in the author's mind that the commissioner fully believed that Mark would be killed if the Devil Society got him and the missionaries would immediately leave his area and he would lose all of his benefits of them being there.

The commissioner was probably intelligent enough to realize that it would be an international incident to the world if his people killed an American boy and it could endanger the millions of dollars of aid that America was giving his country every year. His defense of Mark was strictly for personal reasons and not because Mark was innocent of any crime or that the Devil Society was guilty of murder.

The missionaries knew that one of the highest sacrifices that could be made in the Devil Society was for a member to sacrifice one of their children or a wife to the devil, and some of these men had done just that. If they would do such a heinous thing, then they would not hesitate in forcing Mark to go through the devil rites. The missionaries started to lose hope in the commissioner stopping the Devil Society from taking him. If he was to be saved it would have to come from God and all of them were desperately praying that He would intervene for Mark.

The Devil Society and the commissioner finally agreed to let Mark go if Jim give them $1,000. However, he did not have $1,000 and neither did all of the missionaries put together. Jim would gladly have given them the money, but they didn't have it. Jim told them they did not have that much money and finally they said that since Mark was an unintelligent American boy that did not know their ways, they would let him off if Jim would give them two hogs and fifty dollars.

Jim agreed and gave the Devil Society the hogs and fifty dollars and they left. They still did not seem happy, but all of the missionaries were glad that they still had Mark. It had been a hard day, but things were looking better, or at least the missionaries all thought they were.

Jim and Mary's obedience to God was tested that day as never before, but they had no idea that in a few days Jim's obedience would be tested even harder.

Jim and Mary continued to make plans for Jim to go to Swaziland, but one problem remained: they did not have the money for the plane ticket. After praying about this problem, it came to Jim's mind that he still had all of his tinsmith tools and he could sell them. When Jim and Mary sold their farming equipment before they went to Africa, Jim kept his tinsmith tools and brought them when they came to Liberia. Jim really loved those tools and could make almost anything out of sheet metal with them. He hated to sell them, but if that was what it took to obey God and go to Swaziland, he would do it. Jim got the word out around the area that he was going to sell his tin smith tools. A man from the rubber plantation heard that Jim had tools for sale and he drove to their mission station and asked to see them. The man liked the tools and bought them, giving enough money for Jim to buy his ticket to Swaziland.

Bob was flying to Monrovia to get some supplies the next day, so Jim asked him to purchase the ticket for him. A heavy morning fog delayed Bob's 200-mile flight and he was unable to get to the ticket office before it closed at noon. It opened again at two o'clock in the afternoon, but if no one was in line to purchase tickets, they usually closed for the day after about fifteen minutes. Bob needed to be there right at 2:00 pm. to make sure he got there before they closed.

Chapter 36
The Witch Doctor Tried to Kill Bob

Since Bob missed getting to the ticket office before noon, he went to the mission headquarters in Monrovia. The missionaries were just getting ready to have their lunch when he arrived, so they invited him to eat with them. About halfway through the lunch there was a noise at the door. The weather was very hot and they had the door open to get a breeze, but there was a full-length screen door that was closed, but not locked.

Everyone looked up at the door, and there stood a witch doctor. They could tell he was a witch doctor from his dress and markings on his body. He looked demonic as he stood there, staring at Bob sitting at the table along with about six other missionaries. He looked at no one else, but glared at Bob. Then, in a voice that sounded like the devil himself, he spoke in long, drawn-out words, "I want that man." He was pointing directly to Bob as he spoke. His speech sounded demonic.

It was like Satan himself knew that Bob was there, and he sent this witch doctor to hinder him. Bob did not know what was happening in the demonic world at that time, but today he knows that Satan was trying to stop him from getting to the ticket office that day. God had a series of events lined up in Liberia and South Africa, and getting to the ticket office that day was very important to God's plan. When the other missionaries heard this witch doctor saying that he wanted that man and pointing to Bob, they encouraged him to go out and minister to the witch doctor.

This was an immense delaying trick by Satan, and Bob made the mistake of falling into the trap. God wanted him to purchase a ticket and not to do anything else. However, as a result of the coaxing by the missionaries, Bob excused myself from the table and followed the witch doctor up a small hill about one hundred feet from the mission house. Bob thought he could minister to him, but God was not in it and it did not work. God had called him to purchase a ticket, and here he was standing at the top of this hill facing this witch doctor.

Satan had a plan to delay or kill Bob to stop him from getting the ticket. However, God had a plan for Bob to purchase the ticket and He was going to show the witch doctor that His power in Bob was greater than Satan's power in him. The Holy Spirit spoke to Bob in the still, small voice and said, "Stand still, don't move, and watch what I will do." Bob obeyed and just stood there, looking at the witch doctor.

The other missionaries did not come outside, but stood in the doorway watching through the screen door. The witch doctor walked under a tree and picked up a limb that was about seven feet long. It became obvious to Bob that he was going to use it as a club. Bob stood watching and did not move. He knew that the witch doctor was probably going to try to hit him with the club, but he stood firm, not moving a foot.

The witch doctor walked toward Bob, his eyes glaring with an evil demonic look. When he got within about six feet of him, he drew back his club and swung it as fast as he could to hit Bob in his left midsection. The witch doctor was an extremely strong man, and the speed of the blow was so fast that Bob could hardly see the club as it swung toward his left side. He never flinched or moved in any way.

When the club came close to Bob's left side, it went up and over his head and down at the same level as it was in the original swing. The club was moving so fast that it rotated the witch doctor around at the end of the blow. By this time, his eyes were glaring at Bob with hate as he was preparing for his next blow. He pulled his club way back and swung with what seemed like even more force, this time at Bob's right side. The club's speed was extremely fast as it headed for his right midsection. Once again, Bob did not move, but stood firmly. The second blow did exactly as the first and didn't touch Bob.

Then the witch doctor lifted the club over the top of his head and swung it straight down in a very fast blow aimed at the top of Bob's head. Right before it hit his head, it veered off to his left and hit the ground so hard that a large piece was broken off of the end of the club. With even more hate in his eyes, he lifted the club and made another blow to hit Bob on the top of his head. This time the club veered off to his right and hit the ground so hard that the club was broken into many pieces. After the fourth blow failed to hit Bob, the witch doctor was so confused that he walked away, mumbling something that Bob could not understand.

Who caused the club to veer off like it did on each swing? There was no way the witch doctor could have caused it to veer off on each blow. The club was long and moving very fast and he could not have controlled it like that with such a rapid swing. It was only the Lord who did it, and He probably had an angel deflecting each blow so that Bob would not be diverted from getting that ticket. If any of the blows had hit Bob, he could have been severely injured or killed and would not have been able to get the ticket, which was so important to God's plan for Jim. By just standing there and letting God deliver him, Bob proved to the witch doctor that the power in him was greater than the power in the witch doctor. He knew it, and it left him very confused.

As the witch doctor was walking around mumbling and looking confused, Bob looked at his wristwatch and suddenly realized that he had wasted precious time in doing this. He felt that God was telling him that this was a delaying trick and that he had to get to the ticket office as quickly as he could. Ministering to a witch doctor like this had little value if God had directed Bob to do something else.

Even though it might have sounded like a good ministry, it was not what God had directed Bob to do at the time. The missionaries expressed their disappointment that he was not staying to minister to this witch doctor, but he ignored them and headed for the ticket office. It would take him a half hour to get there, and he did everything he could to make up for the wasted time. He prayed that God would help him get there in time and that he would be able to get the ticket at this late time.

When Bob got to the ticket office, the doors were still open. He walked in and sat down in front of the ticket agent's desk. The agent had no idea that just minutes before a witch doctor had tried to kill him. As professionally as he could, Bob asked for a ticket to fly out of Monrovia to Swaziland in two days. The agent acted like it was impossible to get on that flight due to the short notice, but he did some checking and said that he would be able to book the last seat on that plane. Bob took the ticket and gave him the money Jim had received for his tools.

Even though neither brother knew why, it was in God's perfect plan for Jim to be on the flight to Swaziland that left on the 15th of March. Through strong opposition from Satan, Bob got the ticket, but there was still to be more opposition before Jim got on the plane.

Chapter 37
Jim's Difficult Testing

The day before Jim was to leave Liberia, Bob flew to the Bassa Mission Station with Jim's ticket. He stayed overnight so he could go to the airport to see him off. There were six people going to the airport, which include Jim and his family and Bob. Bob's plane only held four people so they planned to make the two-hour drive-in Jim and Mary's Land Cruiser.

Shortly before Jim was to leave the Bassa Mission Station and fly to Swaziland, some of the Bassa Christian men came to him with a warning concerning Mark. They said it had been reported to them that when the Devil Society men returned back to their village without Mark, the rest of the members were very angry. The members said under no circumstances should the men have let Mark off, and they demanded he be forced to take the Devil Society rites just as their law stated. The Christian men reported to Jim that the Devil Society was going to capture Mark, and if he would not join the Devil Society, they were going to kill him. Jim could see that the Christian men believed the Devil Society would actually kill Mark and this was proof to him that they would do it.

Jim was faced with a terrible situation. The Devil Society was very large, so there were hundreds of them. They were scattered throughout the area, and it would be easy for them to capture Mark. It was no small matter. Jim knew these men would do this if they could, and he knew that God had given him a date to leave Liberia and go to Swaziland. To obey God, he had to leave the mission and go to the airport within a few minutes.

Jim had been willing to give up their land, income, retirement, medical insurance, and leave the home he loved in order to obey God. Now it seemed he was even being asked to leave his son in one of the worst situations he could imagine. This test of Jim's obedience was worse than it was before when the Devil Society demanded that he give them Mark. Jim could have said, "I am not going to go to Swaziland today. I will take Mark and my family and get out of here immediately and go back to America."

Jim's pain over this was almost unbearable. With this extreme pain in his heart, he said to Mary and Bob, "I must obey God, and I will go as

He has directed." Bob could see Jim's pain in his face and he knew how difficult this decision was. As difficult as it was, Bob knew he had made the right one and he was proud of his brother for making it. Bob did the only thing he knew to do to help Jim. He told his brother that he would watch after Mark and make sure he was okay. However, Bob had no idea what to do. Hearing Bob say that he was going to help his son made Jim feel a little better, but he was still very concerned.

With sad hearts, Jim and his family, along with Bob, got into their Toyota Land Cruiser and they drove to the airport in Monrovia. Mary and all three of their children had tears in their eyes as they said good-bye to their husband and father. Jim even had tears in his eyes as he said good-bye to them and his brother. He walked across the tarmac, climbed the stairs leading up into the plane, and took his seat for the long flight to South Africa. The plane's engines started and soon it was in the air. As Jim sat in that plane getting farther and farther from his family, he was nearly sick over the situation with Mark. He knew he would have no way to communicate with them except by letter and it could be a few weeks before he heard what happened to Mark.

On March the fifteenth Jim was heading across the skies over Africa in obedience to God telling him to leave on that specific date. Even though he was crying in his heart, he had obeyed, not knowing this was the start of thousands coming to Jesus Christ and many churches being built and a large ministry to orphans being established in Swaziland.

Jim's obedience to leave Liberia on the fifteenth of March as God directed was extremely difficult for him. As we have said, his obedience was tested, but what about the results? We can now look back over forty years since that difficult day and see that Jim's obedience resulted in thousands coming to Jesus Christ and many churches being built.

Chapter 38
Mark's Escape

As Bob was driving Jim and Mary's Toyota Land Cruiser back to the Bassa Mission Station, he could see that Mary and the children were all very sad that Jim would be away from them for a long time and also worried about the Devil Society finding Mark. There was no doubt in any of their minds that if they found him, they would do exactly as they said they would.

It was a two-hour drive and there was little talk along the way. Bob was thinking about how difficult it was for his brother to leave his family. He could see the pain in Jim's face as he said his good-byes, walked across that tarmac, and got into the plane. Bob did not know it at the time, but Jim wept almost the whole time he was on the flight, getting farther and farther away from his beloved family.

As Bob was driving, he was also praying about what to do concerning Mark. He told Jim he would take care of things with Mark, but he just did not know what to do. Bob felt a huge responsibility with this situation. He felt sure that the Devil Society would try to capture Mark as quickly as possible. Bob knew every village had a Devil Society, so they were a very widespread and strong organization in the jungle. He was thinking and praying about this as he drove, trying to figure out a way to protect Mark.

Suddenly, as he was driving down the road through the jungle, the Holy Spirit spoke to Bob in His still, small voice and said, "You have an airplane, don't you?" Bob almost laughed at the simplicity of the answer he received from the Holy Spirit. He did not laugh out loud, but he did smile inwardly when the Holy Spirit spoke those words to him. God can take something that is so serious and seems to have no answer, and make it so simple! This was one of those times. Bob immediately knew what the Lord was saying. He wished he could tell Jim how simple the answer was, but there was no way for that as he was hundreds of miles away on his way to South Africa and Swaziland.

Bob said, "Mary, just as soon as we get back to the mission, get a bag of clothes packed for Mark as quickly as you can. I will get the plane ready to fly as you do it. Then I will fly Mark out to my mission station. We won't tell anyone where Mark is, so if the Devil Society tries to find out where he is, no one at your mission station will be able to tell them." Mary understood this plan and was happy about it.

Bob knew that their mission station was so far away that the Devil Society would not get word to that area concerning Mark. They also would not have any communications through the jungle that far away, nor would they travel that far looking for Mark. Bob knew the Devil Society would not hurt Mary or the girls, so they would be in no danger. It would only be Mark that they would try to capture and they would not find him.

About one hour later they arrived back at Mary's mission station. All of them already had a long day and were tired, but they had important things to do quickly. Bob wanted to get them done so quickly that if some of the Devil Society men were near the mission station, they would not have time to capture Mark. Just as soon as they drove into the mission station and up to Jim and Mary's house, Bob ran to the airplane.

As Bob was checking the plane out and getting it ready to fly, Mary, Mark, and the girls were quickly getting Mark's things ready to leave. This took about fifteen minutes. By this time Bob had the mission plane ready to fly except for starting it and checking out the engine before takeoff. He did not want to start the engine until the very last minute in case some of the Devil Society men were nearby.

Just as soon as Mark's things were ready, he ran to the plane and quickly got into the right front seat. Bob was already in the plane and ready to start the engine. He shouted the normal, "Clear prop," and turned the starter switch. Almost immediately the engine started with a roar. Bob quickly checked out the magnetos and controls and got his concentration on the takeoff. He applied full power, released the brakes, and the plane shot down the little runway. In about four seconds it came off the ground and they were in the air and over the trees.

Bob kept the plane on a straight-out heading at an altitude just above the trees until they got out of sight. In case any of the Devil Society men were around, he did not want them to see which way he turned after his takeoff. Right after they were out of sight from those on the mission station, Bob turned the Maule to a two hundred-degree heading toward River Cess Mission Station. He and Mark were able to relax some and enjoy the flight.

They were flying over very high jungle, and Bob was watching the compass to keep them on course. Shortly before they reached the mission station, they flew over the Cess River. The river was very wide and there were no bridges that crossed it. There were a few dugout canoes that were used by some of the Africans to cross the river, but in general, people did not go from one side of the river to the other.

Bob's mission station was about twenty miles south of the Cess River, and the jungle in that area was extremely dense. This made travel by foot in that area very difficult. Bob was confident that Mark would be very safe living with his family until Mary and the girls had things ready to return back to Indiana. When they landed the plane at Bob's mission station Tony was there and he was very happy to see his cousin get out of the plane. The two boys had a wonderful time together in the jungle.

Mary and the girls packed their belongings, said good bye to the missionaries and Christians at the Bassa Mission Station, and drove their Land Cruiser to Monrovia. They bought their plane tickets, sold their Land Cruiser, and were ready to fly back to America after three days. During that time, Bob flew Mark to Monrovia and they all returned to America.

Forty-five years after the incident with Mark and the Devil Society the memory of the event is as clear in Jim, Mary, Bob, and Mark's minds as if it happened yesterday. All of these years later the brothers are still amazed that the government official said nothing against the murder and he judged Mark as being guilty because he may have seen the host.

As the author was thinking about how terrible this was, the still small voice of the Holy Spirit spoke to him about his own country. He reminded him of all the abortions that take place in America and that life begins at conception and this is a fact that is firmly supported by Scripture. Abortion kills that life and it is murder! The author's country is performing about 3,000 abortions a day and the government is paying for many of them. This is happening now and America is guilty before God for these murders.

Many, in the author's country, approve of this. Then in addition to that, many in authority protect the abortionist and judge those guilty who see it as wrong and try to stop it.

God was saying to the author that his America is guilty before Him the same as Liberia is guilty before Him on this issue of murder.

Where does this leave us as Christians? To answer this question lets go to Ezekiel 3:8-10.

Ezekiel 3:8-10 (NIV) *8 But I will make you as unyielding and hardened as they are. 9 I will make your forehead like the hardest stone, harder than flint. Do not be afraid of them or terrified by them, though they are a rebellious people." 10 And he said to me, "Son of man, listen carefully and take to heart all the words I speak to you. 11 Go now to your people in exile and speak to them. Say to them, 'This is what the Sovereign LORD says,' whether they listen or fail to listen."*

God was reminding the author that we must be strong and speak against the evil going on in our country just as He told Ezekiel to do to those in his country!

Chapter 39
Move to Swazi and Preach

When Jim boarded the big plane that was taking him to Swaziland, he could not help but remember the vivid dream he had of words in the sky which said, "Move to Swazi and Preach." However, there were two thoughts almost simultaneously running through his mind. One was, "I obeyed God's call and am finally on my way to Swazi!" The second thought was, "I am worried about Mark and the Devil Society." Not for one second was Jim sorry that he had obeyed God, but he could not overcome his fear for Mark. Jim had tears in his eyes for almost all of the 3,000-mile flight. However, when the plane landed in Johannesburg, South Africa God gave Jim peace, but he had no idea what the Lord had for him in Swaziland. He only knew he was to go there and Johannesburg was his first stop on the way.

When Jim's flight arrived in Johannesburg, South Africa, he was to catch another plane from there to Swaziland. As he was walking up to the ticket counter to check in for this flight to Swaziland, a young man stepped in front of him and obtained the last ticket out that day for the Swaziland flight. There was nothing Jim could do, so he had to wait twenty-four hours for the next flight. He knew nobody in Johannesburg, but through a strange set of circumstances of meeting someone in the airport, Jim was invited to spend the night with a white South African Christian couple that he did not know.

Early the next morning, Jim went out to the kitchen, where he met a man and woman who had just dropped in for a quick visit. They were passing through Johannesburg on their way back home to Cape Town, which was about one thousand miles away, and they stopped in that morning for a very short visit. The couple had already talked to the husband and wife who lived in the home where Jim spent the night, and they were told that Jim was on his way to Swaziland. The first thing they said to Jim was, "We hear that you are on your way to Swaziland." He affirmed that he was. Then they said, "About two years ago we met some old missionary ladies from Swaziland and they gave us a map to their mission station." They pulled out a handwritten map drawn on a small piece of paper they had been carrying all this time and gave it to Jim, suggesting he might want to visit them sometime. This couple was in the home with Jim for only a short time before they headed on to Cape Town.

The timing of this meeting was very critical for what God had planned for Jim. The couple with the map had been on a long trip. If they had stopped at their friend's home the day before, Jim would not have been there; if the young man had not stepped in front of Jim at the ticket counter and gotten the last ticket to Swaziland, he would not have met these people. If he had not been invited to stay all night with this Christian couple, neither of them would have met Jim. And if the couple would have stopped to see their friends later in the morning, he would have already been gone.

If Bob had spent even a few more minutes with the witch doctor, he would have missed getting the ticket, and Jim would have missed these people. And most important of all, if Jim had refused to go on the flight the day God told him to, because of the situation with Mark and the Devil Society, he would have missed these people with the map. The meeting with these people was critical to everything that would happen for the next twenty-two years and beyond.

When God told Jim that he was to leave Liberia on March the fifteenth it was extremely important that he obeyed, even when he was so worried about Mark. Jim's commitment to obey God was severely tested and he passed the test. Very few Christians would have done this, but Jim did and he received the map, which was in God's perfect plan for him and for the future plans God had for him and Mary.

Before Jim left Johannesburg, he met a missionary from WEC named Eddie Cain. When Eddie found out he was going to Swaziland, he gave Jim an old Citron car that had about five hundred thousand kilometers on it. The floor boards were so rusted that he could see the ground through the holes! Even though it looked terrible, it ran well and Jim took it. Rather than flying the 250 miles on to Swaziland, he drove there in the car that God provided.

Chapter 40
Bob Could Not See to Land

When Jim flew out of Liberia to Swaziland Bob knew God was in it. He well remembered how, years before this, Jim shared with him his dream with the words, "Move to Swazi and Preach." Bob also remembered how God used the gifts of the Holy Spirit to give them words of direction regarding selling their land, quitting their jobs, and what to do with their money. He also remembered their many prayers together as the Holy Spirit directed them in every step to get them where they were at that time.

It was almost engraved in Bob's mind how the Holy Spirit used prophecy, words of wisdom, words of knowledge, visions, dreams, and healings to bring them from their difficult youth to being servants of God in this foreign country. Yes, it was hard for his brother to no longer be with him in this country, but he knew it was all in God's magnificent plans for them. Jim would now serve God in Swaziland and Bob would continue serving Him in Liberia. Bob was also totally convinced that he and Jim would continue to trust God to direct them with His spiritual gifts.

Bob knew Jim could face dangers thrown at him by Satan while he was in Swaziland, and also against him in Liberia. He also knew that God was not finished with them and He could deliver them from Satan's plans to kill them.

Bob continued to know the dangers he faced daily in his flying. Every jungle pilot he knew thought about this. They all knew that some jungle pilots had died from the inability to see in bad weather or darkness. All of them could fly at altitude on instruments when the visibility outside was down to zero, but they had to be able to see outside to land on the short airstrips in the jungle. If they could not see due to darkness or bad weather and were forced to land, they were probably going to crash and possibly get killed or injured badly. Bob knew this well, but he also knew that they served a God who can make a way when there seems to be no way! This happened to Bob one day and he is still amazed at how God did it.

Bob took off from the airport in Monrovia, one morning with about six hundred pounds of supplies for their different mission stations that were about two hundred miles back in the jungle. He did not have the plane overloaded, but it was heavy enough that he had to have a fairly long runway to land on and get the heavy load stopped. Bob knew Flumpa Mission Station had the longest runway, so his plan was to land there first and unload their supplies. Then he would have a lighter load for the other stations.

When Bob got about forty miles from Flumpa, he saw a dark storm front coming toward their runway from the opposite direction. He did not like what he saw because he could not land on any other runway in the area with the load he had on board. He needed at least nine hundred feet to get down and stop the plane with this load. If the rain beat him there, he would not be able to see well enough to land, and he would be in big trouble. Bob sped the plane up to about 140 miles per hour in an effort to beat the approaching storm. When he was about ten miles from the runway, he saw he was going to lose the race unless the storm front slowed down.

However, it did not and when Bob was about two miles from the runway, he watched the heavy rain come across the Flumpa station and runway. He was flying well over two miles per minute, which made the timing very close. If he had two minutes more, he could have landed the plane and been safe on the ground when the rain came. Bob clearly had lost the race, but there was nothing he could do about it at this time except to trust the Lord to safely get him on the ground someplace.

Bob quickly made a right turn to avoid the rain for a short time so he could still see well as he looked around the area from his plane. He knew the directions to all of the other mission stations in the area, and he could see they were all having heavy rain as well. This eliminated the possibility of going on to a different runway to land. The only area that had clear weather was toward Monrovia where had he just come from, and he did not have enough gas on board to go back. Bob made a slow circle while he was still outside the rain to give him time to evaluate his situation. There was no other place he could land! He did not like his conclusion at all, but he had no other choice. He had to try and make a landing at Flumpa in the heavy rain!

Having no alternative, Bob began flying toward the Flumpa runway at a reduced speed of 120 miles per hour and within seconds was in the rain, which caused his visibility out of the front windshield to decrease greatly. You could compare it to driving a car at 120 miles per hour in a heavy rain with no windshield wipers. Bob could see the runway out of his side window until he made the turn for his final approach; then the runway was so blurred that he could not distinguish the runway from the trees. It just looked like a blurred brown area surrounded by green, and he could not tell where the sides were, nor the ends of the runway.

Bob slowed the plane down and was trying to line it up with the runway for a landing, but he just could not see out of the front, even at the slower speed. From the side windows he could see that he was about twenty-five feet above the trees, but he could not see the exact location of the runway so he gave the engine power to make a go-around.

Bob climbed up to about one hundred feet above the trees and made a left turn in an attempt to land again. He could see the runway out of the left side window as he went by it on his downwind leg, so he thought he would try it again. Bob turned and lined the plane up for a final approach the second time. Once again, the runway looked like such a blur that he could not tell where the edges and ends of the runway left off and the trees began. The runway was narrow so he only had about forty feet on either side of his wings before they hit the big trees. This gave him very little room for error.

If Bob did hit one of the trees, it would most likely spin the plane around and tear off both wings high above the runway, which would cause it to drop to the ground, and possibly burn. Bob knew he was in big trouble, and would probably crash, but he had no other option. He had to land here, so he planned to bring it on down and trust God for the rest.

From the side windows he could see that he was still high and needed to lose some altitude. Bob quickly did a cross controlled slip to get a little lower. He brought his left wing around in front of him in the slip. This meant he was flying somewhat sideways. When he did this, he was looking out of his left side window as he made the sideways slip. To his surprise, he could see the runway perfectly because the rain was hitting the top of his wing, and he was looking at the runway out of his left window, which was below the wing. The wing was a roof over his window.

Bob continued to bring the plane down, but held it in the left sideways slip. With his left wing leading the plane and protecting his side window from the rain, he could see perfectly. He was still heading exactly toward the direction of the runway, but he was flying sideways. He held that heading and lowered the plane until he was about ten feet above the ground directly over the center of the runway. Bob quickly brought his nose around so it was lined up with the runway, cut the power, and landed it, looking out the side windows as he did. It worked perfectly! It felt so good to hear and feel the wheels rolling on the ground. By looking out of the side windows, he was able to keep the plane in the center of the runway as he came to a stop.

Bob very sincerely thanked God that he was safe on the ground. He and He alone gave Bob this way to see. He knew God somehow took control of his flying in such a way as to cause him to be a little high and to put the plane in the left sideways slip so he could see out of his left window. He never would have thought about this. He certainly was never taught this procedure in any private or commercial training he had. God had just taught Bob a new way to land a plane in very heavy rain and He made a way for Bob to see!

Chapter 41
"God, How Can I Fix It?"

One evening Bob flew into a mission station with the intent of staying all night. He barely got out of the plane when the mission's station leader told him they had no electric lights because he had failed to put new brushes in the generator, and the spring steel that pushes down on the brushes had come into contact with the rotating commutator.

This caused an electrical short that burnt deep pits in the commutator. It also left the commutator very rough, and it needed to be smooth in order that the brushes could slide easily on it as it rotated at high speeds. If it were rough, it would wear out the carbon brushes within minutes. The generator was worth several thousand dollars, and the missionary felt very badly because he thought he had totally ruined it and blamed himself for failing to replace the brushes. He knew the mission station did not have funds to purchase a new generator, but at the same time they needed one to run the mission station.

The two missionary men on the station asked Bob to look at the generator. As he walked over to look at it, they walked beside him, telling him they didn't really have any hope that it could be repaired and, as Bob looked at it, he found himself agreeing with them. It looked like it was totally ruined. The pits were deeper and the roughness was rougher than he expected it to be. Bob's first thought was, "There is no way to repair the commutator without dismantling the generator and mounting the commutator on a very large lathe to cut away all of the pits and the roughness."

Bob knew of no place in all of Liberia where this repair could be done. Repairing the generator looked pretty hopeless without shipping it out of the country. If the generator had to be shipped back to the United States or England, the cost would be tremendous. The cost was not the only problem. It would take at least six months to get the generator back, and they would be without power all this time. Without sharing any of these thoughts with the others, Bob just continued staring at the damaged equipment as he prayed, "God, how can I fix it?"

As he stood there, God spoke to him in His still, small voice showing him how to repair the generator right where it was sitting. He was very surprised at the plan God had given him. In fact, he was absolutely amazed at it, but he saw it would work! Bob asked if they had a sharp wood chisel. One of the men said he had a new one. He also asked them to find a two by four that was about twelve inches long and also two C clamps. He knew that nearly every mission station had these.

Then Bob asked if they had a pair of micrometers that he could use to measure the diameter of the commutator, and one of the missionary men said he had brought some from America. On top of that, he asked for a fine file and some fine sandpaper, which they had. The men gathered the items together and brought them to the generator building as Bob stood there looking at the generator and thinking about the plan God had given him.

Bob was planning on making a lathe right where the generator sat. Rather than rotating the commutator on a large lathe, he was going to rotate it using its own bearings and drive it by running its own large engine. Bob planned to use the chisel as a type of lathe-cutting tool. He would clamp the two by four about one-sixteenth of an inch away from the commutator. He would, very carefully, lay the chisel on the two by four and hold it very tightly in both hands at about a forty-five-degree angle with the face of the commutator. Then he would very slowly move the chisel's point into the rotating commutator. By holding the chisel on a forty-five--degree angle, just the point of one side of the blade would touch the commutator.

The chisel point would be like the point of a lathe tool bit coming into contact with the material it was to cut. If this worked okay, the point of the chisel should cut into the rotating commutator a few thousandths of an inch. Bob would very slowly pull the chisel across the two by four letting the point cut the rotating brass on the commutator. This would cut away the rough and pitted surface of the commentator if it all went according to the plan that God had given him.

Bob had to be very careful in doing this, because he could get hurt badly. The engine was very large with a flywheel about four feet in diameter and probably weighed about five hundred pounds. The engine drove three large V belts, and they drove the generator. Bob would have to work in a space right beside those belts. If he accidentally rubbed against them, they could pull him into the pulleys and could cut his arms or legs off in an instant. He also had to be very careful not to get into the spokes of the flywheel, as it could also hurt him very seriously.

The other possible danger would come from the generator itself, because it would be running at full speed when they started the engine. As a result, it would be producing a very high amount of voltage and amperage. When Bob touched the rotating commutator with a steel chisel that he was holding, a high amount of voltage would flow through the chisel to him. That could seriously injure him and it would also blow another hole in the commentator just as the springs did when they touched it. To eliminate this danger, Bob had to disconnect the right wiring from the generator so that it did not produce electricity.

By this time the sun was setting, and it was becoming very dark. One man brought a kerosene lamp and lit it so Bob could continue to work. The light was dim, but it was sufficient for him to see well enough to continue on with his plan. He clamped the two by four in place and disconnected the wires on the generator. The men hand-cranked the large engine and got it running up to speed. With great care, Bob slowly moved himself into the cramped space between the engine and generator and carefully got down on his knees. With the large belts running at a high speed right beside him, he moved his left arm into place very carefully, as it was only inches away from the belts.

Next, Bob took the wood chisel and very carefully placed it on top of the two by four and slid it against the rotating commutator. As he held the chisel very tightly in his hands and slowly pulled it to his left across the rotating commutator, a very thin ring of about ten one-thousandths of an inch per side of shavings came off of the commutator surface just as Bob planned. He was amazed at how well it worked. In fact, it worked about as well as if he had cut the commutator surface on a proper lathe. When Bob finished making the cut, the commutator surface looked very good. He took the file and very lightly filed the rotating surface to remove his tool marks. Next, he took the fine sandpaper and lightly sanded the rotating surface until it was extremely smooth.

After this they turned off the engine and let it stop rotating. When it stopped, Bob took the micrometers and measured the diameter to make sure it was perfectly round. It was as perfect as if he had done it on a lathe. He measured the amount of taper on the surface of the commutator from one end to the other. To his surprise it only had 0.001 of an inch taper per side from one side to the other. A piece of normal paper is 0.004 of an inch, so the taper was only one-fourth of the thickness of a piece of paper from one side to the other. Bob was simply amazed at how accurately it came out. After that he took new brushes that the station leader had on hand, mounted them, and reconnected the wires that he had previously disconnected. They restarted the engine, and the whole mission station came to light. The generator worked perfectly, and every missionary on the station rejoiced and thanked God that once again they had electric lights.

Bob heard the still, small voice of the Holy Spirit as God showed him how to repair the generator right where it sat. God had given him the plan and the ability to cut the brass on the commutator very accurately. Let's look again at Exodus. 31:4-5 and see how this is stated in the Scripture.

Exodus 31:4-5 *To devise cunning works, to work in gold, and in silver, and in brass, And in cutting of stones, to set them, and in carving of timber, to work in all manner of workmanship.*

The commutator was brass. Bob needed to cut it to make it usable. God had given Bezaleel skills in working with brass and also in cutting stones as we see in Exodus. 31:4-5. He needed to cut stones to make them usable. God had given Bob a skill and a plan on how to cut brass to make it usable. He did not have the proper equipment to do this in the country where the generator was located. Bezaleel also did not have the tools we have today for cutting brass and stones. They had not yet developed the materials that we have today for doing this. They also did not have the equipment that we have today for getting the stone out of the stone quarries. Even without what we would call proper tools for cutting and shaping stone, they built what was probably the most beautiful building the world has ever seen. How did they do it? God gave them the skills to do it with the tools they had, just as He gave Bob the plan and skill to cut the commutator on Bahn mission's generator with the tools they had on hand!

Chapter 42
Swaziland: Dream Fulfilled

When Jim arrived in Swaziland, he followed the map that the couple gave him to a very remote mission in a semi-desert area of the country. The mission was so remote that Jim would never have found it without the map. The drive there took him over many miles of very rough dirt and gravel roads. When Jim finally got to the mission station, he turned in and drove up a driveway, which was about a quarter of a mile long, and up to one of the houses. He did not think about it at the time, but God's plan to get him there was fulfilled.

An older lady was outside when he pulled his old car up near where she was standing. She stepped over to the car before Jim had time to get out and asked, "Have you come to stay?" The woman's question shocked Jim. Why would she have greeted him in those words? It was like God had given them to her. Jim did not answer her question, but he knew he had probably come to stay. He got out of his car and introduced himself to her and she told Jim her name was Miss Bonnie. Just then another older lady walked up to him and introduced herself as Miss Adams.

Both ladies invited Jim to come into their house for some refreshment. He knew they were wanting to know why he was there, but they did not ask. He followed them to their house and they went in and sat down. They brought Jim a refreshing drink and, after taking a few sips, he told them the story behind his being there. They listened intently and seemed very amazed as he gave them the details of how God had directed him to come to Swaziland. They were very interested in Jim's very strange story. After that they wanted him to stay and told him there was another small house on their mission and no one was living in it. They really encouraged Jim to move into it that very evening.

That evening the ladies prepared a very lovely dinner for Jim. After their meal they spent the rest of the evening visiting and getting to know each other. The ladies gave Jim a history of the mission, which he appreciated very much. They told him about their background and how God led them there. Jim gave them a detailed background on his family. Through their conversation the ladies became aware of Jim's skills in many areas and this especially thrilled them. They told Jim of their prayers for a man with his skills to come to their mission station.

They knew the mission buildings were needing many repairs and they did not have the skills to fix them. They also knew the Swazi men did not have the skills needed to repair the buildings.

As Jim listened to them tell him about their prayers, he could not help but remember the prayers of the two ladies at the Bassa Mission Station in Liberia. They had prayed for a long time for a man of his skills to come and build a Bible school. Now he was in Swaziland where two ladies had been praying for God to send a man to their mission with his skills. This was more than strange to Jim that this exact thing would happen in two different countries with women who were 3,000 miles apart and did not know each other or know him when they prayed, and that he would be the man with the skills they needed and he would end up in both countries. To Jim, it was much more than just a coincidence, it was a miracle of God. Jim was the answer to the women's prayers in both countries. His thoughts then centered on one thing. He would give his very best to following God's plan and he would try to work at it as hard as he had for Mary and himself when he was on their farm.

That evening Jim met pastor Fagute, who was the pastor of the mission church. He was a delightful man and he and Jim would become very close friends. Jim also met one of the church deacons named Tomba and they would also be close friends. They visited until late that evening and then Jim went to his house and got his first night's sleep at this Swazi Mission Station. Before Jim went to sleep thoughts were rolling over and over in his mind of everything that had happened to bring him to this place thousands of miles from his farm home in Indiana. He thought about how God told him to leave Liberia on the fifteenth of March, then how he met the couple with the map that led him to this mission and the two old ladies who had been praying for a man with his skills to come there.

Jim knew he was finally where God had called him when He spoke to him in the dream and said, "Move to Swazi and preach." Yes, Jim was there and it felt so good knowing he had been obedient to God's plan for Mary and him. However, he could not help but think about Mark and wonder what happened to him. He was wondering what Bob did to help him. Jim knew Bob told him he would take care of Mark, but he could see no way he could protect him from the Devil Society. Jim told himself over and over that he had to trust God to care for his son. He decided that he would write a letter the next morning and give them the address of this mission so they could reply and give news about Mark, and he would give them the details of what happened to him.

Jim was awake early the next morning. He got up, dressed, and walked outside. The sun was just coming up as he walked slowly around the mission. As he was walking, he prayed that God would deliver Mark from any harm from the Devil Society. Then a peace came over him and he felt the Lord was telling him that everything was going to go well for Mark.

After that Jim closely observed the mission station buildings. He was shocked to see that there were fifty buildings on the mission and most needed repairs. The school was huge with 500 children attending. Also, there was a large clinic and a large church building. From Jim's earlier conversation with the ladies he already knew that the generator was not working properly and needed repairs. He also knew that the 400-foot-deep well had no water in it and that getting enough water for the mission was a major problem. Jim was almost overwhelmed with how much work needed to be done and he hardly knew where to start.

Jim decided to work on the generator first. He found that a lot of the wiring was in deplorable condition and that the generator needed some repairs. The repairs took Jim about a week before the mission had electric lights in the evenings. After that he decided to do what he could to improve the water problem. They already had drilled a 400-foot-deep well and did not get any water from it. Jim knew it rained about twelve to fourteen inches a year, but that all came in three months. After some calculations he felt he could build several reservoirs to catch the water from the roofs of many of the fifty buildings. Then he would make them totally enclosed so that birds and animals could not get into them and containment the water. Jim would also have to have pumps so the people could get water from them. This would be a tremendous amount of work and cost a lot of money, but he knew it could be done and he would trust God for the money.

There was a very large river that flowed through the area and people would walk miles every day to get a bucket of water. During the latter part of the nine months of dry season the river dried up. The people would then dig down into the river bed to get some very dirty stagnant water and many people died every year from it.

After some careful planning Jim started digging a very large hole beside the church building. He paid many of the Swazi men to help him dig the hole. This took about a month and then he made a cement floor and walls around the hole. After that he lined the hole with a very thick plastic to make sure it would hold water with no leaks. Then he built a roof over it with no holes for birds or animals to get in. After that he put in a pump and made large gutters around the church roof to funnel the water into the reservoir. The reservoir held about 30,000 gallons of water. After that Jim built some more smaller above ground reservoirs. With almost perfect timing, the three months of rain started shortly after the reservoirs were completed and all of the reservoirs were filled with enough water to last the mission through the year.

It all worked perfectly and Jim believed the Lord gave him the idea and knowledge to accomplish the project. To say the least, the many people who lived on the mission were delighted. This included the missionaries, the families of the clinic nurses and school teachers, plus the 500 children who attended the school. After the first year of making the reservoirs on the mission Jim made many more, and within time, they even had an excess of water. During one very dry year the Swaziland Government ask Jim to furnish water for the whole area. He agreed to do this and the government really appreciated it.

Jim McCauley boarding the plane

Chapter 43
Captured by The Devil Worshipers

One day while Jim was working on building the water reservoirs a man came and wanted to talk to him, so he stopped what he was doing and listened to what he had to say. Jim had met him briefly once before on the mission station, but he knew nothing about him. However, Jim was told by Miss Bonnie that some missionaries were very impressed by this man's Christianity and they paid for him to go to a Bible school in the United States. The man was attending the mission church, but it seemed that Miss Bonnie was somewhat concerned about his Christianity.

The man told Jim that an old man wanted to talk to him and he said it was very urgent. The man wanted Jim to go with him right away to the old man. He told Jim that it was not far so they could walk there. Jim felt this might be something God was wanting him to do so he told the man he would go with him right then. Since he said it was just a short distance Jim did not tell Miss Bonnie or Miss Adams that he would be gone for a while. He thought it would be just a few minutes' walk.

Jim followed the man down the road for a short distance and then he left the main road and started walking through the brush area where there were small flat top trees and high grass. There were hardly any people or huts in the area that Jim could see. The man kept telling Jim that they were almost there so he kept following him. After about thirty minutes Jim started to wonder where he was taking him, but he hated to turn back. He thought the old man might want to make things right with the Lord and he did not want to miss out on the opportunity to pray with him.

After about one hour of walking through the very rough area they were still not there, but the man assured Jim that they were very close. Jim followed him for another hour and then he saw a very large group of men standing a large "U shape formation." Jim immediately started to wonder about what all of this was, but had little choice by this time except to continue following the man. He led Jim through the center of the "U Shape" formation and then the men closed the opening and formed a large circle around him. He could see that they were all armed with long machetes and spears and had evil expressions on their faces.

The man Jim was following led him to a very large man seated on a chair. Jim could immediately tell that he was a witch doctor from his dress. He glared at Jim with a look of hate that could have come only from the Devil. Standing beside him was another very large man holding a long sharp machete. He also was glaring at Jim with an evil expression on his face.

Jim knew he was in trouble. He was a Christian surrounded by devil worshipers who were intent on killing him. Jim was also miles from anyone who could help him and no one even knew where he was and he hardly knew himself. The witch doctor spoke to Jim and said they were going to cut off his hands and eat them so they could get the power he had in them. People had watched Jim fixing the mission generator, doing electric wiring, making the water reservoirs, and doing many other things that they did not know how to do. Word had got around the whole area that Jim could do many things and the devil worshipers believed he had a special power in his hands. They believed if they each ate a small part of Jim's hands; they could also do these things.

The man with the large machete looked like he could hardly wait to cut off Jim's hands. As he was getting ready to do this some of the men started to laugh at Jim and shout, "Preach to us before we cut off your hands. Preach to us before we cut off your hands." All of the men were laughing at Jim and seemed to think it would be fun to hear him preach to them before they cut off his hands. Even the witch doctor joined in with this and told Jim to preach.

When he told Jim to preach the Holy Spirit came upon him in a powerful way and he started preaching. Jim knew it might be his last sermon so he preached as hard as he could with the Holy Spirit leading his every word. After he had preached to them for a while the witch doctor and the man who was going to cut off Jim's hands became very fearful. The man with the knife started screaming in fear. After that he threw the knife as hard as he could and Jim watched as it flew end over end through the air and passed some huts and out of sight.

The man who had thrown the knife did not say one word to Jim after that and neither did the witch doctor. The men standing in the circle around him backed away from the area where he had walked in. Jim did not say a word, but slowly walked away from the witch doctor and the man who was going to cut off his hands. He continued slowly walking through the opening the men had made for him. Not one of the devil worshipers came after Jim and he made the two-hours walk back to the mission station.

What happened? There was absolutely no way Jim could have resolved the situation he was in! Their plan was to kill him! What caused great fear to come upon the man with the knife? He was very strong and evil, but he started screaming in fear. His fear was so intense that he threw his big knife as far as he could. He would never have wanted to show fear before the other men, but this time he could not control it. This just does not happen! He was a very powerful man in the Devil Society and probably feared by most of the members, yet something caused him to scream like a scared woman. All of the other men, including the witch doctor, suddenly had this same fear.

Who were they afraid of? It was the Holy Spirit who brought this on, but their focus was on Jim as the one who was doing it. They were so fearful of him that they wanted him out of there and the armed men opened up the circle so he could walk out. Not one of them communicated with each other, but they all acted in unison to let Jim out.

The power of the Holy Spirit brought this about! The power in Jim was greater than the power in the witch doctor, the big man with the long knife, and all of the other devil worshipers. All of the men were no doubt demon possessed, but the power of the Holy Spirit was greater than all of the power of the demons combined in the devil worshipers.

When the witch doctor tried to kill Bob in Liberia, he found that the power in Bob was greater than the power in him. As Bob just stood still before him, he could not hit Bob with the tree limb. After making four blows at Bob with the limb he was shocked to see that Bob's power was greater than his demonic power. Of course, we know that it was not Bob who had the power to divert each blow, but the power of the Holy Spirit within him.

In Mark 3:14-15 we see that Jesus sent out His twelve disciples to preach His Word. Then in Luke 10:1 we see that He sent out seventy-two. When they returned, they were very joyful and we see part of their report in Luke 10:17.

Mark 3:14-15 (NIV) [14] *He appointed twelve that they might be with him and that he might send them out to preach* [15] *and to have* <u>*authority to drive out demons.*</u>

Luke 10:17 (NIV) *The seventy-two returned with joy and said,* <u>*"Lord, even the demons submit to us in your name."*</u>

Do people get demon possessed in our life time? They most certainly do and I will give a few examples of this.

One time two other missionary couples and Bob and Pat were just starting to have a meeting for about fifty Liberian women. The meeting was outside and everyone was sitting on the ground except the missionary man who was going to have the message. He asked Bob to come to the front and have a prayer for the meeting. Bob stood up and walked to the front and asked everyone to stand for the prayer. Every one stood up and he had a short prayer asking God's blessings on the meeting and on the speaker. Bob closed his prayer with these words, "God. don't let anything of the devil stand here during this meeting." Bob had not planned on saying those words, but they just come out.

When Bob opened his eyes after the prayer, he was shocked at what he saw before him. Several of the women had fallen to the ground and they were squiring around on the ground and flopping their arms and legs, and within seconds they started foaming at their mouth. Bob had seen horses foam at their mouth many times, but this was the first time he had seen humans do it. There were about a dozen women doing exactly as we see in Mark 9:20.

Mark 9:20 (NIV) *So they brought him. When the spirit saw Jesus,* <u>*it immediately threw the boy into a convulsion. He fell to the ground and rolled around, foaming at the mouth.*</u>

Almost in unison, without hardly saying a word to each other, the three missionary couples went to one lady at the edge of the group and stood around her. They spoke to the demon and demanded that it come out of her in the name of Jesus Christ. The demon came out right away and she stood to her feet and raised her arms and started praising the Lord and weeping for joy.

One by one, the missionaries went to each of the ladies who were rolling around on the ground foaming at their mouth and cast the demons out of them. When each woman was delivered from the demons they did as the first woman had and raised their arms and started weeping and praising God.

Each missionary there had been filled with the Holy Spirit and were living a life of death to self and holy before God. When the time came, they were ready to cast out the demons and they knew they had authority over them. Satan wants every person to be fearful of him. He tried this on two people, who lived in a village called Bay-Pee-A, after they accepted Jesus Christ as their Savior. That village was heavy into witchcraft and most of the men belonged to the Devil Society. The two Christians became very fearful because they thought the Devil Society might put a curse on them. Bob heard about this and decided to make the long walk to the village to help the Christians and when he got there, he went to the center of the village to speak. When the people saw him, the whole village came and sat on the ground in a large circle around him. The two Christians also sat with the others to hear what Bob had to say.

As loud as he possibly could, Bob spoke about the power of the Holy Spirit being greater than the power of Satan and his demons. He used Scripture to back what he said and he told the people that the power in him was greater than the power in their witch doctors and those that worshiped Satan. Bob could see the Christians sitting a little off to his left as he spoke. When he made it personal and said that the power in their witch doctors was not nearly as powerful as the Holy Spirit's power in him, he saw fear come over the faces of the Christians. Bob continued to speak on this from about every angle he could using Scripture to back what he said. Finally, he saw the fear on the Christian face turn to one of joy.

Boldly Bob shouted to the witch doctors and devil worshipers that they could not do anything to him unless God permitted it. He knew most of the people were serving the devil and he wondered if one of them would stand up and challenge him, but none did. Bob had two goals in doing this. One was to convince the Christians that the power in them was greater than the power in those who worshiped Satan. The second was to convince the devil worshipers of this also. This gave the Christians boldness and it broke the spirit of fear the devil worshipers had tried to put on them.

One time right after a very large meeting a woman came to Bob and his friend Bill. The woman requested prayer from the two men saying she was seeing fire in her mind all of the time. She related that it was so vivid that she could hardly sleep or work and she could not get away from it. There were about six or seven other women there when she told this to the two men. Bob boldly spoke and said, "This is a demon and we will cast it out right now." There was a chair there and Bob told the woman to sit down and he asked the other women to gather around as he and Bill cast the demon out. Bill was in agreement and they prayed and cast the demon out in the name of Jesus Christ. The demon left immediately and the woman never had a problem like that again.

One evening, a Swazi man that Jim and Mary knew came to their home and told Jim they needed him to come immediately to minister to a demon possessed woman. Jim was very tired at the time, but he went with the man. When they arrived at the house where the woman and her husband lived, they went in. The house was very dimly lit, but Jim could see a few other Christians there and the wife was completely out of control. Jim no more than got in the house when she attacked him and knocked off his glasses. Then she bit Jim's right arm so hard that her teeth cut through his skin and into his muscle. Then she would not let go, but tried to tear out a chunk of his flesh. Two men properly grabbed her and pulled her mouth open and Jim was released. The woman started cursing and talking in different voices.

With his arm bleeding, Jim joined the other Christians and cast the demons out. When the demons left, the woman returned to her right mind and did not even know she bit Jim or any detail of what just happened. After that she became a dedicated Christian and even joyfully visited Jim and Mary a few days later and never seemed to regain any memory about being demon possessed. However, Jim still has vivid memories of it because he still has a big scar on his arm as a reminder.

Does demon possession ever happen in America? Most certainly it does and it is more common that many think. I will go back in time to relate this story. Before Bob quit his job with G.M., he was on a trip for his company and ready to get a motel for the night when the Holy Spirit spoke to him in the still small voice and said, "Go home immediately." Bob did not get a motel, but made the long drive back to his farm home near Kokomo, Indiana. When he pulled into his long driveway, he saw his dad's car parked near his house. He parked beside of his dad's car and right away his dad got in Bob's car.

He was drunk and this upset Bob because he had seen it for so many years. Bob harshly said, "Dad, why do you want to go to hell?" His dad answered, "If you could tell me why all of our boys are getting killed in Vietnam, I would accept Christ!" The tone of his voice indicated that he believed Bob could not answer his question, so he was safe in saying he would become a Christian if he did. The Holy Spirit immediately gave Bob the answer and he knew his dad would be on the spot for accepting Christ. Bob said, "Dad, I will answer that question with one word! It is sin dad, it is sin."

Immediately Bob's dad looked shocked as if he heard something he never expected. He dropped his head and said, "God forgive me!" Instantly Bob heard the Holy Spirit say, "Pray in tongues." Bob was surprised by this, but started praying in the Holy Spirit. Just as he started to pray in tongues, his dad's body was slammed hard, face first, into the windshield, then his head and shoulder crashed hard into the right door window, and his body flew through the air between Bob and the steering wheel and crashed head first into the window on Bob's side and then back into a sitting up position.

Then Bob's dad said, "I love everybody. Have you ever felt that way?" Bob answered, "Yes I have Dad, every day." Bob's dad then put his left arm around Bob and kissed him on his right cheek. This was the first time Bob ever remembers his dad kissing him.

What happened? Bob and Jim's dad was delivered from a demon and Born-Again that evening. When did he get demon possessed? Bob or Jim cannot answer that question, but they can answer the question of how he got demon possessed. His sinful lifestyle and addiction to alcohol opened him to it. Did he look demon possessed? "No." He could carry on farming and doing electrical work etc. and he looked as normal as could be. A person would never think he had a demon, but he did. Yes, this does happen in America.

Incidences of deliverance's like this were too numerous to put more in this book so I will stop here. A major point I do want to express is this. People who get involved in things of the occult or even willful sin can open themselves up to demonic control. This is very dangerous, and if not repented of, it can lead to demon possession. The wonderful thing is this. A Christian, living a life of obedience and death to self, has the Holy Spirit power to cast out demons.

Jim was living in the Holy Spirit and in this power when he followed the man through the wilderness to where the devil worshipers were waiting on him. Jim saw firsthand the power of the Holy Spirit and the Word of God that day. There was no way he could have talked the devil worshipers out of cutting off his hands. Of course, if they cut off his hands Jim would have died very quickly because of loss of blood. They knew this and would have, no doubt, sacrificed his blood and body to the devil. The man who betrayed Jim to the devil worshipers was not a Christian at all, but rather a worshiper of the devil himself. If he was a Christian at one time, he certainly was not at the time he betrayed Jim to the devil worshipers. Judas betrayed Jesus and our Lord said that it would have been better if he had never been born (Matthew 26:24). The man who called himself a Christian and yet betrayed Jim to the devil worshipers might have the same thing said about him.

God had plans for Jim in Swaziland and He was not going to let the devil worshipers stop him. For centuries Satan has tried to stop, delay, or hinder God's plans. Jim's obedience had brought him to this place in God's plans and He would stop Satan's plans to kill him just as He stopped Satan's plans to kill or delay Bob from getting the ticket.

God's plans to save the little girl laying on the dirt dying had not come about yet and He was not going to let a group of devil worshipers stop that either.

Chapter 44
Help for Zenzele Arrived

After Jim's encounter with the devil worshipers he went back to working on the water reservoirs. In addition to this, he was also going into the villages preaching the Gospel. Jim was very busy and tired a lot of the time. but he could not help but remember his decision to work as hard in the Lord's work as he had on his farm when working for himself and Mary. One Sunday he spoke in five different villages and he was very tired. In many ways it would have been easy for him to call it a day and return to the mission to get some rest. It was then that the old drive Jim had when he was on his farm caused him to look at the sun to see if he had enough daylight left to go to another village and preach. He saw that he could go to one more, so the fact that he was tired was not a factor in his mind. He was going to go!

Jim drove his car down a very rough road looking for another village where he could preach. Then he saw one, but it was not located on the road, so Jim parked his car and got out with the intentions of walking to the center of the village. It was a long way to the center of the village and he was so tired that he decided to take a short cut that would take him through a rough terrain that people did not normally walk in.

As Jim was walking through the area, he was shocked to see a little child laying in the dirt. Jim walked over to get a closer look and was very upset at what he saw. The child was a little girl with no clothes on and laying in her own feces and urine with insects crawling over her little body and fly eggs in her eyes, nose, ears, and mouth. Also, the odor coming from her was almost overwhelming. Jim's anger flared up within him at what he saw. How could anyone let this happen? Jim knelt down to take a closer look at the child. She appeared to be about eight years old and she was still alive. He was very angry with whoever was responsible for leaving this child!

Jim quickly walked on to the center of the village and immediately started asking about the little girl and why the people left her laying in that remote area. He talked to several people and no one seemed to even care about the child. Then he finally found the little girl's parents and they were both drunk. In fact, nearly everyone Jim talked to was drunk. Some of the villages made beer from their maze (corn) and this village was one of them. The local people called these villages, "Beer villages." Nearly every person who lived in a beer village would be very drunk by Sunday afternoon and this was the situation Jim found in this village.

Jim asked the parents why they left their daughter lying in the dirt. They replied that she was sick and was going to die. Jim asked them why they did not take her to the mission clinic. They replied that it was too far to walk. This infuriated Jim because it was only about one mile to a place that they could easily get a bus or a ride in a passing car to take her there. Jim begged them to bring their little girl to the mission clinic, but they refused. After trying to persuade them to get medical help for their child he gave up. By this time Jim's anger was overwhelming and he decided to do what he could himself.

Jim decided against taking time to preach in that village and walked back to the little girl. He looked for a small stick that had a point on it. Then he got down on his knees and started to carefully use the point of the stick to remove the fly eggs from the child's eyes, mouth, nose, and ears. He was especially careful when he removed the fly eggs from her eyes because he did not want to damage them. This took Jim about one hour and the child was still alive when he finished. He had a bottle with a small amount of pop in it that was in his truck. The pop was about like our Sprite. Jim slowly got a small amount of it down her throat. Not once did her parents or anyone else ever come to see about the little girl when Jim was there.

Even though the little girl was dying, Jim knew if he took her with him to the clinic, they could arrest him for kidnapping, so he drove as fast as he could back to their mission. When he got there, he went directly to the Swazi nurse. Jim told her about the little girl and asked her to go to the village with him to treat the child. She agreed and he drove back to the village as quickly as he could.

When they arrived at the village, Jim took the nurse to the child. The nurse carefully examined her and said she had malaria. She gave her some medicine for the malaria and Jim helped the nurse get a little nourishment in the child. This was very difficult for Jim and the nurse, but they had to leave her laying exactly where she was so Jim would not get into serious trouble with the law. Jim and the nurse were very troubled by leaving her there because of the dangers that could happen to her through the night. There were several wild animals in Swaziland that would eat the little girl right away if they came upon her during the night when many of them prowl. Among those are the lions, leopards, jackals, and badgers. There are also many very poisonous snakes in Swaziland that would bite and kill the little girl if they came upon her, and huge snakes that would eat her.

Through the night Jim thought about these dangers and could hardly wait until sun up to drive back to where the little girl was lying to see if she made it through the night and to give her some of the malaria medicine and some nourishment. When Jim got back shortly after daylight, she was still there but did not look any better. After giving her the medicine and nourishment, he had to leave her there, but he planned to come back later in the day to treat the child.

For several days Jim went back to the village twice a day to give the child medicine and nourishment. She started to improve and get her strength back and this was a blessing to Jim. The parents, however, would do nothing to help their little daughter and she lay there for many days.

The Swazi Christians on the mission station saw how Jim was going to the village twice a day to feed and care for the child. They also knew he could not move her or he would be in serious trouble. One day Pastor Fagute and Tomba went to the village and brought the little girl back to Jim. Since they were both Swazis, they could do this, but Jim could not because he was a foreigner. When they returned to the mission station, they came to Jim carrying the child and said, "Here is your daughter."

Since Mary was not with Jim yet he got one of the Swazi women to care for Zenzele. She continued to gain health and strength and after about a month of being properly cared for, Zenzele was back to being a normal little girl.

The statement below was quoted from Chapter one when Zenzele was laying in the dirt dying.

If the little girl was to be helped it would have to be God who did it because no one else would. Also, her help would have to come quickly because she was near death.

Zenzele's parents had no desire or willingness to save their own daughter from a terrible death. No normal human being could do this, but they did. No normal village could allow this, but they did. When

Jim told the villagers about the little girl laying in the dirt, not one person cared enough to get involved or help her. This is what happens to devil worshipers and many in that village worshiped him. Sad to say, substance abuse can cause the same thing. The normal mother or father will love and care for their children. Bob and Jim saw through the years how people who get addicted to drugs and alcohol do not love and care for their children as the normal parent does. Their desire for drugs and alcohol is far above meeting the needs of their children.

There is absolutely no logic for why Zenzele's parents did this, but one of God's people from a far-off land got involved and this made a huge difference in the little girl's life. What does this mean? There are areas where Satan is worshiped as he was in that village and it effects the culture in that area. What can change this? Many times, Bob and Jim saw this. When people came to Jesus Christ in repentance, their whole life changed. Some had worshiped Satan, some were on substance abuse, and there were some who did both, yet their whole life and desires changed to serving God with all of their hearts, which included being good parents, sons, or daughters. These people can and will made a difference in the culture where they live.

About five years before this God summoned a man from a far-off land to fulfill His purpose for saving little Zenzele. That man obeyed God's call and during those five years He used the man in many places and then got him right to where Zenzele was lying in time to save her life.

Isaiah 46:11 (NIV) *From the east I summon a bird of prey; from a far-off land, a man to fulfill my purpose. What I have said, that I will bring about; what I have planned, that I will do.*

As was said above, God had plans for little Zenzele even when she was lying in the remote area of Africa covered with insects and having fly eggs in her mouth, ears, nose, and eyes. He also had plans for little Bobby and Jimmy as they were in mental anguish because of the way their parents were living. All three suffered as children due to substance abuse. They had this in common. However, all three had something else in common when they grew up. They did not remain in the lifestyle of their parents, but became dedicated Christians, serving God with all of their hearts and obeying Him in everything He directed!

Chapter 45
Ministry in Liberia Finished

Shortly before Jim left Liberia to go to Swaziland, Bob and Pat, along with Tony and Tanya, moved to the River Cess Mission Station to take the Hodgson's place so they could go back to their home in Canada for a yearlong furlough. Bob continued his flying from there and his ministry in the villages to preach the Gospel and treating the sick people intensified. Many were coming to Jesus Christ as he went, plus God continued to send the money in to fly the plane on the aviation medical evangelism flights. About two months after Jim left Liberia to go to Swaziland Bob received a letter from him giving details of where God led him and what he was doing. Bob knew Jim had no contacts in Swaziland and knew no one there, but he also knew the Lord had a plan for him and He would bring it about. The main thing Bob knew was it was very important that Jim got there on the 15th of March, which he did. From Jim's letter, Bob saw the hand of God leading him step by step. Bob missed his brother and knew it would probably be a long time before they saw each other again. However, Bob knew Jim's main calling of God was to go to Swaziland and preach and he was there doing that.

Four months before the Hodgson family would return to Liberia, Bob and Pat had to make a decision about Tanya's schooling. They had two choices. They could send her to the mission school in the Ivory Coast and it would be four months before they saw her again. Or they could send her back to her grandparents in America and she could start her school along with the other students she would be going to school with when they returned to America. Bob and Pat decided that sending her to live with her grandparents would be the best. They prayed about how they could do this because she was too young to fly there on her own. God blessed and a missionary couple from another mission said they were returning to America and they would take care of getting her home. Bob and Pat knew this was God's answer, so Tanya returned to America and stayed with her grandparents for the four months and went to school from there.

Tony continued doing his high school through correspondence and received his diploma. This was a big day for him. He did not have one day in a normal high school, but did it all through correspondence. Pat had a big celebration on the mission station for him. Mike had finished his high school by correspondence about two years before and his mother did the same thing for him. Shortly after he graduated, he went back to Indiana and started going to college at Purdue University.

The mission needed someone to take Bob's place flying when they went home after five years, so a couple named Dwight and Nancy Land came to Liberia and Dwight was going to be the new pilot when Bob left. Bob still continued flying just as he had, but he took Dwight on every trip teaching him how to be a jungle pilot. During that time, Bob noticed that no money was coming in for the evangelistic flights into the villages and soon the fund was almost broke.

When Bob made his last flight into a village to preach the Gospel and treat the sick people, the flight cost was exactly what was left in the airplane fund. The fund finally went broke on Bob's last flight. Bob well remembered his prayer about God supplying the money to use the airplane for evangelism and how God had sent in the first $100. He also well remembered how he had tried as hard as he could to break the fund and he could not do it. Bob was absolutely amazed at how God kept the money coming in until he made his last flight.

The mission then officially turned the plane over to Dwight. At that time Bob had made about 3,500 jungle flights. He had loved his time flying as a jungle pilot, but he believed that this was the end of his time of flying in the jungle and God was going to use him in another way. Bob watched closely as Dwight got in the plane and flew out of the airstrip where Bob was standing. He had a sad feeling in his heart knowing he would never fly that plane again. A few days before the Hodgson's returned to River Cess Mission Station, Bob, Pat, and Tony, left Liberia and flew back to America.

God had used Bob and Pat to win hundreds to Himself in Liberia. Also, He had used Bob to preach the Word and treat hundreds of people who were sick in the villages. This resulted in saving the lives physically of at least 350 people. Then in addition to that God had used Bob to help Jim build the Bible school in the mid-1970s and it is still going on to this day. Now, all of Bob's ministry in Liberia was finished, but God had a future ahead for him that was going to be even greater than it had been in Liberia.

Chapter 46
Back Home Again in Indiana

Bob, Pat, and Tony's first desire, after returning to Indiana, was to see Michael and Tanya. It was so refreshing to see both of them and have their family again in the same location. Mike's parents could immediately see that their beloved teenager was now a young man. Right away they rented an old house in a small town near Jim and Mary's home and their family all moved into it. Now it was exciting to have their family all living in the same house again. It would be short lived however.

Mike had finished two years at Purdue University and made the choice to become an electrician. He had written to his parents while they were still in Liberia asking for their permission to change his goal from engineering to being an electrician. They gave him their full approval to do it and he was now an apprentice electrician. God blessed Tony the first day he went out looking for a job and he got one working in a tool and die shop as a janitor. Tony was disappointed with his job, but his dad was elated. He told Tony to get to work 15 minutes early every day and start to work right away and get the place as clean as possible. One day they will need someone to cut steel on a milling machine and they will ask you to do it. Listen very carefully and do exactly as they tell you to. This can lead to an apprenticeship as a tool and die maker. Tony did exactly as his dad told him and he did get an apprenticeship as a mold maker in a large plastic molding business. Bob and Pat were elated with how God had blessed both of their sons with good jobs.

A few days after moving into their rented house, Bob and Pat heard a knock at the door and when they opened it, there stood Jim and Mary. Jim had just flown back to Indiana from Swaziland. It seemed so unusual to both families that the brothers had returned to Indiana at nearly the same time. Neither one of them had planned this timing. It soon became obvious that God had planned it, and they could clearly see it from what was about to happen.

The brothers and their wives spent about two hours just getting to know what God had done with each of them. Jim also told Bob and Pat he was only going to be home for three weeks and then fly back to Swaziland. Jim was kept very busy for the three weeks visiting family and friends he had not seen in four years. During this time, he was driving through the small town of Windfall where he did his banking before he and Mary went to Africa. He saw the president of the local bank and his wife walking down the street. He was the one who offered Jim a job of being the president of one of his banks. Jim stopped and greeted the banker and his wife. They both were very happy to see him.

Jim had a large burn on his arm and they both noticed it and asked what had happened. He told them that his old car in Africa got very hot and boiled over and burnt his arm as he was checking it. They asked Jim about the car and he told them that a man had given it to him and it had about 300,000 miles on it. Much to Jim's surprise the bank president and his wife gave him a very large sum of money to buy a new one. Jim had not asked them or even thought about them giving the money to him. He believed and still does that God brought this about. He knew Jim needed a reliable vehicle to use in the ministry and that he did not have the money to buy one. God just took care of it for him. Jim thanked the banker and his wife for the gift. After that they talked for a few minutes and said good bye to each other.

Shortly after Jim told Bob and Pat that he was returning to Swaziland in three weeks, the Holy Spirit told Bob in the still small voice that he was to go with Jim to Swaziland. Bob shared this with Pat and she agreed, so they told Jim and Mary. Jim was elated and hoped Bob could go back with him. Both brothers felt Mary and Pat should stay with their children in Indiana for two months and then come to Swaziland. Jim also said it was nearly impossible to get a permit to live there as a missionary. The Swaziland government required that a person have a job to live in the country. However, the two old ladies got permission for him to stay there as the manager of the mission station.

Jim said he had talked to a man who had a large contract with the Swaziland government to spray the swamps using an airplane to kill the tsetse flies. When the man heard that Jim's brother was a jungle pilot, he said he would hire him as sprayer pilot if he came to Swaziland. He would also take care of getting him permission to stay in the country. As Jim and Bob talked about this, they agreed that it would be a way for Bob to be there and the two of them could work as missionaries when Bob was not flying. From that moment on the brothers made plans to go in three weeks. They both were totally convinced this was God's plan for them.

When the banker and his wife gave the large sum of money to Jim, he had enough to buy a pickup truck and purchase his ticket to return to Swaziland. However, Bob did not have a ticket, nor did he have the $1,800 needed to purchase it. In fact, he had very little money at all. Somehow this did not brother Bob and he continued on with all of his plans to fly out on the given date with Jim. Bob had seen God furnish so much money in different ways before this that he was not worried about the funds. He had total confidence the money would be there when he needed it.

Then one day a pastor, whom Bob did not know, felt he should take up a collection during his mid-week prayer service. He also felt God would give him the name of the person he was to give the money to at the service. There were only 34 people at the prayer service, but the collection came to exactly $800. Bob's pastor was at that service and he asked prayer for Bob. When he did this God spoke to the church pastor in His still small voice and said, "That is the man to give the money to." They gave the $800 to Bob's pastor and the next day he gave it to Bob.

That same day Bob went with his pastor to visit one of his farmer friends. Bob did not know the farmer and hardly talked to him about his missionary ministry. They only stayed a short time at the farmer's house and most of the conversation was on farming. When they left the farmer's home, Bob's pastor gave him a $1,000 check from the farmer. Bob had never even mentioned to the farmer that he needed any money. Money for the ministry did not come up in the conversation at all.

Bob thought about it for a short time after receiving the $1,000 and realized that God had provided the exact amount of money he needed to buy the ticket and he did it in one day. He was not surprised at all because he knew God was going to supply. Right after that Bob went to a ticket agent and purchased his ticket. The day quickly came and he and Jim said a sad good bye to their children, because they knew it would be a long time before they saw them again. The wives then drove them to the airport in Indianapolis, Indiana and the brothers flew to Johannesburg, South Africa.

Chapter 47

Brothers in Swaziland

Shortly after Bob and Jim arrived in Johannesburg, Jim purchased a new pickup truck, which they drove to Swaziland. When they arrived in Swaziland, they had to go through customs in the capital city of Mbabane. Since Jim was already listed as having a job of managing the mission, he went right on through customs with hardly any questions asked. Because Bob did not have a job the custom officer gave him three weeks to find one. If he did not find one, he would have to leave the country immediately. After leaving the customs office Jim took Bob to meet the owner of the flying business. After talking to Bob for a very short time, he said he would hire him as a sprayer pilot and for him to come back the next day.

Jim took Bob to meet a pastor and his wife who lived in Mbabane. As they were talking, the pastor and his wife told Bob that they were leaving in a few days and would be gone for two months or more. They said they would like to have Bob live in their house until they returned. It would make them feel better about leaving if they knew someone was watching after their home while they were gone. The house was beautiful and once again Bob could see how God planned ahead of him and had a lovely home he could live in. This was a wonderful offer for Bob and he gladly took them up on it. Since Bob had a place to stay, Jim drove on to his mission, which was a two-hour drive away.

The couple gave Bob a very lovely bedroom where he could stay, and after a delicious meal and visit for the evening he went to his room. Bob knelt down and had his first time of prayer in Swaziland. The Holy Spirit clearly spoke to him in the still small voice and said, "You are not to take the flying job, but I will give you a job using your engineering and machine shop skills." Bob was somewhat disappointed because he really wanted to be flying. However, he fully submitted to the directions from the Holy Spirit.

The next day the pastor talked to Bob about his background in engineering and machine shop skills. Bob told him he had been a senior engineer for General Motors and also was a journeyman tool and die maker and he could operate all of the machine shop machines. The pastor told Bob he had a friend who owned a machine shop and he wondered if Bob would like to meet him. Bob felt this might be what God wanted him to do and he told the pastor. He took Bob to meet his friend and he interviewed Bob and said he would like him to come back the next day for a test. Bob agreed and the next day the shop owner gave him a piece of bar steel and told him to make a bolt and nut with a very difficult thread. Bob did the work and the bolt and nut turned out perfectly. The shop owner seemed very pleased and almost surprised that Bob could make it. He hired Bob as his shop foreman.

Bob could hardly believe that he had just arrived in the country and was now foreman over a seventy-man machine shop. It was by far the largest machine shop in Swaziland and in that whole area of South Africa. God had just given Bob a very good job and a good salary and a lovely home that was only about a quarter of a mile from the machine shop. In addition to that, a plantation owner, who Jim knew very well, had a very nice used car he wanted to sell at a very reasonable price. Since Bob had a job, he was able to buy it. This made it possible for Bob to stay in the country and also to minister with Jim when he was not working.

Bob had no trouble leading the men in running the equipment because he knew how to do it himself. There was one problem he had that was somewhat difficult. Bob had both black and white men working under him and he hardly knew what the word apartheid meant until he had lived there for a short time. He grew to hate it and to see the injustice in it. It seemed daily he saw the hate between some of the whites and some of the blacks. Not every person white or black was involved in this, but enough were that it caused problems that Bob was not used to. Bob tried to do his job in leading the machine shop work and also in being a peace maker. In doing this, it seemed he was receiving some respect from both sides.

Bob worked at his job five days a week and, on Friday after he got off of work, he made the two-hour drive to Jim's mission. The two of them would go from village to village preaching the gospel. English was the official language and all of the schools were taught in English. As a result, nearly every village had some younger person who could interpret for them into the Swazi language. They were seeing many come to Jesus Christ as they went. Also, many had never heard of God's plan of salvation and some had never heard of Jesus Christ.

When Bob was working at his job, Jim would take his Toyota pickup truck out on the rough dirt roads to minister by himself in the villages. There were many widows and poor people in the villages, and he faithfully took cornmeal and other food items to them when he went. Every Sunday morning Jim would start driving early in the morning, making trip after trip to the different villages, picking up people and taking them to church. He usually had about twenty people in the back of his pickup truck. Many times, the little truck was so fully loaded that it looked as if it could not go, but it always did. After church, he would make trip after trip taking the people back to their villages.

One Sunday a woman, who was about thirty-five years old, went to church in Jim's truck along with a load of other people. She had her three-week-old baby with her, so Jim had her and the baby sit in the front so she and the baby would be more comfortable. After church, Jim returned this woman along with the rest of the people back to their own area. The woman had a bad case of malaria and died that night. Jim was told about this right after it happened, and it really shook him up because he had no idea if she had accepted Christ as her Savior. Jim was in deep grief and blaming himself for not talking to her about the Lord before she died and he feared she might be in hell for eternity.

The little house Jim was living in had two small bed rooms, a small kitchen and a living room. That night Jim went to his bed room and Bob to the one he used when he was there. Jim was still very concerned about the eternal destination of the woman who died. He was heartbroken that he had not talked to her about the Lord when she was in his pickup truck. Bob knew this and was concerned about Jim recovering from his feeling of guilt.

Both brothers went to sleep and about half way through the night Bob suddenly woke up. He was completely awake when he saw a bright colorful vision against one of the walls in his bed room. It was a very vivid scene about four feet long and three feet high and it stayed against the wall for about one minute. The scene had a message in it for Jim that said he could rest easy because the woman was right with the Lord when she died.

After about a minute the scene disappeared and the room returned to darkness, but Bob continued to be fully awake thinking about it. God had just given him a message for Jim that would be very important for him to hear. Bob wondered why God gave the vision to him rather than

Jim. To this day Bob does not know the answer to this, but he does know God did it. Very early the next morning Bob told Jim about the vision. Jim never questioned why God gave the vision to Bob, but he was very relieved, knowing the woman was saved and she would be in heaven for eternity.

1980 Jim McCauley building a church in Swaziland

Chapter 48

The Boy I Saw in My Dream

There were numerous times in Jim's life that God has directed him with a dream. We see in the New Testament that God did it back then and He still does it today.

Joel 2:28 (KJV) ***"And afterward, I will pour out my Spirit on all people. Your sons and daughters will prophesy, your old men will dream dreams, your young men will see visions.***

Matthew 2:12 (KJV) ***And having been warned in a dream not to go back to Herod, they returned to their country by another route.***

Matthew 2:13 (KJV) ***When they had gone, an angel of the Lord appeared to Joseph in a dream. "Get up," he said, "take the child and his mother and escape to Egypt. Stay there until I tell you, for Herod is going to search for the child to kill him."***

Matthew 2:19-20 (KJV) *[19] **After Herod died, an angel of the Lord appeared in a dream to Joseph in Egypt [20] and said, "Get up, take the child and his mother and go to the land of Israel, for those who were trying to take the child's life are dead."***

One night the Holy Spirit gave Jim a vision in a dream of a little Swazi boy. Jim saw the little boy's face very clearly in the dream and knew exactly what he looked like. The Lord spoke to Jim in this vision and told him when he saw this boy, he was to take him to the mission and He and Mary were to raise him as their own child. Jim shared this dream with Bob. The day after the dream, Bob and Jim went out preaching in the villages. As they were driving down one of the secondary roads looking for a village to preach in Jim saw a very small dirt trail that led off of the road they were on. Jim felt the Lord wanted him to turn onto that small trail and drive down it.

After about fifteen minutes of driving on the very winding and rough trail they came to a village Jim had never been to before. He stopped his truck in front of the first hut they came to and a little boy came to Jim's window and stared at him without saying a word. Jim looked at him and was shocked to see the exact face he saw in his dream. Jim knew without any doubt that this was the little boy God told him to take to the mission and raise. With the boy still looking at him, Jim spoke very loud to Bob and said, "This is the boy God showed me in the dream! This is the boy God showed me in the dream!"

Even before they got out of the truck a woman came walking towards them. The brothers got out of the truck and Jim greeted her. Jim and Bob could tell from the expression on her face that she was very burdened about something and wanted desperately to talk to them. She told the brothers a very strange story. She said her husband was poisoned and died a few days before this. She said her husband's evil brother did it because he wanted his brother's cows. In their culture, wealth was measured by the number of cows a person had and the woman's husband had many. Also, in their culture, if the father died the cows went to the oldest son. If he died, the cows went to the deceased man's brother. The woman felt the brother would kill the boy and then he would own all of the cows.

Jim knew that using poison to murder someone was common in Swaziland so the story sounded logical to him from that standpoint. Jim also knew the law and she was right that the cows went to the oldest son if the father died and if the son died, they went to the oldest brother. The mother had no place in the inheritance process. Since God had already showed Jim in the dream that he and Mary were to raise the boy, Jim believed the woman's story and that the boy's life was in danger.

The woman told Jim the boy's life would be saved if he would take him to the mission and raise him there. Jim and Bob could see she loved her son very much and was in great fear for his life. They also knew she would miss being with her son, but she was willing to give up being with him to save his life. Right then Jim told her he would take the boy and raise him on the mission. She was very pleased about this. Jim also told her that she could come to the mission any time she wanted and visit her son.

The woman knew that the evil brother would not dare come to the mission and try to kill the boy. Jim also knew this and that the boy would be safe with Mary and him. The brothers also knew that as long as the boy was alive the evil brother could not legally get the cows. The mother could have some of her other children or friends look after them. The mother told her son he was going to live on the mission station and he was okay with this. A few days later Jim came back to the village with pastor Fagute and Tomba and they helped him take care of the details for the boy to come with them to the mission station.

The little boy's name was Mandla. When they arrived back at the mission station Jim took Mandla and introduced him to his future missionary mother. Mary already knew about Jim's dream and fully accepted Mandla as the boy God directed them to raise. As time went on the little boy's mother came to visit him about once a week. This was a very enjoyable time for both of them. The evil brother never got the cows he wanted and Jim and Mary never heard of him again. Mandla grew into a very fine Christian man who loved Jim and Mary. He also loved his mother and appreciated how she had been willing to let him go to the mission to save his life. Then most important of all, he became a very dedicated servant of Jesus Christ. After the boy came to live with them, Mary and Jim now had two Swazi children, Zenzele and Mandla. However, God would soon give them more children to raise.

Today Mandla is a grown man and has a son who is the age he was when he went to live with Jim and Mary. He still loves them very much and occasionally calls them on the phone from Swaziland. Mandla has a very good job working for the government in water purification. He is also a very dedicated Christian.

This all had to have been in God's plan for Mandla and He (God) used a man from a far-off land to bring it about. As we look at this, we see that it was in God's perfect plan for Jim and Mary to be there to raise Mandla. It could be said this way, "It happened because of God's plan and man's obedience."

Chapter 49
Bob Stopped a Murder

God worked out all of the details for Mary and Pat, along with Tanya, to go to Swaziland two months after Bob and Jim went there. Within the two months all of their children, who would be staying in Indiana, had good jobs and could support themselves. Jim and Mary's children could live in their home. Pat found a very nice seventy-foot-long house trailer she could afford to buy for Mike and Tony. It was located in a good model home park near where they worked.

The day came when Pat and Tanya said good bye to Mike and Tony and Mary said good bye to Mark, Belinda, and Debbie. God also supplied the money for their tickets and they flew to Swaziland. Shortly before they arrived Bob rented a nice house near his work and he, Pat, and Tanya moved into it. Mary went to the mission to live with Jim. Bob and Pat, along with Tanya, would spend every weekend with Jim and Mary on their mission station.

Bob's job as foreman of the large machine shop continued to have challenges due to the apartheid between some of the men. The hate between some of the blacks and whites had been ingrained in them for so many years that it became a part of their culture. There were even two wash rooms and the whites were to use one and the blacks the other. Bob did not know this when he started to work there so he went to either one when he needed to go. After doing this for a few days, he was informed by one of the whites that he was not to go in the washrooms for the blacks. This shocked Bob, but he decided it was best to do what the man said. After Bob had worked there for a few months a small group of black men told him they wanted to have a meeting with him after they got off work. Bob had no idea what this was all about, but he told them to come to his car after work.

After work Bob walked to his car and a small group of men were there waiting on him. One of the men spoke for the group and said, "Umfundisi, why do you treat us different than other white men?" Bob had noticed long before this that the men started calling him "Umfundisi." At first Bob did not know what this word meant. Then he found that it was a Zulu word meaning endearing father. It could also be used for a priest or teacher. The way the men were using it was in the context of showing respect and appreciation for Bob.

Bob answered their question by telling them that all men are equal in God's sight. He is no respecter of person. He loves all men the same and God wanted all men to love each other as He did. Bob said he was a Christian and he did not put one man above another. The black men really appreciated what he told them. After that the black men seemed to all have a love for Bob, even though he was their foreman at work.

About a month after this, Bob and the shop manager were walking across the yard from the main building to the welding shop. As they got close to the welding shop, they saw a Zulu man named Joe (not his real name) standing outside of the building just looking around. Joe was one of the welders and he usually wore a vest open at the front. One could tell from looking at Joe's upper body that he was ultra-strong. He looked like a weight lifter. When Bob and the manager got close to Joe the manager said, "Joe, get to work."

Immediately Joe hit the manager with a very strong blow to the front of his face. The blow was so hard that it splattered the manager's blood on Bob. He was shocked at what he just saw happen right beside him. The manager's body flew backwards about six feet and hit a parked car and fell to the ground. Bob looked backwards for about a second as this happened and then he looked back at Joe. He took off running to the open door of the welding shop and grabbed a bar of steel that was about two feet long. There were about six or eight Swazi or Zulu men right beside of the open-door watching Joe. It was obvious to Bob from the look on Joe's face and his actions he planned to kill the manager.

Bob's immediate thought was the men near the open door would try to stop Joe, but Bob quickly saw they all had smiles on their face as if they approved of what was happening. The thought flashed through Bob's mind, "They are not going to even try to stop Joe from killing the manager. They are happy about it!" In an instant of time another thought flashed through Bob's mind, "I am the only one to stop Joe from killing the manager. If I try, I might be killed also!"

The manager was still laying on the ground bleeding as Joe was running at him with the bar of steel raised above his head to make the fatal blow." Bob quickly jumped in front of Joe and lifted both of his arms out from his body much like a basketball player would do in a defensive way. Bob knew he could immediately be hit by the bar of steel because he could see that Joe was extremely angry. Joe did not hit

Bob, but tried to go around Bob's left side. Bob instantly jumped to his left in front of Joe and loudly shouted "No Joe." Again, Joe did not hit Bob, but quickly tried to go around Bob's right side. With both arms still held out Bob jumped in front of Joe and again shouted, "No Joe!"

Bob was very surprised to see Joe stop and lower the bar of steel to his side. He was also looking at something behind Bob. He very slowly tried to keep one eye on Joe and look behind him to see what he was looking at. Bob was very happy to see the manager running as fast as he could towards his car. He jumped in and quickly drove away. Joe slowly turned around and walked back to the open door of the welding shop and put the bar of steel back where he got it.

Bob did not say another word to Joe, but walked back to the main building where his office area was and continued on with his work. That evening the manager and the machine shop owner had a long talk and decided it was best not to fire Joe.

Why was Bob able to save the manager's life that day? The black men appreciated him very much because he treated them as equals. Many of them had such a high respect for Bob that they called him the very endearing name of Umfundisi. It is now Bob's belief that Joe had enough of a respect for him because he treated the blacks well and that resulted in him not hitting Bob with the steel bar. The fact that the blacks had a high respect for Bob probably saved his life. He also believes the incident helped him with the whites because they saw he defended one of them even though it could have resulted in his own death.

God used Bob's quick decision to save the manager's life to enhance his testimony with both ethnic groups of men. Was it in God's plans for Bob to save the life of the manager? Most certainly it was. It brought glory to God in the fact that one of His servants was willing to defend someone even when it meant he possibly could have been killed.

Chapter 50
A Voice from Heaven

On the weekends Bob, Pat, and Tanya, would make the two-hour drive to Jim's mission station and the brothers would go into the villages teaching and preaching the Word of God. They were ministering in many different villages in the area, but had purposely stayed out of a terrorist training area due to the dangers involved for them if they went in there.

Many of the people they preached to did not even know who Jesus Christ was. They asked one man if he knew who Jesus Christ was and he got a very serious look on his face as if he was thinking intently. He then pointed in a certain direction and said, "I am not sure, but maybe he lives down the road this way."

Hundreds of people made decisions to accept Christ as their Savior after they heard the Word of God. Most of the people knew little about the Creation story and man's fall due to the sin of Adam, or that Jesus Christ died for their sins. Often the brothers had to start at the beginning and tell the story about God's plan and what Jesus Christ did for every person. The people were very open to listen and respond to the Word.

The terrorist area that they had purposely stayed out of consisted of about two hundred and fifty square miles. After they had ministered in the different villages around the terrorist training area for many months, Jim told Bob that he felt God wanted them to go into that area and preach the blood of Jesus Christ and repentance in every village. The brothers talked about doing this, but Bob wasn't sure they should go into that area.

The terrorists were not only teaching the Africans to kill white people, but also to kill any African who was friendly to the whites. They tried to make examples out of the Africans who showed any friendship to the whites by killing them and their families. Many white farmers in the nation of South Africa had already been killed and the terrorists had started their evil work in Swaziland, so Bob and Jim knew the seriousness of going into the area.

A few days before the brothers started talking about going into that area, Jim and Bob preached the Word of God in a village that was

253

located near the terrorist area. Shortly after they were there, a group of terrorists came running through the village with their guns blazing. They shot every person they could: men, women, and children. Some of the residents of the village were able to run and escape, but sadly, many were not able to get away in time and were shot. Many were wounded and eleven died on the spot from the gunshot wounds. The brothers do not know how many died later. Bob and Jim felt there was a good possibly that the terrorists killed all of those people because they were friendly to the white brothers.

As Bob prayed and thought about them going into the terrorist area, it came to his mind that for two white guys to go into that area would be like two Jews going into a Nazi training area and preaching. They probably would be killed. It was not safe for them to go in there, and they probably would be killed unless God protected them. Bob also had another problem. By this time, he had changed jobs and was working in a plastic molding shop for a man who had escaped out of East Germany. The shop owner was a wonderful Christian and he and Bob often talked about spiritual matters. He and Bob also became very close friends. He was hungry for the Word of God and questioned Bob on many different aspects of the Bible. He respected Bob and Bob respected him. He grew up in a Communist country and Bob in the United States, yet they had an excellent friendship in Jesus Christ.

God also used the shop owner to teach Bob plastic molding. Bob had served an apprenticeship as a tool and die maker and had also been a senior tool engineer for General Motors. His German friend was an expert in plastic molding. Bob knew little about plastic molding and his friend knew little about sheet metal tools and dies. He wanted to learn all he could about building sheet metal tools and dies so he could expand his business into those areas. He told Bob he would teach him how to build plastic molds if Bob would teach him how to build sheet metal tools and dies. Bob agreed and every day the two men gave each other equal time of teaching, hour for hour.

By the time they finished their teaching and learning time together, Bob's friend became an expert in tool and die skills and Bob in plastic molding skills. Bob's German friend then started to quote sheet metal tool and die work from a local industry that used a lot of sheet metal parts. It opened his shop up to thousands of dollars worth of new business. At the time, Bob only did this teaching to be friendly, but little did he know God was teaching him an engineering skill from this German that would be of extreme value to him in the years to come.

The government gave Bob a work permit to stay in the country as long as he had a job. If he stopped working at his job, he was supposed to be out of the country within one week. They wanted to know Bob's whereabouts at all times. It was not a problem to minister with Jim on the weekends as long as he was back on his job on Monday morning.

The law in that country was very strict, and many people were in prison for many years because of some very small infractions. If Jim and Bob went into the terrorist area full-time, Bob would have to quit his job, and if he did not leave the country in one week, he would be in violation of their immigration laws. If the police caught him, he would surely go to prison for a long time. On top of that, if the terrorists caught the brothers, they probably would be killed. This was not a good situation, and Bob was desperately praying about what to do.

Early one morning he was praying about them going into the training area. Suddenly Bob heard Jim's voice calling him. It was so clear! Jim was calling for Bob with a tone of desperation in his voice that meant come quickly, I need your help. It was Jim's voice, and it sounded as if he was right outside their house. Bob wondered why he had made the two-hour trip from his mission station to their home in the city so early in the morning. Something was wrong, and Jim needed Bob's help immediately.

Pat was still in bed; Bob woke her quickly and said, "Pat, Jim is outside." Bob ran outside, expecting to see Jim's pickup truck in the driveway, but it was not there. Surprised by this, Bob knew Jim had to be someplace outside and he needed him immediately. He ran around the house, expecting to see Jim in the yard, but he was nowhere to be found. Suddenly, Bob stopped looking and realized the Lord had spoken to him using Jim's voice. This time it was not a still, small voice of the Holy Spirit Bob was hearing, but an audible voice from heaven!

Since it was mainly Jim's feeling that they should go into that area, Bob knew God was confirming it to him by using Jim's voice calling in this desperate tone, meaning come and help me now. Bob had just heard an audible voice from heaven! He did not know if it was the Lord or an angel, but he did know he heard a voice from heaven confirming to him that they should go into the terrorist area and preach the blood of Jesus and repentance in every village.

Bob knew then that he was to resign from his job and they were to go back into the terrorist training area, no matter how dangerous it was. Jim was right in his convictions that God wanted them to do this. In an audible voice, God gave Bob the confirmation that he had been praying for. Bob needed this confirmation because of what he was facing if he quit his job and went in this area, and God graciously provided it.

Bob had just finished building a plastic mold in the tool and die shop and was ready for his next job when God spoke this confirmation to him. The timing was perfect as far as Bob's job was concerned, because he could leave without putting his friend's work in jeopardy. His friend was also low on work at the time, so the timing was perfect to resign.

Bob told his friend what God was directing him to do. The shop owner immediately realized the seriousness of Bob leaving his job and told him he would have to report him to the authorities within a week or they would put him in prison. Bob understood this and called him by his name, saying, "I totally understand you have to report me. I don't want you to get into trouble. You must do what you have to and I must do what I have to."

Shortly after that Bob left his job. He knew he could never go back to it and probably would never see his friend again here on this earth. Bob has never seen him since that day, but he knows he will in heaven. Right after this, Jim and Bob went back into the terrorist area and started preaching the simple message that God had given them.

Pat and Tanya stayed in their home in the city and worked quickly at getting rid of their belongings, except for a few necessities they would need. She also notified the landlord that they were leaving so he would not be upset. The work took Pat about a week, and Tanya was a big help to her mother in getting the house ready to move from.

That week Pat and Tanya had quite a scare, however. One day a man came to the back door, broke the lock, and came into the house. Pat and Tanya ran toward the bedroom. There was a door in the hallway that had a lock on it (which was on the bedroom side of the door). As Pat and Tanya were running for the bedroom, Pat slammed the hallway door and managed to get it locked before the man rammed the door from the other side. The man continued to ram against the hallway door, but was unable to break the lock or the door. Pat started to pray and rebuke Satan because she had a strong feeling that he, Satan, was leading this man to do this as an attack against them for what they were doing to obey God. The man gave up after a time, and stole a few things out of the house and left.

After closing up the house, Pat and Tanya came to the mission station and stayed there, waiting for Jim and Bob to finish ministering in the terrorist training area. Pat and Mary knew the dangers they were facing and daily prayed for them.

There were many small villages in the terrorist area, and Jim and Bob knew the Lord was leading them to preach in everyone. The task was great, but they felt the Holy Spirit was telling them to do this job quickly. The brothers also knew that sooner or later the terrorists could catch them or the government would catch Bob. They felt they should divide up, Bob would go into some villages and Jim would go into others. This way they could cover many more villages in the same length of time. They were traveling in Jim's pickup truck to the different villages. They would usually park it in a location between two villages, and Bob would walk to one and Jim to the other. When the villagers saw a white guy walking into their village, they would always come out to see them and hear what they had to say. This gave the brothers a wonderful opportunity to give them the Word of God. When the people heard the simple message of the blood of Jesus Christ and repentance, many made a decision to become Christians.

The brothers did not know exactly where the terrorist camp was, but they did know it was in the area where they were preaching. No doubt they ran into some of the terrorists in the villages, but they did not know who they were, as they would have looked like any other person who lived there.

One day as Bob was walking down a path that led into a village, he saw two African policemen in the village. By their uniforms, he could tell that they were from one of the larger cities. They were in this very remote area looking for something or someone, and Bob felt it might be him. He knew if they saw him in this remote area, they would question him, and Bob did not want that. He was near a mud hut located right at the edge of the village when he saw the policemen. No one had noticed him walking into the village yet, so he quickly stepped behind the mud hut and stayed there until the police left. After they left, Bob stepped out and walked into the center of the village. The Africans greeted him very favorably and listened closely as he taught the Word of God.

Every day, as the brothers went out, they knew that they could be shot that day. Since the terrorist goal was to kill whites, Jim and Bob qualified, and they could easily be targets. Most of the terrorist killing was done by hiding in the bushes and shooting their victims from a distance. Many of the white farmers, who were shot, never saw the person who shot them, and the brothers knew they could be victims in this exact way. They knew God had called them there, but they also knew many people in the Bible and missionaries of their day had been killed in God's service. In spite of this knowledge, they continued to preach day after day. Jim and Bob were willing to die in God's service, but they were not willing to disobey their wonderful Lord because of fear.

Two months passed and finally there were only two villages left that Jim and Bob had not preached in. One was about a mile walk up a tall hill from the road they were driving on. The other village was about a mile walk down into the valley from the road. They decided that Bob would take the village on the hill and Jim would take the one in the valley. They parked the truck beside the road, and each of them walked to their village to preach.

When Bob walked into the village, all of the people came to see him. It was strange for them to see a white man walk into their village, but they all listened as he preached the simple message to them. Bob well remembers a blind girl listening so intently to him as he explained the Word of God. When he was finished with his teaching, she said she wanted to accept Christ. Bob led her in the sinner's prayer and she accepted Jesus as her Savior. He told her that an African Christian pastor from the mission church would come to visit her. He also told the village people where the African pastor lived and where the church was, and asked them to please come to that church. They did this with each group of converts.

Bob said good-bye to the villagers and started his walk back down the hill. The sun had gone down by this time and it was starting to get dark, but Bob could see well enough to walk. About halfway down the hill, the Spirit of the Lord came upon Bob and spoke to him in a still, small voice saying, "Get out quickly because they are looking for you."

Bob knew that he had to get out of the country as quickly as possible because he was a wanted man and would be in serious trouble if he delayed leaving.

Jim had also finished preaching in his village and they met at the truck at about the same time. The brothers discussed their day as Jim made the long drive on the dirt roads toward the mission station. Both of them had a very good feeling in their hearts that they had obeyed the Lord in spite of the dangers, and they felt good that they were both still alive. No doubt, many of the men who heard them preach were terrorists, but God had protected them.

In time, the terrorists left the area. Later Jim went back there, and he and the African Christians built several churches there. Today there are hundreds of Christians living in that area. Many of the ones the brothers led to Jesus are leaders in those churches, and the blind girl is still going on with the Lord. God used Jim and Bob to make a difference in that whole area.

As they were driving back to the mission, Bob told Jim what the Holy Spirit had spoken to him as he walked down the hill. The brothers agreed that Bob, Pat, and Tanya had to get out of the country as quickly as possible. Bob still had a major problem that concerned him. To get his exit permit out of the country he had to go to five different government agencies and have his papers stamped for approval. There was no way around this. They would each check their records to see if he had violated any laws while he was in the country before they would stamp his exit papers as approved. If any of the offices saw he did not leave the country within a week after leaving his job, Bob was in big trouble and could still go to prison.

As Bob thought about this, he also thought about a friend of his in a neighboring country who was in prison for a year and a half for putting some posters up about a Christian young people's meeting. Bob knew these things could be very serious. He was somewhat anxious for what he still had to do.

With some anxiety, Bob went back into the city and to the first government agency. It had been two months since his friend had to turn him into the immigration office for violating his work permit. Bob felt the paperwork showing his violation would surely have reached that office within those two months. With dread, Bob walked up to the large desk, handed the officer his papers, and asked him for an exit permit. The official looked at Bob's papers, got up and went over to a large record book, and took a long time looking at it. All kinds of thoughts were going through Bob's mind as he stood there watching him look into the record book. What would he say if the official asked Bob where he had been for two months? Bob could not lie to him, and he certainly would be angry if he said that he had been back in the terrorist area for the time. This would certainly open him up to all kinds of questions and problems.

After the official finished looking in the record book, he came back toward Bob. His demeanor was not happy, but Bob could not tell what he was thinking. With the same expression on his face, the official picked up a large rubber stamp and brought it down on Bob's papers. He signed and dated them, saying nothing as he handed them back to Bob. The official had approved them; Bob's violation had evidently not reached this office yet. He was relieved, but he still had to go through four more offices like this one before they could exit the country.

As Bob went to each of the other four agencies, he anxiously awaited as they went through their records to see if he had done anything wrong while he was in their country. They all ended up stamping his papers, signing and dating them, stating Bob was not wanted for anything and they could leave the country. When the last official stamped Bob's papers and signed them, it was like a heavy weight was off his mind, and he knew they could go home. What had happened? Was their system so slow that Bob's work-permit violation had not been recorded in any of these agencies? Maybe God had blinded their eyes to it? Bob does not know what it was, but he does know that God had again delivered him from what could have been a terrible situation.

Now that Bob and Pat had their exit permits, they were able to get their tickets, and were very relieved to be free from the pressure they had faced. They said good-bye to Jim and Mary and a few other Christians and were soon on the plane heading to the United States of America. When they arrived in New York, Bob had a strange feeling. He even asked himself what it was. He thought for a little bit and realized that for the first time in over two months, he felt free because he no longer had the thought of possibly being killed, being a fugitive, or going to prison. They were back home!

Bob and Jim had risked a lot to take the Gospel into the terrorist area. Even though they knew this at the time, they were obedient and went into that area preaching the blood of Jesus and repentance. Were the results of their obedience worth the risk? Yes they were! Before they went, hardly anyone in the area knew about Jesus Christ and now, over forty years later, it is a flourishing area for Him! Yes, the results of their obedience justified the risks!

Picture from Zenzele's wedding

Chapter 51
God's Plans for Each Brother

When Bob and Pat said their good bye to Jim and Mary in Africa and boarded the plane it would be the last time they ministered together in Africa. Jim and Mary continued ministering in Swaziland with Zenzele and Mandla to raise. God not only had plans for Jim and Mary to raise those two children, but also nine more. I won't get into all of the details, but nine more children came into their lives with desperate needs that required Jim and Mary to also take them to raise. This meant that they had eleven Swazi children to care for along with maintaining the mission station, building many water reservoirs, and ministering in the villages.

From the time Jim started ministering in Swaziland he drove himself very hard, as he had on his farm and in Liberia. Satan did many things to discourage or stop him from ministering, but Jim kept on going regardless of the difficulties he and Mary faced. During this time God gave Jim a vision in a dream, which included a story about an old ship at sea. Jim knew this was a word of encouragement to him from God and it was so special to him that he wrote it down. It is copied below.

I'll See You Through

Jim McCauley

I had a dream one night as God was speaking to me
I saw a lot of ships, one was in a storm at sea
Many others were at dock where everyone could see

The one way out in the sea rolling and tossing in such a raging storm
And all alone it seemed
It went beneath the water then came up
Only God could have redeemed

Flashing lighting, howling wind, and oh such waves
still it does not sink
It never dropped anchor to ride out the storm, but just kept on going
and God said, "Now stop and think.

This ship is you, and I will see you through

No time to anchor and ride out the storm which will not soon end
Just keep going, the cargo cannot wait
and you I did send.

Those other ships chose to stay by the dock
all neatly tied in a row
But they're not doing anything
just sitting there all for a show

They all could have been used of me
but chose to sit there and be the norm
Rather than go out at sea
carry my cargo and face the storm

So my son, just keep on doing whatever I tell you to do
and remember I'm always there and I will guide you and see you
through."

But I kept on looking at those ships along the dock
so beautifully painted and lettered all the same
The old ship at sea, battered and painted dull gray
and didn't even have a name

Then the Lord said to me, "Listen to me
for there's more for you to see
About those beautiful ships tied along the dock,
and the plain old ship out at sea

The strength of a ship is not in the nice paint
and the name on the side
Often these cover the flaws
and a multitude of errors do hide

But rather how it's made within
honest and true, no errors or sin
And that's why the ship at sea
many souls will win

Those ships standing along the dock
look so very strong

> *But fact is, they're sitting in the sand*
> *been there so long*
>
> *So don't be weary or fearful of the storm*
> *lighting and roaring waves, away at sea*
> *For I'll see you through*
> *and from every snare set you free."*

Jim would daily go into the villages and preach in the center of the village or under a tree to get out of the hot African sun. When he had about 250 converts in a village, he would build a church. As time went on Jim started mentoring eleven converts teaching them the Word of God and how to preach. Some of these were their own Swazi children. When they built a church Jim would always work physically with them. He would never ask the Swazis to do anything he would not do himself. Jim taught them every detail of building a cement block building with a cement floor and mental roof. He put a special emphasis on making it level and square. As time passed, the disciples learned the Word of God and how to teach and preach it and also how to build very good church buildings just as Jim had.

One time, Jim was working on top of the rafters of a church they were building. He slipped and fell about eighteen feet and landed on the cement floor. It knocked him out and when he came to his Swazi disciples were in a circle around him waving empty cement bags up and down as fans to cool him in hopes that this would help him regain consciousness. When he came to, he lay there for a few minutes and got up and climbed to the top of the rafters and started to work again. His disciples were amazed and said, "Look at him, he just fell eighteen feet on cement and is back up there working again." As the Swazi men saw Jim's work ethics, they started to call him, "The Machine" because he could continue working hard for long periods of time without seeming to get tired. This was their respected name for Jim and they loved him as their father.

Building the churches in the different locations almost always became a place of ministry as well as building. Some people would walk long distances with a sick person and ask Jim and his disciples to pray for them. One time a very ill woman was brought to them and they asked Jim to pray for the woman. He was covered with sweat and dirt and his hands had so much cement on them that he hated to touch the woman. Jim got an empty cement bag and wiped off one finger and with the tip of it he touched the woman on her forehead and asked God to heal her and He instantly did. As they were building one church, they had so many people healed that they nicknamed it the miracle church. In addition to that, when some people walked by as they were building, Jim or his disciples witnessed to them about Jesus Christ and they accepted Him as their Savior and were born again.

One morning as Jim drove into the church lot where they were building the "Miracle Church" a lady was waiting on him with a very skinny little girl. When he got out of his truck the woman said to him, "My child has TB. and will not even eat anything. I took her to doctors, but she is no better. Please pray for my child!" Jim and the men working with him prayed for the child and asked God to heal her in the name of Jesus of Nazareth. A few days later Jim and Mary saw the little girl and her mother and they were so blessed to see that the little girl was very active and the mother was very happy. The mother spoke to them in her broken English and said, "Baby well, baby eat now."

One day a Swazi lady showed up at the church they were building. She was a teacher and well known by the pastor. He said to Jim, "Please pray for this lady as she can no longer teach school because she has terrible sounds in her ears. Some people had prayed for her before, but the loud sounds in her ears continued. Jim talked to the lady about the Lord and she repented of her sins and accepted Jesus as her Savior. He also asked her if she had been involved in witchcraft and she admitted she had and that she had some witchcraft charms. Jim told her she had to repent of being in witchcraft and to give them her charms so they could burn them. She supposedly gave them all of her charms and they burnt them. Even after this the loud sounds in her ears continued.

After this God gave Jim a word of knowledge and he said to the woman, "I think you are lying. Now where is the rest of your charms?" The teacher looked very shocked at what he just said to her. After a moment she admitted she did have one more charm. Jim told her there was no reason to even pray for her unless she brought that one last charm and they burnt it. She left later that day and returned with the charm. The charm was something you could hide in your hand yet it totally stopped the miracle of healing God had for her. She handed Jim the witchcraft charm and then he said to her, "Now you must, in all sincerity, repent of lying to God and also to many people about this. You must also repent of putting part of your trust in the devil."

The Swazi teacher did just that and in prayer they broke the power of the satanic item. After that they burnt the charm. Jim's hands were very dirty from working so he rubbed the tip of one finger clean on his shirt and simply touched her on the forehead as they prayed. Instantly God healed her and the loud noise in her ears stopped. Her hearing was completely back to normal. After that she went back to teaching and Jim is sure she learned a valuable lesson. A person cannot dabble in the things of Satan and have the blessings of God at the same time.

At sundown on a Thursday before Easter Jim drove the final roofing nail on the Miracle Church. Jim and the men helping him were doing their best to get the new church ready for Good Friday, Saturday, and Easter Sunday services. Jim preached on Good Friday morning and many came to the altar after the message. Most of them just wanted a closer walk with the Lord Jesus.

After the service was over, the pastor brought three ladies to Jim and said, "All three of these ladies really need healing, please pray for them." One lady was actually weeping due to pain across her shoulders. Her pain had been going on for a long time and the doctors had not been able to help her. They talked to her about the Lord and were satisfied that she was living for Him. Then the pastor, Jim, and Mary laid their hands on her and prayed for her healing. Then they went to the next lady who was having severe pain in her legs and she could not walk well. They talked with this lady just as they had the first woman and prayed for her healing. Then they went to the third lady and she could not hear well enough to understand what they were saying so they prayed for her healing as they had the others. After that Jim and Mary left and drove back to their home on the mission station.

That evening they drove back to the church for the Good Friday evening service. As people were arriving the pastor came to Jim and Mary very joyfully and said, "Do you remember these three ladies?" They were the three ladies they prayed for that morning, but they looked entirely different. Their countenance had completely changed from a look of being in severe pain to smiles of victory and joy.

The lady with the severe pain in her shoulders was totally set free and had so changed that she looked like a different person. The second lady they prayed for who was having severe problems with her legs was walking like a young person and was full of joy. The third lady they prayed for could now hear every word very correctly. This changed her entire life. She now had the ability to communicate with her family and friends etc. It would also help her in being a witness for the Lord and His miracle working power. Jim and Mary gave God all the credit for this and say that it was Him alone who did it!

Jim and Mary saw God do many miracle healings, but this one is very special.

One day Jim and one of their Swazi sons named Simon went to a village to preach the Word of God. A lady came to them and said, "Would you pray for my child since his eyes are closed?" This was her way of saying, "He is blind." As always, Jim and Simon checked to see if she had consulted a witch-doctor before talking to us. They knew she had to be honest and repent if she had been in any witchcraft or had any witchcraft medicine of fetishes. From experience, they knew God would not heal the boy if she did not do this first. They found that the woman was not in this sin and they prayed that God would heal her son and let him see. They did not see evidence of this immediately, but still believed God for a miracle of healing for this blind boy.

The next time they came back to this village the mother brought her son to them saying, "My son is healed!" Jim will never forget how the little boy looked at him with his beautiful brown eyes. Jim thanked God for this boy's healing and gave God all the glory for it.

One day a government car drove into Jim and Mary's mission station and a chauffeur started to help a government official get out of the car. Jim immediately saw that the official could not walk and one of his legs was in a cast. Jim and a few other men carried the man into the church. They could tell that the official's legs were in very bad shape because they smelled terrible. The official told Jim and the others he had a problem with his legs and wanted them to pray for him.

He had been in a very serious car accident and severely injured his legs. He was treated by several of the best doctors and hospitals in South Africa, but his legs would not heal. He had even started to smell badly as the infection and decay worsened. It became obvious to the government official that he was never going to walk right again and he was possibly going to die. He had heard about people being healed at their mission station and decided to seek God for his healing.

Even though the man was a government official Jim and the other Christians still went through all of the procedures they did with other people, making sure he was not into witchcraft and had accepted Jesus Christ as his Savior. After this they prayed that God would heal him. Then they carried him back to his car and his chauffeur drove him away. A few days later he made the two-hour drive back to the mission station. However, this time he was driving himself; bringing his wife and children with him. He got out of the car on his own and walked to Jim in a normal way. God had totally healed his legs. He came back to say, "Thank you" even though he knew it was God who healed him through the name of Jesus Christ of Nazareth and of course so did Jim and those on the mission station.

The man was wearing a pin of U.S.A. and Swazi flags. He took it off and, while singing the American National Anthem, pinned it on Jim. Praise God he walked away without any limp at all.

The pin is of two flags. One is an American flag and the other is of a Swaziland flag. This pin means a lot to Jim because he knows what God did to bring this event about. Jim still wears this pin to church and other places. The official was very famous in Swaziland because he wrote their Swaziland Anthem.

Through the years Jim and Mary continued to see God do miracles and deliverance from demons just as we read about in the Book of Acts. Jim also continued to work endlessly and God prospered their ministry. Thousands came to Jesus Christ and today there are well over 8,000 Christians and 42 churches in the area of Swaziland where God directed them. After being in Swaziland twenty years, all of their Swazi children were adults and supporting themselves. Jim and Mary believed God was directing them to return to America and to let their disciples take over the Swaziland Ministry they had started. By then their disciples were preaching and making disciples themselves and building churches on their own.

Jim and Mary are living back in their home in Indiana and enjoying their children, grandchildren, and great grandchildren. They are still very involved in supporting the ministry in Swaziland and especially a ministry to orphans whose parents died from AIDS.

When Bob and Pat returned from Africa WEC Mission asked them to be Mid-West representatives for them and they accepted the offer. This meant they would speak about missions in churches, Bible schools, and Bible colleges throughout the Mid-West. They also would assist and encourage young people who were interested in being missionaries.

God also spoke to Bob in the still small voice during that time saying, "I want you to have an Apostle Paul ministry." Bob's immediate thought was that he was to have a preaching ministry filled with signs, wonders, and miracles. God spoke back and said in His still small voice, "Preach My Word and support yourself by working as Paul did." This surprised Bob, but he fully understood it. We see in the verses below that Paul not only preached the Word, but he also supported himself through building tents.

Acts 18:3 (NIV) *and because he was a tent-maker as they were, he stayed and worked with them.*

Acts 20:34 (NIV) *You yourselves know that these hands of mine have supplied my own needs and the needs of my companions.*

1 Corinthians 4:12 (NIV) *We work hard with our own hands. When we are cursed, we bless; when we are persecuted, we endure it;*

2 Thessalonians 3:8 (NIV) *nor did we eat anyone's food without paying for it. On the contrary, we worked night and day, laboring and toiling so that we would not be a burden to any of you.*

Bob thought about this for a short time and he came up with three conclusions. The first was he knew he had time to work at a job when he was not speaking. Most of their speaking engagements were in the evenings or on weekends and he could still do most of those. Pat was a very good speaker and she could do it during the day. The second was he could support his family. The third was he could have a testimony as a working man who was serving Christ with all his heart. Many people in the work force never go to church, but Bob believed he could reach many of them by being on their level.

After prayer, Bob believed God was leading him to get a job in a local plastic mold building shop called Hewitt Tool and Die. The shop owners, Ed and Linda Hewitt, were friends of his and they hired him as their shop foreman. This job required the same skills that Bob learned in Swaziland from the man who had escaped from East Germany.

Back then, Bob never thought he would use the skill of building plastic molds, but God's knew years before that he would need that skill to fit into the plans He had for him. He would now be using that skill every day on his job as a foreman in a plastic mold building shop.

Not long after Bob went to work at Hewitt's, Ed became a turned-on Christian for Jesus Christ. He also was baptized in the Holy Spirit and started sending a tremendous amount of money into the world to spread the Gospel. God used Ed's testimony as a Christian business man to other business men that a preacher would never touch. God prospered Ed's business and he built a new large building and purchased many new plastic molding machines. He continued to build plastic molds and molded millions of plastic parts for many companies. God not only prospered Ed's shop, but He also prospered Bob and he became well known to many companies as a very knowledgeable foreman in building molds.

God used this in Bob's favor and later He told him in the still small voice to send in an application to General Motors for a senior engineering job in plastic molding. Before Bob did this he told Ed how God had directed and he fully understood. After that Bob hand wrote a very unprofessional application on a small piece of paper for an engineering job in plastic molding and sent it to the local GM. plant. They called him the next day for an interview and hired him at a very high salary. Three weeks later Bob went back to work at GM. and Ed's oldest son took over Bob's foreman job.

Having a job as a senior engineer seemed to enhance Bob's speaking. He could speak as an engineer who was on fire for Jesus Christ and also as a jungle pilot and missionary. Even though Bob was working in an occupation God was using him and Pat in a powerful ministry, which was led by the Holy Spirit. Below is an example of how God used Pat.

One day a woman, who lived about a hundred miles away, called Pat and said she was having deep emotional problems. She had heard about Pat and wanted to talk to her about her problem. Pat agreed and the woman made the long drive to see her. When she arrived, Pat invited her in and the two sat down across from each other. The woman started to talk about her problems and Pat stopped her. The Holy Spirit immediately gave Pat a word of knowledge about the woman.

Pat boldly said, "You are in a sexual relationship with your pastor and you will never get over your emotional problems until you repent of it!" The woman was shocked when she heard this and she knew the Holy Spirit had revealed this to Pat. She immediately started to cry and admitted it was true and repented of it. The woman never intended to tell Pat about this, but the Holy Spirit did. The counseling session quickly ended with a victory because Pat heard the still small voice of the Holy Spirit.

Even though Bob and Pat were fully dedicated to obeying God they still had a crisis that was ultra-serious. Again, I will quote Isaiah 43:2.

Isaiah 43:2 (NIV) *When you pass through the waters, I will be with you; and when you pass through the rivers, they will not sweep over you. When you walk through the fire, you will not be burned; the flames will not set you ablaze.*

God uses the term, 'when you' which means we will pass through difficulties, but He promises to be with us when we do. Bob and Pat were suddenly faced with a crisis they did not plan for and did not want. Pat developed cancer and after eight months, with her family present, she passed away. Through the eight months the doctor said she had no chance of recovering and yet she had peace through it all because God was with her. Even though she had been used of God and was obedient to Him she still passed away and is now in Heaven where she will be forever. After this, Bob and his children went through a difficult time of grief for many months.

Time passed and then God spoke to Bob that he was to call a woman he hardly knew and propose to her. She had been a missionary and also went through a crisis and was left with two children to raise with very little income. Her name was Esther Werdal and she lived 700 miles away from Bob. Esther was originally from British Columbia, Canada and she had also been a missionary with WEC Mission and served in Africa. Esther and Pat were friends and occasionally they wrote to each other and her children and Bob's children knew each other.

Bob obeyed God and called Esther and proposed and they were married four months later. Esther could speak Ukrainian, some Russian, and was also educated in Canada and attended Prairie Bible College. Esther was a four foot eleven-inch-tall hard driving woman in everything she did, including God's work. Bob and Esther also worked with WEC Mission as Mid-West representatives and later they got involved in Christian work in Russia.

God prospered Bob in his engineering job and through the gifts of the Holy Spirit gave him four inventions in plastic molding. One invention alone saved his company three million dollars the first year and a million every year after that. Bob became well known in his company and plastic molding shops throughout the Mid-West. One engineer from Wisconsin later told Bob that his name was like a legend in plastic molding. All of this resulted in Bob receiving a very high salary and a good retirement income.

God had a plan to start a seminary in Moscow and to start a large ministry to street children and children in prison in Russia. God's plan included using a woman who would not give up when faced with very difficult situations, which would include living in bitter cold places in Russia. She would also have to go into the sewers to minister to the street children and into the prisons three or four times a week to minister to the children and youth. This would include waiting for hours outside of the prisons in the bitter cold and being exposed daily to diseases such as T. B. and AIDS and other things such as lice and sewer gas. This woman had to continue in her ministry in spite of threats from the Russian mafia and many other difficulties. Even though she was beautiful, she had to be rugged and fearless in what God was calling her to do. This woman was Bob's wife, Esther.

While Bob was still working in engineering, Esther went to Russia and pioneered a ministry to street children and children in prison in Russia, which is still going on to this day. Bob and Esther were very involved in sending about a million dollars worth of food, clothing, and medicine to the Russian Christians and God supplied about two million dollars over a twenty-year span to support the ministry to the children in prison and street children. Also, they were very involved in starting the first seminary in Moscow. Esther and Bob first got involved in Russia in 1991 and were very involved in that ministry for over the next 20 years. Esther was there 26 times and Bob 23 times. Through the years many children, youth, and adults came to Jesus Christ and were born-again.

Bob's second book, "***God's Faithfulness: A Journey in Trusting***" is about Esther's life of growing up in the forest of British Columbia and their ministry in Russia and at home.

As was said in the beginning of this book, God has plans for every person's life no matter what the situation of their birth or childhood was. The key to having God's plans come about, is obedience to Him in everything a person does. This obedience might cost a vast amount of time and a great sacrifice of money and the things you love the most.

Fifty years later we could ask the brothers this question, "You know you could have been worth a lot of money if you had not obeyed God. Also, you faced death and lived in very difficult conditions during some of this time. Would you do the same all over again?" The brothers are still alive and in sound mind and able to correctly evaluate the results of their decision they made fifty years ago.

Bob's answer to the above question is, "When I was thirty-five years old, I totally committed my life to obeying God and being a living sacrifice for Him. Obeying God included living a holy life because this is what He wants of His servants. That was fifty-one years ago, and at that time I had no idea what His plans were for me and my family. I can now look back and see that thousands of souls in Africa, Russia, and America heard the Word of God and many will be in Heaven for eternity as a result of my decision to obey God. In addition to that, hundreds of lives were saved physically as a result of our medical flying ministry in Africa. Also, the Bible school we built in Liberia is still going on and a countless number have heard the Gospel as a result. Many street children in Russia had a good life and many came to Christ as a result of our ministry there.

Then in addition to that God blessed my children just as He said he would. Also, He has taken care of all our needs and He still is. I have had a very exciting life and I would not trade it for any amount of money. I attribute having a wonderful and joyful life to living in obedience to God in everything, which let His plans for my life to come about. Yes, I am glad I did it and I would do it again!"

Jim's answer to this question is this, "I would probably be dead today if I had not obeyed God. As I look back and see the results of what God did with me during the last fifty years, I see this; A Bible school was built in Liberia and is still going on. Thousands have heard the Word of God and a countless number have been born-again in Liberia as a result. Mary and I made many disciples in Swaziland, who went out preaching the Word of God. The church went from about 150 to well over 8,000 where God sent us in Swaziland and it is still progressing. Also, forty-two churches have been built and paid for.

God blessed our three children in America and the eleven we raised in Swaziland. One was little Zenzele, whom I found dying in the remote area of Swaziland. God has also taken care of our needs through these last fifty years. I would gladly do it again, even knowing that I would have been very wealthy if I would have lived. Through the years being obedient to God at all cost was my desire and goal and it still is. Yes! I would do it again."

God used these brothers in His plans and He was able to do this because of their obedience!

Bob McCauley   5-22- 2020

Bob and Esther on their wedding day